D1605942

JEWELLERY MANUFACTURE
AND REPAIR

Jewellery Manufacture and Repair

Charles A. Jarvis FGA

N.A.G. Press
an imprint of Robert Hale · London

© *N.A.G. Press Limited and Charles A. Jarvis 1978*
First published 1978
Reprinted 1981
Reprinted 1990
Reprinted 1994
Reprinted 1997
Reprinted 2001

ISBN 0-7198-0052-8

Robert Hale Limited
Clerkenwell House
Clerkenwell Green
London ECIR OHT

Printed in Great Britain by
St Edmundsbury Press Limited, Bury St Edmunds, Suffolk
Bound by Woolnough Bookbinding Limited

Contents

Foreword

by Eric Bruton FGA

The making and correct repair of individual pieces of jewellery has not succumbed to the short-cut methods of the technological age. Even jewellery made in quantity by lost wax casting techniques requires, in most cases, a master pattern to be made by traditional methods. This book sets out the traditional practices that have been used for centuries and are still being used today by individual craftsmen in London and Birmingham, as well as in many other centres over the world. It does not offer any short cuts to the high degrees of skill needed, but does give step-by-step instruction which can lead the reader, who intends to make a living from the craft, or just to excel at it as a hobby, to a high level of professionalism.

Some classes and many books have been devoted to making jewellery by quick methods that rely upon attractive design at the expense of craftsmanship. With the 1970s, this period has largely ended, except for frivolous work, and there is a strong movement back to the traditions of high quality in construction, whether the design be traditional or contemporary.

In this book, emphasis is deliberately on methods that are almost universal and have been tested over centuries. Undoubtedly a fluorescent or spot light has replaced the magnifying flask of water on nearly all benches, the bench itself may be partly of stainless steel, and the stool one designed originally for typists, but the principles, and even the shape of the benches, remain the same. Some jewellers, particularly amateurs, have a self-contained blow lamp and others one using gas-oxygen; but few jewellers who have acquired the knack of soldering small parts with a mouth blowpipe would forego its flexibility and sensitivity for a modern counterpart.

It is hoped that readers of *Jewellery Manufacture and Repair* will not only take pleasure in learning these ancient skills, but will find that employing them gives a fresh and continually increasing joy in producing jewellery of the highest quality to add to whatever merit it may have in design.

ERIC BRUTON FGA

1. The Jeweller's Workshop and Tools

Making jewellery by hand is divided into three distinct processes—in fact, three distinct trades:

(1) *Mounting*—that is, making the actual article of jewellery from the precious metal, building it up to suit the gemstones which are to be set therein;

(2) *Setting*—that is, actually fixing the stones in their appropriate place in the finished product; and

(3) *Polishing* or *Finishing*—It is intended to deal with mounting first, then setting, and thirdly polishing.

The Workshop

The workshop itself is of great importance, and attention must be paid to heating, lighting and cleanliness. A craftsman cannot do his best work if he is sitting in a draught, or is feeling uncomfortably cold; neither can he do well without unnecessary strain if lighting is bad or ineffective. The same applies to craftswomen, of course. Therefore the position of work-benches and the arranging of artificial lighting must be carefully considered. The bench itself, for instance, should be fitted under a window or windows, whichever is appropriate, bearing in mind that many jewellers' workshops are small and choice is limited; but as the best light is daylight, every possible advantage should be made of it, and so the flat side of each three- or five-seat bench is fixed directly under a window.

The window should be fitted with a good blind which, while allowing ample light to come in, is yet able to stop the glare of the sunlight. A good roller blind is far more convenient, and less messy, than the often used method of sticking paper to the windows when the need arises—although

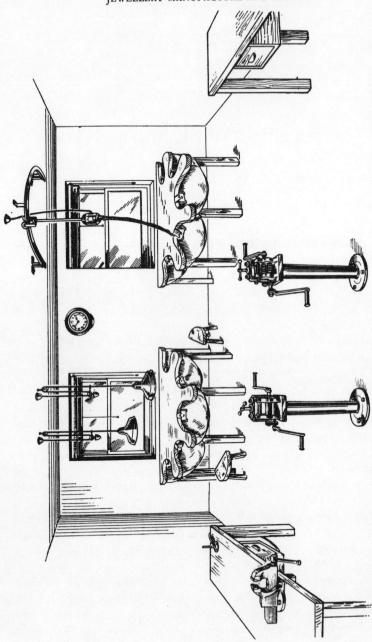

Fig. 1. An ideal workshop with jewellers' benches under the windows and two rough work benches at the sides, one with a fitter's vice. Notice that the jewellers' bench on the right has a drill with flexible drive running on a rail so that it can be passed from one man to another. The push-button switch for the drill is at the chuck end which gives easy control.

even this serves an essential need. Direct sunlight is damaging to the eyes, and one cannot possibly see the work being handled when working under such conditions.

According to the size of the workshop, the convenient placing of universal equipment (e.g. hand-rolling mills, vice, and rough-work bench) has to be borne in mind. The sketch (Fig. 1) shows a general view of a well-appointed workshop. The same principles apply even if the workshop is for a single person with a single bench. There should be space for a large bench for general work and for the other necessary equipment.

The Work-bench
The work-bench itself may be made for use by one, three, five or more people, even sometimes for ten. This results in a large oval bench, easily accessible all round. This large bench creates certain difficulties in making full use of natural light, as such a bench cannot be too near a window. Use is sometimes made of a glass roof or skylight, but this presents many obvious difficulties. It is more usual for a work-bench to have five places.

Each bench is made of 2 in (50 mm) beech wood. Taking as an example a 'five-seater', as they are usually called, its flat side is 7 ft (2.1 m) long, its legs or supports are of 2 in (50 mm) square timber and are situated one to each arm-rest—that is, one on each side of a work-place (Fig. 2).

Each work-place is a semi-circular recess in the bench, usually 18–20 in (46–50 cm) wide by 11 in (28 cm) deep, and fitted with a boxwood peg or pin against which to work. When purchased, this peg has a square end and is

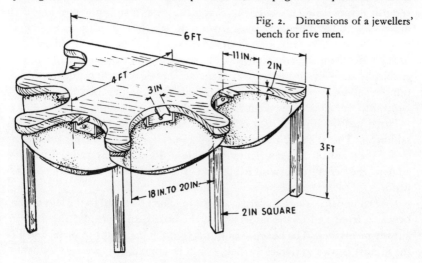

Fig. 2. Dimensions of a jewellers' bench for five men.

3

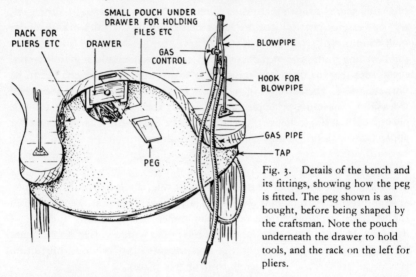

Fig. 3. Details of the bench and its fittings, showing how the peg is fitted. The peg shown is as bought, before being shaped by the craftsman. Note the pouch underneath the drawer to hold tools, and the rack on the left for pliers.

tapered down to about ⅛ in (3 mm) thick. This must fit absolutely rigidly into the chiselled-out socket, as it would be quite impossible to work on a peg which moved or was not perfectly firm when the craftsman was filing against it.

The sketch of the individual place (Fig. 3) shows the means of fitting the peg with the sloping side at the top so that the end nearest the bench is about level with the bench top. It is usual, and always advisable, to shape this peg roughly before fitting it securely to enable the jeweller to begin working. It is impossible to lay down any standard way in which to do this, as everyone works slightly differently, but generally speaking it is best to cut off about 1 in (25 mm) from the end, and roughly shape a 'V' in the centre. This will enable the craftsman to start working against the peg where it is thicker, as the thin end is useless anyway. One soon finds that the peg becomes steadily worn into the most convenient shape for the person using it.

Fitted just underneath each place is a drawer for sundry small tools and oddments. This is about 10 in by 8 in by 4 in (25 × 20 × 10 cm), and when closed the front of the drawer should be about 2 in (50 mm) under the front edge of the bench, otherwise it obstructs the freedom of movement of the hands.

Draped underneath each place is a pigskin which is affixed to the legs of the bench in front and to the underside of the board, and includes the drawer already mentioned. The purpose of this is to catch the scraps of metal and all the filings, known as 'lemel', which, it will be appreciated, are very valuable in the jewellers' business. It also serves to catch any gemstones or piece of work which may be accidentally dropped and makes it easy to retrieve.

It is also very practical to use a metal tray specially produced for this purpose; in fact in some ways it is even better than the traditional pigskin. The metal tray is made from galvanised iron sheet, the same shape as the semi-circular work place, with an open section at the back to allow for the use of the drawer beneath the bench-peg area. The bottom of the tray is slightly curved to help the lemel, etc to accumulate in the centre. The total depth is approximately 10 in (25 cm). The craftsman sitting working at the bench will have his legs underneath the tray, so it cannot be too deep. The tray is fixed by means of a screw to the underside of the bench and also each side to the bench supports (Fig. 3).

The main point in favour of the tray is that it is not damaged as easily as the skin, and would therefore last many years longer. It also protects the legs from lemel which could burn the worker if a hole were made in the skin by dropping hot metal in it, or by accidentally tearing it.

Tool Storage
A useful addition to the drawer is a piece of similar pigskin, nailed to the underside, loosely enough to allow files and other small tools in constant use to be always at hand, ready for use.

On the right arm of each place on the underside of the bench is a gas jet with tap, with the usual type of fitment to permit rubber tubing to be attached. This forms the means of supply to the blow-pipe, which is also readily to hand on the right-hand side. The blow-pipe is usually hung from a strong wire made into the form of a hook, fixed to the top of the bench, as can be seen in Fig. 3.

The blow-pipe itself will be described later when dealing with tools and equipment.

On the left-hand side of the curved work-place is a very simple but effective tool rack for the numerous pairs of pliers which are found to be necessary. This consists simply of a stout iron wire (about 20 gauge) about 6 in (15 cm) long, with an extra inch or two at each end turned over at right-angles and ending in a circular eye, through which screws can attach it to the bench.

The Stool
The jeweller sits on a three-legged stool with a semi-circular seat, as seen in Fig. 1. Three legs have the advantage of being always firm on the floor and, even if the floor is not quite level, will not allow the stool to rock, as four legs would. The stool is very simple but strong, being of 1¼ in (30 mm) beech. The

legs, $1\frac{1}{4}$ in (30 mm) square, are firmly fitted into round holes in the stool top, the tops of the legs being rounded to fit. Each leg is then wedged tightly with a narrow wedge-shaped piece of wood driven in from the top into a previously made saw-cut in the centre of the leg.

The height of the stool depends upon the person using it, as it is necessary to sit correctly and comfortably. The best guide is that, when seated, the top of the jeweller's shoulder should be about 4 in (10 cm) above the level of the top of the bench. If the stool is too high, the man's back will be bent, and he will be looking down too much on to his work. If it is too low, the man's arms will be in a too much raised position. Neither position is comfortable.

Tidiness in the Workshop

It is important to keep a workshop clean and reasonably tidy for purposes other than appearance. A workshop which is kept tidy will be an added incentive to all who use it to return all small tools for general use (such as draw-plates) to their proper place after use, and this alone saves time. However, the true reason is that precious metals are being used and, however careful one is to avoid wastage and to prevent scraps of metal and filings or lemel from falling to the floor, this does occur. Indeed, an amazing amount of precious metal is temporarily lost in this way. For instance, each time a craftsman gets up from his stool for any purpose, even though he first brushes his hands to remove filings, some will remain and are probably deposited on the floor during the time spent away from the work-place.

Pieces of used sandpaper which contain fine gold dust are dropped on to the floor, and although perhaps one may think the amount lost from a piece of sandpaper dropped on the floor to be so small a quantity as to be negligible, it is in fact extremely important and valuable. Every effort should be made to recover the gold from this dust and dirt by various means which will be mentioned in detail later, and until they can be dealt with in the appropriate way, all floor sweepings should be kept in bins provided for this purpose.

Artificial Lighting

Good light is of the utmost importance and as we in this country are well aware, daylight sufficiently good for the work a jeweller has to do is not always available. Quite apart from winter mornings and evenings there are many dull and overcast days when use has to be made of artificial light. It follows, therefore, that this is a very important part of the equipment of each work-bench. If the light is wrongly placed or inefficient, it is obvious that a very great strain on one's eyes will result.

There are two types of lighting in fairly general use and it is debatable

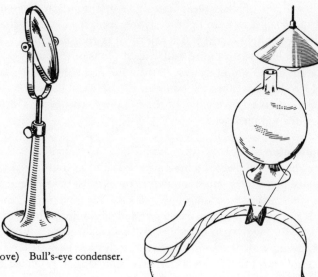

Fig. 4. (above)   Bull's-eye condenser.

Fig. 5. (right)   A globe type of condenser.

which of them is more satisfactory. The older method consists of an ordinary 100-watt lamp inside a plain, shallow cone-shaped shade, which, by means of a shot-loaded porcelain (or plastic) container to balance its weight, can be raised or lowered as necessary. This is used in conjunction with either a bull's-eye condenser (Fig. 4) as shown, or a globe filled with water to which has been added a small quantity of copper sulphate sufficient to give the water a very pale blue tinge. This avoids the glare which would result from using pure water and tends to make the light less harsh without destroying its efficiency (Fig. 5).

The condenser or globe is so placed between the worker and the lamp that the light is concentrated on the board peg where the actual work is being carried out, giving a circle of light of approximately 4 in (10 cm) diameter, the remainder of the work-place having sufficient light to show small tools, etc, which are required.

Another and more modern type of lighting is the fluorescent daylight tube, fitted so that it may be raised when not in use. This is necessary because if it were permanently low enough to be the most effective when lights were on, it would be very inconvenient at other times and would, in fact, considerably detract from the effectiveness of daylight by creating shadow.

7

The advantage of fluorescent lighting is that no water globe or lens is needed and one has an even light, fairly free from shadows. Its disadvantage is that the actual light on the board peg is not as good as with the older type. Against the older type it can be said that the globe or lens takes considerable space on the bench and in the case of the water globe there is the danger of a breakage with the resultant flooding of the bench, tools and work. It is a matter for individual choice, but of the two there is probably a little more in favour of the old method.

The Blow-pipe

To the right of each place is a blow-pipe which is one of the items of equipment which play a very important part in the making of jewellery. There are various types, either the mouth-operated gas blow-pipe or oxygen-gas type. Choice is a matter of personal preference and convenience, but it is very useful for at least one oxygen blow-pipe to be available for the particular purpose of dealing with platinum. The need for this will be more apparent later.

It is also practical and useful to have air pressure provided from air-cylinders or from a rotary blower, instead of from a mouth blow-pipe; the pressures of the former can be controlled by a circular knob similar to the gas control. Special blow-pipes of this type are obtainable. For a small workshop, or in a self-employed situation, it is more convenient and equally effective to use a bottled gas cylinder and one of the blow torches specially made for use with bottled gas. The pressure and control of flame size is very convenient with one small control knob. A selection of blow-pipe jet-ends is available; they are easily changed to provide very large, or very small flame pressure. Each of the jet ends has considerable variation and control, but it is still necessary to change the jet to suit the actual item for which the torch is being used. This will easily be understood after reading more about the actual work of soldering, annealing, etc in Chapter 3.

The mouth-operated pipe, as Fig. 6 shows, has a circular control knob for the gas. The control can be operated by thumb and finger while holding the blow-pipe in the right hand and directing the flame on to the work. The amount of air pressure used is controlled simply by the breath pressure and mouth of the operator.

The oxygen-gas type is similar in appearance although slightly different mechanically (Fig. 7). The small thumb-operated lever controls both gas and oxygen simultaneously and the proportions of the oxygen and gas mixture are regulated by means of the controls situated nearer to the source of supply, eg, oxygen pressure from the cylinder, etc, and the gas by means of the tap under the bench where the rubber tubing is attached.

8

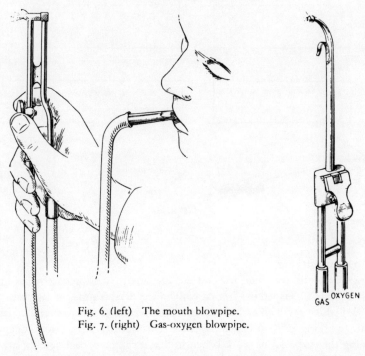

Fig. 6. (left)   The mouth blowpipe.
Fig. 7. (right)   Gas-oxygen blowpipe.

Both types of blow-pipe have a small by-pass gas tube to provide a pilot
light which is left continually burning while the blow-pipe is likely to be
needed. Experience and continual practice are needed for the best use to be
made of either type, and after the necessary practice one can become so used
to either that the most intricate job of hard soldering can be done. However,
it is still felt by many that the mouth-operated blow-pipe permits an extra fine
adjustment and control of pressure which is an advantage on some small
soldering jobs.

A good selection of draw-plates of the more usual shapes, eg, round,
square, half-round and knife-edge is necessary for odd items which it is necessary to make at times. Of course, one can take advantage of the experience and
service offered by most bullion dealers and order shapes and thicknesses of
wire which are most useful and so avoid a lot of hard work in hand-drawing.
Even so, it will be apparent that small pieces of wire will be needed other than
those purchased and so it will be necessary to draw them down as required.
A fitter's vice on the rough work-bench and a pair of strong draw-tongs are
all that are necessary for most purposes, although other mechanical means are
available if more or thicker materials have to be drawn (Figs. 8 and 9).

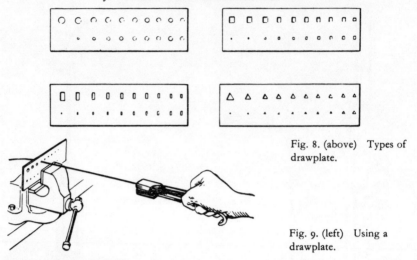

Fig. 8. (above) Types of drawplate.

Fig. 9. (left) Using a drawplate.

Drilling Equipment

Drilling has to be provided for and usually this is done by means of the flexible shaft drill suspended from a convenient place above the worker. A good idea which saves no end of time and inconvenience when several crafts-men are working on one bench together is to have the drill on a runner, following the shape of the work-bench so that it can be passed quickly from man to man.

This was shown clearly in the diagram of the workshop layout (Fig. 1). The motor for the drill is about $\frac{1}{8}$ or $\frac{1}{16}$ hp and has a flexible shaft about 3 ft (90 cm) long running through a protecting cover to the chucks attached to the end. Control is by means of a push-button at the lower end of the flexible shaft at the place where it is held (Fig. 10).

There is also the very primitive drill stock which may, however, still be used with satisfactory results. This is of the hand-operated type, spinning in opposite directions with each downward pressure (Fig. 11). There is a differ-ence in the type of bit which has to be used inasmuch as the electric drill uses the ordinary steel twist bit of which a good range of small sizes are useful, whereas a spade or needle drill bit is used for the hand-operated drill stock. These are made quite easily by hand, and an ordinary needle is as good as any other type of steel for this purpose, otherwise a broken twist bit can be used satisfactorily. In either case this is done by first softening the part to be used by heating on a charcoal block and allowing to cool very slowly. The end is then flattened to give a slight spade-like shape and the cutting edges roughly shaped as in Fig. 12. Next it must be hardened, but first it should be

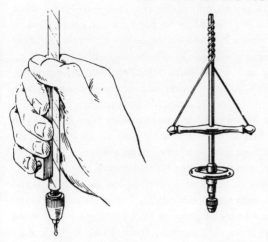

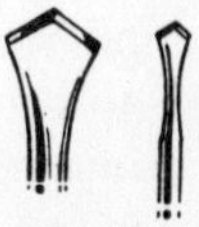

Fig. 10. (left) How the chuck end of the electric drill is held.
Fig. 11. (centre) The jewellers' drill stock.
Fig. 12. (above) Flat drills.

emery-buffed to get it clean and then dipped in oil to keep it so during heating. Immediately the end is heated to bright red, it is plunged into a waiting pot of cold water. It ought now to be hard and should be tested with an old file. If not, the same procedure tried again will probably be successful.

Next it must be tempered by warming slightly after again coating with a thin film of oil. This time warm the top first until a band of colours moves down towards the end. When the portion just a fraction of an inch before the cutting edge becomes straw-coloured, plunge again into water. The bit is then ready to be sharpened. As the bit revolves in both directions, it is made to cut in both directions. Each edge of the spade is sharpened on the oil-stone so that it is V-shaped, as shown in Fig. 12.

Jewellers' drills still have their uses, although generally superseded by flexible shaft electric drills.

Other Tools

Next we come to the small tools which are every working jeweller's constant companions. Each man usually provides his own according to his choice, but generally speaking choice does not vary very much.

A saw-frame is indispensable and practice in its use is vital, as many intricate jobs are done with it, and could easily be ruined by lack of skill in manipulation. The frame itself is quite a simple arrangement as Fig. 13 shows. Usually it is made adjustable for length, but not very much use is made of this facility. The purpose, of course, is that if a saw-blade breaks near its end the frame can be shortened and the saw-blade used again for a while.

A variety of different cuts of saws are available from 6/o to the very thick No. 7, but the range used by the jeweller is usually between 4/o and No. 2.

Several pairs of pliers with various shaped noses are essential, the most important ones being flat-nosed, half-round, flat-points, and round-points. Other tools include a small pair of shears and a pair of nippers (top-cutters or side-cutters); a small hammer with either a domed pane and flat pane, or with cross pane and flat pane (Figs. 14 to 16); a tapered steel triblett (Fig. 17) for ring work—this is about 12 in (30 cm) long and tapering from about 1¼ in (30 mm) diameter to ⅜ in (9.5 mm) throughout most of its length apart from 3 or 4 in (7.5 –10 cm) left parallel as a handle; and a ring size stick (Fig. 18) which is a tapered gauge conforming to a set standard of ring sizes along its length. It is similar to a triblett, but is very much lighter, being hollow and made of aluminium or steel, with a wooden handle. This is marked off along its length with an equidistant series of grooves each bearing a letter of the alphabet by which its size is known. The sizes run from A to Z and it is quite a simple matter when dealing with rings to denote the required size. There are also in use sets of size rings to enable a person's finger size to be established. These consist simply of metal rings made in sizes exactly corresponding to those on the size stick, and these can be tried on the purchaser's finger. This is usually done by the retailer, of course. An easy means of conveying the size required is thus established, eg, size 'L' or size 'M½' denotes an exact measurement which on all size sticks should be invariable.

Rolling Mills

Two larger pieces of equipment for the jeweller's workshop are the hand-operated rolling mills and the draw-bench for heavier wire. Rolling mills are an absolute necessity in any jeweller's workshop and, although designs and details may differ according to the manufacturer's individual choice, they vary but little in their principal features. The most important things are that the rollers of the flat or sheet rolling mills are properly flat and smooth. This depends to a very considerable degree upon how they are used and cared for. They must also be adjusted correctly so that both ends of the rolls are milling the same thickness. More will be mentioned about this when dealing with the actual process of rolling down metal. The 'square' mills are almost identical in construction but the actual rollers are grooved, as shown in Fig. 19, to form squares in between them, of decreasing size from approximately ⅜ in (9.5 mm) downwards. These grooves should be so formed that wire after milling (assuming that it has been milled correctly, of course) is reasonably square and with fairly good corners.

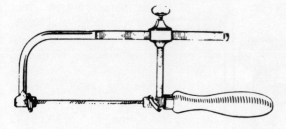

Fig. 13.   Jewellers' saw.

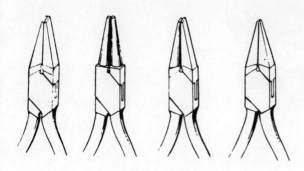

Fig. 14. (above)   Pliers (L to R). Flat nose, round nose,
half-round and flat, and pointed nose.
Fig. 15. (below)   Shears.
Fig. 16. (bottom)   Side-cutting and top-cutting nippers.

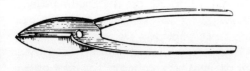

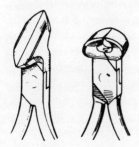

Fig. 17. (right)   Triblett.
Fig. 18. (far right)   Ring
stick.

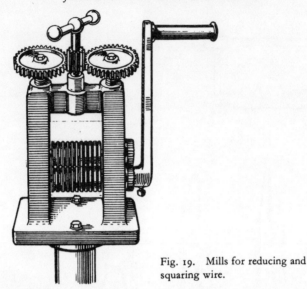

Fig. 19. Mills for reducing and squaring wire.

The Draw-bench

The draw-bench is not an essential but is none the less very useful on occasions when wire has to be drawn down and is too thick or perhaps there is too much of it to be pulled down by hand using only the draw-tongs, draw-plate and vice. It is quite often the practice to purchase wire in various thicknesses from the bullion dealers, so that any which has to be drawn will not have to be drawn down very much, and only as much as can be done fairly easily by hand. However, the faithful old draw-bench is a good standby.

As the illustration (Fig. 20) shows, this is quite simple in its construction, consisting of a very stoutly made bench whose legs are spread fairly widely to give it more stability. Two stout steel pillars are vertically fixed at one end, with a space of about 1½ in (38 mm) between them. The draw-plate is placed behind these, with the point of the wire to be drawn protruding between them, enabling it to be gripped by the draw-tongs. A stout leather belt, one end of which is fixed to the drum on the axle of the 'windmill', has at its other end a triangular steel loop. This loop is placed over the upward-curved ends of the draw-tongs gripping the wire, and so upon turning the 'sails' of the windmill, pressure is brought to bear upon the tongs. The shape of the loop at the end of the belt causes an inward pressure, thus making the tongs grip the wire, while also drawing the wire through the plate. Even wire of considerable thickness can be drawn down by this method.

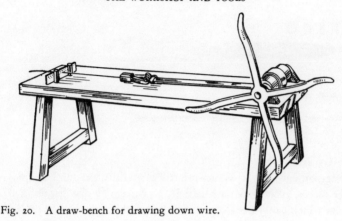

Fig. 20.   A draw-bench for drawing down wire.

The Boss or Wig

For the purpose of heating metal, both in soldering and annealing, a very useful addition to one's equipment is an iron binding-wire 'boss'. There are times when this is more useful than the accepted (and, of course, essential) charcoal block. A boss, or wig, can be made quite easily by pressing together very tightly a tangled mass of soft iron binding wire and hammering it so that a fairly compact, circular pad of about 3 in (75 mm) diameter and $\frac{1}{2}$ in to $\frac{3}{4}$ in (12–20 mm) in thickness results. From soft iron wire of about 18 to 20 gauge (either three or four pieces) a stem is twisted as shown in Fig. 21, the ends being used to form loops overlapping the edges of the boss itself. The purpose of this is mainly to save wastage of heat through its being conducted away, as would happen with a more solid article. I remember a very young apprentice once trying to anneal a small piece of metal about the size of an old sixpence by placing it on a 6 in (15 cm) square slab of $\frac{1}{4}$ in (6 mm) steel plate and blowing upon it with the gas blow-pipe and, after a considerable time, wondering why it was not getting hot! For soldering parts together which need to be more carefully placed, then, of course, the charcoal block is the better of the two.

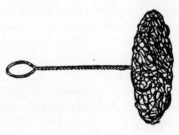

Fig. 21.   A binding wire boss or 'wig' for soldering.

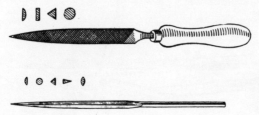

Fig. 22. Two types of file, with several sections. That on the left is a needle or Swiss file.

Tweezers and Files

Tweezers, or 'corn-tongs' as they are still often called, are used for picking up smaller pieces, placing parts together, and generally for handling work in progress which cannot be so well handled with fingers. It is useful to have two or three pairs, including one pair especially kept for picking up gemstones, which will be necessary when making an article for which stones are provided. These differ from the general-purpose tweezers in that they are not so pointed and have lightly grooved holding surfaces to keep the stone from slipping.

Files are very important and a good selection must be kept by each worker. The indispensable ones are half-round, three-square (a name by which a triangular file is always known although it is not technically correct) and flat. Each of these is in the 'hand-file' size, approximately 6 in (15 cm) in length (the length of a file is the length of the blade, not including the tang) and supplied with a small wooden file handle. Varying grades of 'cut' are available from oo—very fine—to No. 4—very coarse—but usually one or two around the centre of the range are found sufficient for most purposes. Again, shapes and widths vary according to the makers and it then becomes a matter of choice, after practice, for the individual worker to decide which he prefers (Fig. 22).

'Needle' files, which are the small ones essential for the jeweller, vary considerably and a good wide selection is very important. The most usual ones are half-round, three-square, knife-edge, sage leaf (or double-half-round), and round, in varying cuts. These have a cutting surface of about 4 in (10 cm) and a plain round handle of slightly shorter length; a separate handle is not really necessary and most workers use them just as they are (Fig. 22).

Other Equipment

A piece of slate or a manufactured dish will be required for borax which is used as flux. It must in fairness be said that the old-fashioned piece of slate serves its purpose excellently and is still favoured by many. A lump of rough

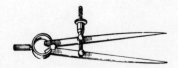

Fig. 23.   Dividers.

crystal borax is without doubt the most satisfactory type to use although borax cones and powdered borax are available. For jewellery, only small joints are usually to be soldered, and the flux used has also to be very fine indeed. With crystal borax rubbed on the wetted slate, this is produced to perfection and can be made to the thickness required very conveniently. A small bottle of water is obviously needed to provide the necessary fluid and must be readily to hand. Any bottle with a hole pierced in the screw top serves this purpose.

Together with these, each jeweller will find that he adds odd items as he progresses through apprenticeship. For example, he will find a spitz-stick useful for marking where drill holes are to be made. He will also provide a pair of dividers—about 4 in (10 cm) type—to mark out distances (Fig. 23), and a small ruler. One could go on naming the small items which are added to each man's tool kit, and find a place in his drawer under the bench, but the most important ones have been mentioned and the question of tools can be left there until it may be necessary to describe some of them and their uses more thoroughly when dealing with particular processes.

2. The Jeweller's Metals

The modern jeweller uses a fairly wide range of metals—or, more correctly, of precious metals—ranging from those in the platinum group to silver. Thanks to the efforts of research metallurgists, alloys having special qualities for different purposes are now available.

The jeweller who is constantly working with these various alloys gains by experience considerable knowledge of them and their working properties, how best to deal with them when soldering and performing other operations and (usually by a number of accidents in early training!) just how much heat they will safely bear. It is useful for some purposes and interesting to know, for instance, that platinum has a melting point of 1755° C (3190° F) and palladium about 200° C (390° F) less, but when the craftsman is actually heating them in the course of his work, he has no means of knowing just when a particular temperature has been reached. After gaining experience, however, he can judge by looking at his metals when heated and watching their colour how near to melting point the work is.

As this book is intended to be chiefly practical, much detail of the metallurgical properties of metals will be avoided, but some knowledge of the properties of metals and the uses to which they can be put is valuable.

The Platinum Group
The platinum group includes platinum, palladium and rhodium, together with lesser known metals such as iridium, ruthenium, and osmium. Only the first two are of importance to the manufacturing jeweller, although rhodium is used in a particular finishing process known as rhodium-plating. This will be mentioned when dealing with finishing; at the moment we are concerned with

the metals which the craftsman uses for fashioning.

Platinum is without doubt an ideal metal for jewellers. It has a fresh white colour which it always retains, being untarnishable and unaffected by the atmosphere and its contents. Having been highly polished, this metal will retain its finish to a very remarkable extent. Its colour and ability to resist tarnish make it the perfect metal for showing off to best advantage the gem-stones which are set in it. From the point of view of the working jeweller, it has everything in its favour as it does not oxidise when heated, and is thus easy to clean and to solder. It is very malleable, that is, capable of being moulded into various shapes without cracking, but is not so soft that it bends too easily and so has little strength. Add to this its very high melting point and it will be seen that this is indeed a perfect metal.

Platinum, as used in jewellery manufacture, is of an accepted standard of not less than 95 per cent pure, the usual grades being around 97 per cent pure. The remaining small percentage of the alloy is usually copper in platinum for jewellery manufacture, as this slightly improves the colour. For a harder metal, platinum is alloyed with iridium or rhodium.

Palladium

The other important metal in this group is palladium which is fast gaining favour and it indeed has many features which make it an important metal. One consideration is that its cost is very considerably less than platinum.

Palladium is a white metal, strongly resembling platinum in appearance and colour, though rather darker. It bears a very high polish and retains it well in the alloys now available, although it does not quite equal platinum in this respect. Anyone who is used to working with these metals can distin-guish, usually without very much difficulty, between the two. An easy test is to drop a spot of iodine on it; upon evaporation, a black stain will be pro-duced on palladium but not on platinum.

Commercial palladium is alloyed with gold, silver, nickel, copper, or combinations of them to produce the most effective working metal. From the jeweller's point of view, it is quite a good metal to use, being malleable almost to the same extent as platinum, but generally speaking it is harder. It does not have the capacity for resisting oxidation when heated as platinum and so needs a little different treatment when soldering.

Other Members of the Platinum Group

Very little mention need be made of rhodium as it takes no place in actual manufacturing processes; it is sufficient to say that it is a white metal closely resembling platinum but with a slightly yellowish tinge, and having a melting point even higher than platinum, approximately 1950° C (3540° F).

One peculiarity of some palladium alloys is that, when heated to a certain temperature (dull red), they oxidise; but beyond that temperature become white again. Palladium also has the power of absorbing gases to a considerable degree, especially hydrogen, even when solid. When molten, this takes place to an extent that causes the metal to spit when solidifying.

Platinum and palladium differ very greatly in their specific gravity, platinum being 21.4, which is very high. In fact, platinum ranks with the heaviest of all metals. Palladium in its pure state has a specific gravity of 11.3 which is but little more than one-half that of platinum. The great importance of this difference will be appreciated more in the notes on 22 carat gold that follow.

Gold and its Alloys

The different types and qualities of gold alloys in use to-day are quite remarkable: different shades of colour, different grades of hardness, and suitability for different purposes, together go to form an extremely wide range of alloys. The quality of gold, which is of great importance, is denoted by the carat mark and also expressed as a decimal quantity.

The origin of the word 'carat' is not clear but usually it is ascribed to a Greek word which is variously described as Karob, Keration, etc, this being the name of a seed which was used as a weight by the ancient Greeks. This word carat is used in America as well as on the Continent (though spelt karat there) and denotes the proportion of gold contained in an alloy. Pure gold is 24 carat, and thus 22 ct gold is 22 parts gold, 2 parts other metals; 18 ct gold is 18 parts gold and 6 parts other metals, and so on.

Legal Standards

It is quite possible to make an alloy of any carat from 1 to 24, but the standards used in this country are 9, 14, 18, and 22. Only these standards are legal and hallmarking is, of course, a guarantee required by British law that the gold has been assayed and contains the required proportion of pure gold. In Eire, the standards are 9, 12, 14, 18, 20 and 22.

The quality is also expressed as a decimal figure in the punchmark which is applied at the Assay Office to which articles are sent for the appropriate testing, and to be stamped officially according to their quality. Any articles sent to the Assay Office which do not reach the required standard, are broken up and returned as scrap.

Here is a table which gives the equivalent decimal expression of carat standards:

Carat	Parts Fine Gold	Alloy	Decimal Equivalent
24	24	0	1.0000
23	23	1	0.9583
22	22	2	0.9166
21	21	3	0.8750
20	20	4	0.8333
19	19	5	0.7916
18	18	6	0.7500
17	17	7	0.7083
16	16	8	0.6666
15	15	9	0.6350
14	14	10	0.5833
13	13	11	0.5416
12	12	12	0.5000
11	11	13	0.4583
10	10	14	0.4166
9	9	15	0.3750

Gold in its pure state (24 ct) has no place in manufacturing jewellery owing to its extreme softness and lack of strength. Any article made from pure gold would be quite unable to stand up to any wear, and would bend with moderate finger pressure. The highest quality in general use is 22 ct which is usually reserved for wedding ring manufacture. Even the addition of such a comparatively small proportion of other metals (in this case usually silver or copper, or both) has a very considerable effect on the hardness and workability of the gold, as will be seen when it is realised that pure gold is almost as soft as lead and 22 ct is very much harder, even though still comparatively soft to work with.

Weight and Cost
The addition of other metals also has a considerable effect on the specific gravity of gold. In its fine or pure state, gold has a specific gravity of 19.3, that is to say it weighs 19.3 times as much as an equal volume of water, and when alloyed with other metals (invariably of much lower specific gravity) this figure progressively decreases as the quantity of added metals increases.

This is an important factor when one considers that the price of an article is assessed partly by its weight and that 22 ct is, very roughly speaking, twice as heavy as 9 ct.

Gold of 22 ct is also more than twice the cost of 9 ct per oz troy, and one can see that the cost of two identical articles in those particular metals will be in the relation of approximately 4 to 1—a very considerable difference!

A very wide range of other metals is now used for alloying, according to the purpose for which the finished gold is required, and for what effect it may be wanted.

Colouring Effect

Within the past few years, progress has been made in the manufacture of jewellery articles of two or more colours, particularly in such articles as sleeve links, cigarette cases, and fancy bracelets. Most of these are of 9 ct gold, as such quality gives much greater scope to the bullion dealer in the addition of different coloured metals, there being 15 parts of alloying metals to only 9 parts of gold. Although such colouring effects are possible, there are other considerations, and such physical properties as hardness and malleability cannot be completely sacrificed to obtain the required colour.

The colouring is achieved mostly by the addition of silver and copper in varying proportions. For example, the addition of silver produces a paler alloy until a point is reached when about 60 per cent silver is added and the result is quite white and has the colour of silver itself. The addition of copper adds a reddish tinge, again according to the proportion added, until a 9 ct gold containing pure copper 15 parts and gold 9 parts would have a very reddish coppery appearance. Nickel has a very powerful whitening effect on gold and is used a great deal in the production of white golds.

It should be noted, however, that the colouring effects are only tints, apart from white gold, which can be truly stated to be 'white' in the sense that any metal is white, eg, platinum, silver and nickel. However the terms 'green' gold or 'red' gold do not strictly describe the colour which one could perhaps imagine from its name. To see the colours to advantage, one needs to have the metals alongside, as can be done in an article of two or three coloured golds.

For manufacturing purposes it is necessary to give to gold a greater hardness than it possesses in its pure state and to effect this, the metals which are added to it are blended to achieve the most workable result. It is rather interesting to note that the addition of silver alone hardens gold until a maximum hardness is reached at approximately 50 per cent of each. Beyond that, the alloy becomes softer until finally the softness of pure silver is reached. The hardest alloy that can be achieved by the addition only of copper and silver is of the proportion 50 per cent gold, 25 per cent silver, and 25 per cent copper. This proportion of metal would not be legally usable in the United Kingdom because it would be 12 ct, which is not acceptable for hallmarking.

Anyone now responsible for production, repairs and remounting of jewellery should contact the nearest Assay Office to obtain full details of the legality of precious metals because a new law came into force from January 1975 concerning the essentials of having items hallmarked. Other metals are also used to produce harder alloys and no doubt each refiner has his own particular secrets regarding the quantities added.

Working Qualities

So much for gold generally. Now just a little about the different standard golds that the manufacturer uses most.

Next to 22 ct comes 18 ct. Generally speaking, this is one of the best golds to work with. It has a good rich yellow colour, is soft enough to enable it to be moulded and shaped, has a high enough melting point to enable a variety of solders to be used and takes a good polish. It also has hard wearing qualities.

White gold has a remarkably good white colour, the hard varieties being capable of taking a wonderful polish, but is extremely hard to work with, and sometimes brittle.

Nine ct 'yellow' and other colours are suitable for most work, being malleable and usually a little harder than 18 ct, which allows them to be used in some cases where springiness is required. White gold of 9 ct varies very considerably in hardness according to its alloyed contents, the softest being almost the same as silver. Harder qualities take a much better polish but are not so satisfactory from the point of view of the setter who has to affix stones in them. Special alloys are made for articles which are to be enamelled, and there is no doubt that the already wide range of metals available can and will be extended to cover even more special purposes as time goes on.

Silver

Silver is a metal which is used for jewellery, but usually it is more strongly associated with the silversmith for production of larger articles, such as trophies, plate of various kinds, and high quality articles of utilitarian purposes, such as fruit bowls, cutlery and candlesticks. In the jewellery trade, it is used by manufacturers of small jewellery bearing imitation stones, or mass-produced articles of a much cheaper nature than the type of work which it is intended to deal with in these pages. Indeed, it may be said that the manufacture of this type of jewellery, often referred to as 'fashion jewellery', is quite a different proposition from that of precious jewellery, and is best left to those who specialise in it. Much of the gem-set jewellery of the Victorian era and a little earlier, was made in silver and backed with gold (and no one will doubt the craftsmanship shown in such pieces), but since the days when platinum became available, this practice has steadily declined.

From the point of view of colour, workability, and polish, silver is a metal which has much in its favour. It is quite soft, in fact rather too soft for many purposes in jewellery; if used alone, it is very light in weight having a specific gravity of only 10.5 as compared with 19.3 of fine gold. It is also very much cheaper than gold and other precious metals, which makes it a very good metal for the apprentice to try his first work on. One of its biggest disadvantages is its tendency to tarnish easily, especially in the sulphurous atmosphere of towns.

Precious Metal Substitutes

Regarding the substitutes for precious metals, little needs to be said here because, although rolled gold and gold fronted metals are used to a very great extent in cheaper jewellery of the mass-produced type and good class imitation jewellery, they again are only used in specialist manufacture, and take but little or no place in hand-made jewellery where individual articles or, at least, comparatively small numbers of articles of one pattern are produced. It will be realised that such items as spring-expanding bracelets, Milanese bracelets, etc of rolled gold are articles which have their own particular processes of manufacture.

In passing it may be remarked that the term 'rolled gold' ought not to be used as loosely as it usually is, for it should be applied only to metal which consists of gold of not less than 9 ct quality soldered or sweated to a base metal, and then rolled together simultaneously until the required thickness is reached. The term is often wrongly applied to gold applied by electro-deposition processes.

Solders

Solders of various qualities and having a widely differing range of melting points, are of the greatest importance to the jeweller who will have many joints to make in the construction of an article. Each joint must be strong and, in many instances, will need to be made with a solder which has a sufficiently high melting point to withstand the heat of subsequent soldering without falling apart. At the present time it is quite true to say that a solder for any purpose desired can be obtained from bullion dealers who, with their wide experience and constant research, have made such an extensive range possible. Gone are the days when a manufacturer had to make his own alloys according to his needs.

Quite satisfactory solders can be made in small quantities by varying mixtures of gold, silver, copper and zinc, but it is usually far more satisfactory for ordinary purposes to purchase them ready made. A practice which is probably still in use, and from which a useful guide may be formed, is that of adding a small quantity of silver to gold scrap of the carat quality which is to be soldered. This procedure lowers the melting point and gives a solder that will usually flow freely when melted, but whose carat quality will be slightly lower also. Usually the colour of the solder will be rather paler than the metal on which it is used.

The method usually recommended is to add 5 grains (0.324 g) of silver (fine silver, of course) to each pennyweight (24 grains, 1.6 g) of the gold. For example, if solder for 14 ct gold is required, then 5 grains of silver are added to each pennyweight of 14 ct gold scrap. The actual melting point will be dependent upon the composition of the gold used; that is to say, the proportion of gold and silver already used in the alloy, but the addition of fine silver as stated will undoubtedly lower its melting point sufficiently for the purpose required.

As a result of an order, issued by the Assay Office in 1909, to the effect that solders used on 9 and 15 ct gold articles submitted for hall-marking must be of the same carat quality as the article itself, zinc and cadmium, which have very low melting points, came into use as an additional alloying metal for lower quality solders. Generally speaking, solders for higher quality metals (eg, 18 ct and 22 ct) are of slightly lower quality than that of the gold for which they are intended.

White Gold Solders

The white golds used in this country are usually 18 ct and 9 ct quality and, as the alloys are usually composed of gold-nickel with small additions of silver and copper or of gold with palladium and other metals, special solders are prepared for them, usually from the same metals as the alloy, but in different proportions. These solders are more difficult to work with (and even more difficult to make, indeed it is an expert's job), owing to their contents. The whiteness is maintained by the use of nickel which not only has a high melting point but is also very brittle. Unless special treatment is given and careful alloying arranged, a very brittle and almost useless solder will result. Manufacturers of solders will, of course, have their own guarded secrets as to the manner of making good usable solders in varying white gold qualities.

Platinum Solders

Special solders for use on platinum are prepared by the refiners, and seldom does the craftsman or manufacturing jeweller attempt to make his own. Broadly speaking they contain platinum, palladium, gold, silver, copper and sometimes other metals in small quantities. Usually they are palladium alloys with melting points varying between 950° C and 1600° C (1742–2912° F), and it is generally only those with the higher melting points which contain platinum.

The colours of solders, particularly on platinum work, are important and the best colours usually result from solders made with varying proportions of platinum, gold and silver, or palladium, gold and silver. The amount of platinum or palladium is regulated according to the desired melting point. It is perhaps a rather remarkable fact that the deep yellow of gold quickly gives way to the white of platinum (or palladium) upon the addition of a comparatively small amount of the latter. For example, an alloy of 30 per cent of platinum and 70 per cent gold is only very slightly yellow, and an increase of platinum to 40 per cent, results in a metal (or solder) which has the colour of platinum. This applies even more in the case of palladium, where a mixture of only 20 to 30 per cent of palladium to the remaining 80 to 70 per cent of gold results in an almost white metal. It helps to explain what is often a puzzling factor, i.e. how such white metals result from varying alloys containing gold.

Copper in small quantities is usually present in platinum solders as it alloys readily with platinum or palladium and, as long as the amount of copper is kept below 10 per cent, the solder will not blacken on heating. So it will still retain that quality peculiar to platinum, that of staying clean and white while soldering, which is of very great help to the manufacturer or craftsman.

3. Techniques of Metal Working

The jeweller will always have to roll down sheet and wire to the thickness required for his particular job in hand, because it would be virtually impossible to carry a stock sufficiently large to make this unnecessary. Usually, the manufacturer will purchase his metals from the bullion dealers in various useful thicknesses, from which they can easily be rolled or drawn to exactly the size required.

Rolling is a fairly simple process, but one or two points might well be worth mentioning. Dealing firstly with sheet metal, the most important point is that it can be rolled only a very little each time it is put through the mills; any attempt to do the job quickly, by trying to reduce it, say, 0.01 to 0.015 in (0.25–0.38 mm) at each run through the mills, only results in hard pulling for the operator and excessive strain on the mills themselves.

It is understood, of course, that we are dealing only with hand-operated rolling mills of the normal type for workshop use. It is mostly a matter of judging how much thinner a piece of metal can be made each time by the size of the sheet being milled. Frequent annealing is necessary or the metal will become increasingly hard and many of the metals used may tend to split. It is advisable to anneal them after every three or four times through the rollers.

Another important point is to see that the surfaces of the rollers are quite parallel, otherwise the metal being rolled will be thicker one side than the other. With the type of mills which are adjusted for thickness by one central control adjustment (Fig. 24), this is quite easy as the rollers remain properly set, once adjusted, until subject to wear; but with the type which has two controls, one at each end of the actual rollers (Fig. 25), much more care has to be used.

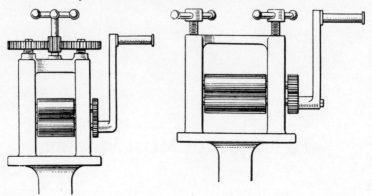

Fig. 24. Mills with central pressure control.

Fig. 25. Two pressure controls on a mill.

It is quite easy to see that mills are not properly adjusted if the metal comes through the rollers curved instead of straight (Fig. 26). The side towards which the metal is curving is the one which is being stretched more, and so spreading more. If metal is found to come through the rollers in a very uneven and irregular fashion, there is little doubt that the mills themselves need regrinding or some other drastic treatment (Fig. 27).

Milling down strip or metal which is needed to be a particular width as well as a particular thickness is usually done from square wire, and here practice alone can help one to know just how much the width of a piece of square wire will increase whilst being milled lengthwise. It does increase considerably, and the amount of width increase is regulated slightly by the amount of thickness reduction at each time through. For example, suppose that a piece of square wire is being milled down for a special width and is found to be not quite approaching the width needed. If it is annealed and then rolled considerably thinner in one squeeze through the mills, it will be found that the width increase is a little more. This means of gaining width is, however, very limited.

When rolling down square wire, particular care must be used to avoid 'burr' on the edges or corners of the wire due to milling down too quickly

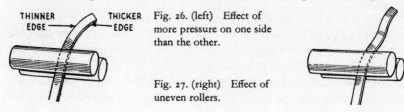

THINNER EDGE →   THICKER ← EDGE

Fig. 26. (left) Effect of more pressure on one side than the other.

Fig. 27. (right) Effect of uneven rollers.

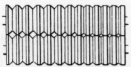

Fig. 28. The metal should eventually come out of the rollers as centre. At each pass, turn the metal through 90° so that the edges shown left and right in the centre sketch are top and bottom at the next pass. On the right is shown the effect of too much pressure.

(Fig. 28). If it should appear, it must be filed off before any further milling is attempted. The process of rolling down in the square mills is fairly simple and, provided one remembers to anneal the metal frequently and to turn the wire so that opposite corners are milled each time through, no difficulty should arise. When a piece of square wire is put through square mills, it will be roughly the shape shown in Fig. 28, which is exaggerated for clarity. On its next time through, it should be turned so that the two corners which were between the rollers are actually in the grooves of the rollers themselves. This will assist in avoiding 'burr'.

If metal is rolled with too great a reduction at one pass, the result will quite probably be as shown in Fig. 28, and it will be obvious that if any attempt were made to roll this back into the square wire, faulty metal would result, and probably disaster to the work for which it is intended.

Wire Drawing

Very little requires to be said about wire drawing as the draw-bench described in Chapter 1 was self-explanatory. The method of using a draw-plate affixed in the vice and a pair of hand draw-tongs is equally simple. In either case, once again, frequent annealing is important.

The wire to be drawn is first filed to a point at one end or, more exactly, just sufficiently tapered to allow the end to be put through the appropriate hole in the draw-plate (starting with the largest, of course). The end should protrude through the draw-plate just far enough for a good grip to be obtained with the tongs. It can then be pulled through. A little oil on the wire helps, and a steady even pull is much better than a snatch or jerky pull which is more likely to result in broken points or broken wire.

Soldering

Without doubt, soldering is the process used most of all in jewellery manufacture. Let it be understood at once that any reference to solder or soldering is to *hard* solder—that is to say, silver soldering, gold soldering, etc—which is quite different from soft soldering (i.e. lead soldering, or using other solders with very low melting points). Soft soldering has no place in jewellery

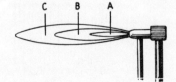

Fig. 29. Zones of the blowpipe
flame.

manufacture, except in a very few minor instances which need not be
mentioned here. To a greater extent, it is used in some kinds of jewellery
repairing, but even then only in cases where it is impossible to use hard
solder.

Soldering with a blow-pipe is a matter which needs practice and considerable experience for one to become efficient. See an experienced jeweller
doing this and notice how easy it appears. The solder runs just where it is
supposed to (allowing for the few exceptions, of course) and the whole
process seems effortless. But watch someone not used to it, and see the
difference! Work is often ruined by bad soldering. One must remember also
that with soldering, as with the other operations in jewellery manufacture,
there is no real short cut. Any amount of advice will not take the place of a
little actual experience, but nevertheless an understanding of the process can
help.

Whether produced by bellows or the mouth-operated blow-pipe, the
flame employed is similar and contains three distinct zones (Fig. 29). A
is a non-luminous core consisting of a mixture of air and unburnt combustible
gas. This core has a relatively low temperature. B is a luminous core composed of burning gases, and C is the outer core which is non-luminous and
free from combustible materials.

The outer core, which is sometimes known as the oxidising flame, will
rapidly tarnish or oxidise the metal, which is very detrimental to a good flow
of solder on to the surface of the metals which are being joined. The inner
core A has the lowest temperature and is equally unsuitable for soldering.

The greatest heat and cleanest flame are in the core B, particularly at its
outer point where it joins core C.

To ensure adhesion of two metals, several points must be observed.
Surfaces of the metals must be clean and remain clean during the heating
process (clean in this case meaning free from oxidation as well as from dust
and dirt generally). Also, the solder must remain clean.

A flux has to be used to satisfy the need for keeping the surfaces clean
throughout the heating. The flux used for jewellery is borax. As previously
mentioned, the rough crystal borax rubbed to a smooth-white cream on a
piece of slate wetted with water is the most suitable. Borax, in addition to

keeping surfaces free from oxidation, has a low melting point, becoming liquid when heated, which wets the surfaces and, as soon as the required heat is reached, assists the solder to run cleanly throughout the joint.

Both surfaces to be united must reach the temperature at which the solder will melt. It would be quite useless heating the solder only, or just one side of the joint.

Preparing the Joint

To enable this heat to be obtained, it is necessary that the surfaces to be soldered should be in such a position that the blow-pipe flame can be directed freely on to both sides and to the metal in close proximity to the joint.

The surfaces must be very close together—in other words, there must be no gaps between the surfaces that will need to be filled with solder—and all along the joint, surfaces must be touching. Surfaces must be clean and preferably filed to give both cleanness and just a little roughness to help the solder to adhere.

Just a smear of borax is needed and the joint is ready for the solder to be placed on it.

With jewellery it is invariably most satisfactory to cut the solder being used into small pieces, or 'paillons', of a suitable size, rather than to use the silversmith's way of having strip solder to hand and applying it to the heated joint. Only sufficient solder to fill the joint is required: to apply a large piece is only wasteful and messy, as it has to be filed off afterwards and serves no useful purpose. The tendency at first is always to use too much solder. Practice will of course tell how little to use. A small brush (a child's paint brush size) used for applying the borax to the joint can also be used to apply the solder as it will serve the dual purpose of applying borax to the solder and at the same time picking it up. The piece of solder can then easily be deposited on the joint.

Before beginning to blow with the blow-pipe flame on to the article, it is necessary to dry off the moisture from the borax slowly. This is best done by directing the flame—using a little air—on to the joint until the borax has become quite dry and white and then by steadily increasing the amount of air pressure and applying the hottest part of the flame already described. If the heat is applied too quickly, the borax will bubble and the paillons of solder will simply fall off. When the parts around the joint reach the appropriate heat, the flame can be directed on to the actual joint and solder a little more fiercely, and the solder will then melt and flow through the joint.

It is a matter of choice and expediency whether the soldering is carried out on the charcoal block or on the wire boss, or even while held in tweezers.

This will depend almost entirely on the job being done. For example, if a part is somewhat delicately balanced and it is necessary to keep it flat, then probably the charcoal block will be most suitable, but if it is a bigger item where the ends to be joined are quite securely in contact, such as a signet ring being joined at the back, then the binding-wire boss will serve best.

Again, where it is necessary to apply heat underneath an article to avoid overheating the part being soldered to it, use of the binding-wire boss may be most practical.

Applying the Heat

Take as an example soldering a safety catch on to a bar brooch. If one were to blow straight away on to the catch, it is easy to see that the catch would get so hot that it would melt very quickly while the bar brooch would only just be getting warm. It is imperative, therefore, to make sure that the bulkiest and most solid part be heated first and, when the melting point of the solder is nearly reached, a gentle blow on the more flimsy part will be sufficient to raise the temperature to the critical point (Fig. 30).

It is an advantage to be able to use the mouth blow-pipe in such a manner that will enable a continuous pressure to be maintained rather than a series of short puffs, and the better one is able to exercise the necessary control, the better also can one handle the more difficult jobs of soldering. To keep a constant flame one has to be able to breathe in while still blowing into the blow-pipe. At first this may sound quite impossible, but with practice it can be done, and when once the ability has been acquired one can go on maintaining a steady, continuous pressure for a considerable time. Breathe in deeply through the nostrils and then, filling the mouth to its full capacity and expanding the cheeks, close the back of the throat. With the mouth thus full of air, a steady blow can be regulated by the cheek muscles into the blow-pipe, while a fresh supply of air is being taken in via the nostrils. One can also release surplus air from the lungs via the nostrils while still maintaining the pressure from the mouth. It really amounts to using the mouth as a sort of reserve supply which is brought into use when it is necessary to take in a supply of air through the nostrils.

The great advantage of having this control over one's breathing is noticed particularly when soldering a delicate piece of work where it is necessary to localise the heat and do the soldering fairly quickly before the heat begins to spread too far around the job. If one has to keep stopping for breath, precious seconds are lost, in which the vital part loses heat and other parts receive it. This method of breathing is well worth practising until it can be done quite easily and almost without conscious effort.

Fig. 30.   Heat the bulk of the metal before the small catch.

Annealing Methods

Annealing is a process to which some attention should be given, because it affects the working properties of metals very greatly. Work can proceed much more satisfactorily with metals which are correctly annealed than with those which are under-annealed or over-annealed. The term simply means 'softening by heat', but different metals respond in different ways.

When a metal is heated, a change in its crystal structure takes place. The crystals from which the metal is formed, re-form themselves from the elongated crystals, which result from rolling, hammering, etc, into crystals more normal for that particular metal or alloy. Beyond a certain point the crystals increase in size and, if this is continued too far, the result will be a weakening of the metal without increasing its malleability, and a roughening of the surface will also become apparent.

A suitable temperature for annealing most gold alloys (excluding white golds) is in the region of 600° C (1110° F) and temperatures between 600° C and 650° C (1110–1200° F) cover most of the alloys used in jewellery manufacture. Figures, however, do not help very much under normal workshop conditions so it is more helpful to state that this temperature is represented by what might be described as a dull red heat.

The annealing should be regular and all parts reaching the same temperature. Over-annealing, that is, getting the metal too hot, is more harmful than under-annealing, especially if too high a temperature is reached in various patches. Nothing is to be gained by keeping a piece of metal at the annealing temperature for a length of time; it may, in fact, be harmful in some cases. It is sufficient to reach the appropriate temperature and then immediately remove the source of heat and allow the metal to cool.

An important point also is that as far as possible oxidation during the annealing should be avoided. Most gold alloys contain a varying proportion of copper, which is most susceptible to oxidation. If reasonable care is not taken, not only will the surface of the metal become oxidised, but the copper oxide will also tend to penetrate the metal, causing the large crystal grains to separate. This results in a film of oxide at the edges or 'surfaces' of the crystals and faulty metal will result during any further attempts to roll or bend the metal.

'Over-oxidation' may again be the result of overheating, and also may be caused by the use of the end of the flame furthest away from the blow-pipe (zone C in Fig. 29).

Gold alloys will always become surface-oxidised during heating with the blow-pipe, but this film is not necessarily injurious if it remains on the surface. It is not necessary to remove it by pickling before continuing to work with the metal.

It is advisable to quench metals of yellow gold alloys in cold water or pickle, rather than to allow them to cool slowly, but this should be done only with the metal at a lower temperature, which is best described as a 'black heat'. In other words, when all traces of red heat have faded away and there is, in fact, nothing in appearance to denote that the metal is hot.

If plunged into cold water (or pickle) at a high temperature, such as red heat, the metal may crack owing to the rapid contraction. This applies particularly to metals containing nickel or zinc (chiefly white gold). In fact, it can be broadly stated that white golds can wisely be left to cool slowly, while yellow (or red) golds are better quenched. It is very necessary to quench 18 ct yellow or red gold when it has cooled as far as black heat to get the best result of annealing. If allowed to cool slowly, it will form brittle compounds which separate during the cooling, causing brittleness in the metal.

Need for Pickling

Pickling is a term applied to the acid treatment of metal during manufacturing processes for the purpose of removing the coating of oxide produced by annealing and also for removing the borax which was used as a flux during soldering. When very large quantities of metal are dealt with, such as by refiners, special methods of annealing which keep the metal free from oxidation are used, and pickling is thereby rendered unnecessary. However during the manufacture of articles, when soldering has to be done in normal atmospheric conditions, oxidation is unavoidable. Considering also the presence of borax, it will be seen that pickling must be done at certain stages throughout the work. It is wise to avoid pickling unnecessarily as a certain amount of surface metal is lost each time, and one could say that, as a general principle, one should do as much work as possible to the job in hand before pickling.

The most usual pickle for workshop practice is made up of one part sulphuric acid (often known as oil of vitriol) to six parts of water. This strength is varied according to individual choice, but one may take the above as a good average. The solution is usually kept in a lead pot, or lead-lined vessel, and may be used hot or cold. If used cold, the container can be left in a convenient spot without having to make any arrangements for heating the solution within it; and if work in manufacture is dropped into the solution while still hot (only black-hot, of course), it will be cleaned immediately and can be removed and rinsed. The loss of water from evaporation will also be very much less if the pickling solution is kept cold instead of being constantly heated. Cold pickle is satisfactory on cold work, but the work will have to be left in the solution for a rather longer time before it becomes clean.

On the side of the heated pickle is the advantage that one can put cold work into it, and it will be cleaned much more quickly than by cold acid. This is even to greater advantage for work which bears precious stones, because such stones must not be put into pickle while they are hot under any circumstances. Many gemstones must not be pickled at all, but more about that at a later date; suffice it to say now that it is often necessary (particularly in the repair section) to pickle the stones as well as the article and, if put into hot pickle, they will be cleaned without delay.

Safety Precautions

A very important point about making up the pickling solution is that acid must be added to water, and not water to acid as a violent chemical action takes place, and the solution can easily boil. Unless care is taken, damage or personal injury may result. Pickle also has a very damaging effect on clothes, and any spots which may be splashed on to one's clothing usually result in a hole appearing there before long.

After work has been removed from the pickle, it must be thoroughly rinsed in clean water to remove all traces of acid and then dried by the most convenient method—*not* using towels. The best method of drying work is in boxwood sawdust which has been kept warm and dry in a bowl or other suitable container which should be placed over a hot-water urn or boiler, the urn thus serving a double purpose (Fig. 31). However a piece of cloth kept at hand will, if necessary, serve to dry work after rinsing. Incidentally the holes which soon appear in it will serve to stress the point mentioned, that this solution is damaging to clothes, because even after rinsing quite often, some acid will remain in crevices.

The solution must be changed at fairly frequent intervals as it would otherwise become overladen with copper which it has dissolved from the

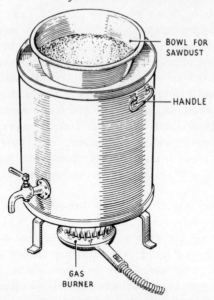

BOWL FOR
SAWDUST

HANDLE

GAS
BURNER

Fig. 31. A hot water urn, for washing work that has been pickled, is also used to warm the boxwood sawdust for drying.

surface of metals, and thereafter work would not be properly cleaned, but would come out from the pickle stained and patchy. This applies particularly to silver with which it will be found that, although the 'black' surface is removed, reddish (copper) stains will be left on the metal instead.

It might be mentioned here that pickle should not be thrown away, but should be watered down and washed through the filters where all other waste water goes as it will undoubtedly contain lemel which adheres to work, as well as particles of other metals which are taken up in the solution.

Buffing

The name 'buffing' applies to the process of sandpapering work to smooth it ready for the first processes of polishing. Quite often people refer to 'buffing' on a polishing lathe using one of the many types of mops which are required for the process. This, however, is not what is meant by 'buffing' in connection with the manufacture of jewellery. Sandpapering would perhaps be a more correct word to use, but we can just as simply use the old names which have been in the trade for many years.

When an article of jewellery is in its final stage as far as the mounter (or maker) is concerned, after filing up has been completed, surfaces must be made smoother and prepared for the 'crocusing' or preliminary polishing.

It is done firstly with sandpaper, No. 1 grade being the most satisfactory for general purposes. When necessary, this can be followed with emery paper, beginning with No. 1 and using finer grades as far as necessary according to the job in hand.

Two kinds of buff sticks are necessary, one being triangular with each side approximately $\frac{1}{2}$ in (12 mm) and just a little longer than the width of a sheet of sandpaper, and the other a round stick of about $\frac{7}{16}$ in (10 mm) diameter and the same length as the first.

A third can be added but is not essential—namely, a flat buff stick of about 1 in by $\frac{3}{16}$ in (25 × 4 mm). On these sticks the sandpaper buff is made. Buffs are a very important part of the equipment. Good work can easily be ruined by the buffing, and this failure can easily be contributed to by a badly-made buff.

The round buff is fairly easy to make and simply needs a little practice to get the sandpaper rolled very tightly round the stick. When this has been done, the roll can be bound in the centre with a few strands of binding wire.

The three-square buff (as it is generally known) is not quite so simple, and needs considerable practice to make, although it appears to be a perfectly simple matter. Starting with the sheet of sandpaper, cutting surface downwards on a flat bench, the edge of the buff stick is placed along the edge of the paper. A mark is scored along the sandpaper using the inside edge of the buff stick as a guide, and using a penknife or sharp-edged scraper to impress a line on the back of the sandpaper. This is to permit it to be folded so that the corners are kept sharp and angles accurate which is necessary to make efficient use of the buff stick into sharp angles of the work. Then the sandpaper and stick are turned so that the next face of the stick is resting on the sandpaper. Another line is scored, making sure that the stick is kept firmly in place. Again the stick and paper are turned together and the process continued until the sheet of sandpaper is used up. The centre is then secured with binding wire as with the round buff. When scoring along the edge of the stick, it should not be done so deeply that the paper tears through, but just deeply enough to make a sharp, clean angle. If this is done correctly the result should be a good, sharp-cornered triangular buff, very firm, and tight upon the stick (Fig. 32).

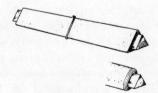

Fig. 32. (top) A correctly made buff.
(right) An incorrectly made one.

It can easily be seen now that each end of the buff (round or otherwise) can be used until the sandpaper has lost its surface, when the top layer can be removed leaving a fresh layer underneath and so on until the whole has been used. The importance of good, sharp corners and flat surfaces on a buff cannot be too strongly emphasised. It is not possible to keep work sharp and flat and corners accurate when buffing with a badly-made buff. After the filing up has been completed and carefully carried out, the same care *must* be used in buffing, to ensure that the same accuracy is maintained. On particularly fine work or sharp-cornered work, eg, a ring with step shoulders, it is always advisable to use fine emery paper until a perfectly smooth surface is obtained.

When doing small work on which it is not practical to use a buff of the dimension named, one has to improvise according to the need. For example, to sandpaper inside a small curve, a small piece of sandpaper can be cut and rolled round the handle of a needle file. Similarly, to buff small, neat corners, etc, a piece of sandpaper can be held on a three-square needle file, making, in effect, a small, three-square buff.

Discretion must, of course, be used as to how far fine buffing is carried out, according to the type and value of the work in hand. A point worth mentioning with regard to platinum work is that nothing is lost by spending a little extra time in buffing, even with super-fine emery, and making the work perfectly sharp, because platinum is a difficult metal to polish (although it takes and keeps an excellent finish). If the job in hand is worthy of being made in platinum, it is certainly worthy of the extra time needed in good buffing.

Filing

Only a few points need be mentioned here about filing, because without any doubt good and accurate use of files comes from practice and more practice.

To file a surface flat is not by any means as easy as it may sound. For example, to file a series of steps on the shoulders of a ring and have them finishing accurately angled with both sides alike and the proper size is a matter which depends upon good use of the files and wise choice as to which files are used. A very good result could not be expected after using a coarse-cut (say 'O' cut) file, and then trying to sandpaper from that stage. One must obviously use a much finer cut, probably a cut 2 or 3 needle file.

One of the major points with filing, whether it is with a hand file or needle file, is to keep it firm and rigid in the grip (Fig. 33). It is also important to ensure that the work which is being filed is quite firmly held. Taking as an example filing the top of a signet ring flat (or it could be filing the top of a

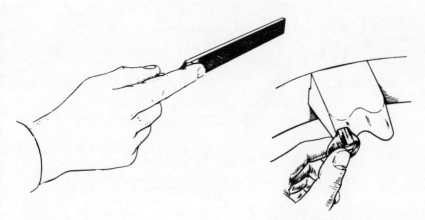

Fig. 33.   How to hold a file.

Fig. 34. Holding the work
against the board peg.

setting flat), there is always a tendency to file the side nearer to the worker
a little more heavily than its opposite side, or vice versa.

In moving the file backwards and forwards there is a tendency to raise and
lower the elbow and so alter the angle and pressure of the file. This has to
be cured to file accurately. Now a file cuts one way and that is on the 'pushing' stroke or when the file is crossing the work from its point to its handle.
When the file is returning, no pressure should be applied to it; in fact, it
should be lifted from the work, but it is usual and sufficient to allow the file
to return smoothly over the work whilst maintaining the same angle.

Full use should be made of the length of the file in use, employing not
little rapid strokes, but steady firm ones using a stroke as long as the file
will reasonably allow. The work is, of course, in the meantime held firmly
against the board peg in its most convenient place (Fig. 34).

Make each stroke deliberately, keeping the file with the handle firmly
gripped in the palm of the hand and the first finger placed along the upper
side. The file must be kept in one line with the forearm, not allowing it to
waver while in use, the wrist being kept firm. With practice one can achieve
the steady stroke necessary. It is a good idea, even after years of practice, to
turn the work round and file it from another direction, wherever this is
practicable, to ensure that the same amount is filed off from each side.

When using a large file, some craftsmen prefer to keep the thumb on top
of the handle as this tends to lock the wrist, which is sideways, and prevent
rocking of the file. This helps in the production of flat surfaces.

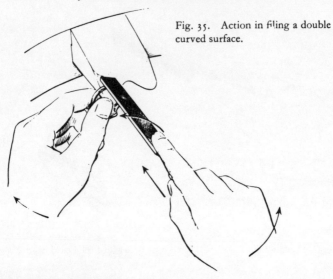

Fig. 35. Action in filing a double curved surface.

Filing Curved Surfaces

When filing a curved surface, the most important point again is smoothness and evenness of the filing action, plus having control over the movement of both file and work. In the case of a ring shank (the back part of the ring which encircles the finger), it is better to keep both the work and file moving smoothly to obtain an even curve and even roundness to the shank. The ring is held between thumb and finger, and at each file stroke gently turned in the opposite direction to the movement of the file, while the file, still kept rigidly in the hand, is used with a rolling and curving movement by turning the wrist gently while the file is moving forward on its cutting stroke. By doing this, bumps and unevenness are avoided (Fig. 35).

It is probably clearer now from the accompanying illustrations that a jeweller works against a bench peg because it permits free movement of the hands underneath the peg, whilst providing a stable and rigid place against which work can be held. The hand holding the work is thus not obstructed by the edge of the thick bench, as it would be if one tried to work directly upon it without the extension provided by the peg.

Filing inside a curve, as, for instance, inside a ring, is again best done with the file moving along the curve as well as across it. The curved surface of a half-round file will, of course, be the most suitable to use. In this case the ring is held slightly differently. The thumb and first finger are again used, but with one on each edge of the ring, and with the ring held in a different position on the peg (Fig. 36).

Doming

Doming, which in its strictest sense means making a domed (that is convex or concave) shape, is generally used to indicate shaping or fashioning of surfaces which are not to be left flat. The easiest of domed surfaces are those required for a circular cluster ring head or any similarly-shaped circle. This is done by using a doming die (or block) which is usually a cubic block of copper or sometimes mild steel, each face being about 2 in (50 mm) square, with a number of various-sized indentations or 'reversed domes' on each of its six faces.

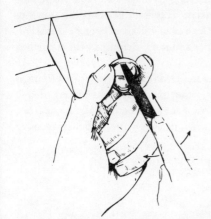

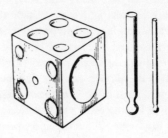

Fig. 36. (left)   Filing inside a concave surface.
Fig. 37. (above)   Doming block and punches.

In conjunction with this, a set of punches with spherical ends, also of various sizes, is used (Fig. 37). This, of course, makes simple doming easy. The circle of metal, previously annealed, is placed in a suitable dome and the punch of corresponding size placed on it and tapped with a hammer until the metal assumes the required shape. With other types of shaping, however, such as a flower shape, the doming block has only limited use, and a lead cake is used instead. This is a cake of lead about ¾ in (20 mm) thick, usually round and fairly flat. In this one can make almost any required shape or part of a shape. By using the various doming tools and punches one can slowly achieve the required design.

Taking as an example a flower, whose centre is sunken and whose petals curl outwards, it would first be necessary to lower the centre of the metal for the job by using one of the punches and the lead cake which is flat. Then, reversing the metal, each petal can be domed separately on the lead cake with a smaller punch of the appropriate size. After annealing, this can be repeated as far as is necessary, lowering the centre a little more and doming the petals more at each stage until the required shape is achieved.

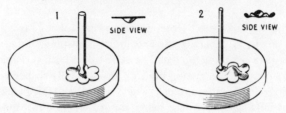

Fig. 38.   Stages in doming a flower shape on a lead cake.

The lead cake being very soft, it is quite easy to make a suitable shape in it before actually starting to shape the metal. This is done with the punches used for doming. The impression on the lead cake will soon become distorted, of course, and will have to be made deeper and more definite again at various stages in the shaping process (Fig. 38).

This is only one example, but shows a method that can be applied to most shapes. With more complicated designs, other methods have to be added—such as sawing out a small section to allow a shape to be partially made—but this can be detailed more appropriately when dealing with particular types of floral work.

4. Single Stone Rings

Having dealt with most of what may be described as 'general processes', that is, processes which do not apply to any particular type of work, it is now necessary to describe procedure and techniques for more particular items. One can truthfully say that each individual item, each type of ring or brooch, etc, demands its own special technique or method of manufacture, and it would be quite impossible to describe fully *every* possible item one might be called upon to make, for the simple reason that new designs are constantly being devised, and therefore methods have to be altered a little to deal with them in the most expedient manner. However, there are practices and methods applied to rings, for example, which could be utilised for any other ring of similar type. For example, a cluster ring, although its shape may be changed, still has to be made in a certain similar manner. For convenience, therefore, work will be divided as far as possible into groups or types, beginning with the different kinds of rings.

Each ring may be briefly described as having a head, which is the settings holding the stones, and a shank, which encircles the finger. There are several types of shanks and heads, each of which is interchangeable and so, for, convenience, I will deal with heads first, followed by shanks and finally methods of soldering the two together, in Chapter 6.

The simplest type of ring is that which is used as a simple mount for a fairly large (usually 'semi-precious') stone for a dress ring. It consists of a bezel, separate claws, usually four, six or eight soldered on the outside, and a shank (Fig. 39). To make this, the bezel (or collet as some prefer to call it) has first to be made.

There are several points to be considered, such as how deep and how thick must the metal be? For a stone of, say, $\frac{1}{2}$ in by $\frac{3}{8}$ in (12 × 10 mm) oval, 9 gauge is a good standard to use, this giving strength without being unduly heavy, and a little variation can be made according to whether the stone is large or small. The depth of the metal depends to a considerable extent on the depth of the stone to be mounted, the rule being that the culet (or point at the base of the stone) shall not protrude through the back of its setting, to prevent it from scratching the finger of the wearer. With a stone having a flat back, such as an opal or turquoise, this problem will not arise, and the only consideration then is the best proportionate depth for the size of the stone.

Continuing to use as an example an oval stone of $\frac{1}{2}$ in by $\frac{3}{8}$ in (12 × 10 mm) with a normal depth, metal of 7 lignes (4 mm) wide (1 inch = 40 lignes) should be sufficient. This would also be a suitable width if the base of the stone were flat, as it would give a well proportioned height to the setting. The term 'setting' simply means that part of the work which actually supports and holds the stone.

Making the Bezel

Now to the actual method of procedure. Having got the strip of metal to the dimensions decided upon, it must next be curved edgewise so that, when the bezel is made, the gap in it will be wider at the top than the bottom. This is not as difficult as at first may be thought if one sets about it in the right manner; if not, then the metal becomes wrinkled on its inner side of the curve and unsatisfactory to work with.

Fig. 39.   Parts of a finger ring.

Fig. 40.   Modified pliers.

Take a pair of half-round pliers and file a groove at the base of each jaw (Fig. 40), i.e. one curved and one flat face. This pair of grooves is very useful and does not render the pliers useless for other ordinary purposes if they are kept down to the base of the jaws. The metal is held edgewise in these two grooves in the left hand (assuming that the worker is right handed) and a pair of blunt 'flat points' (flat-nosed pliers) in the right hand can be used to pull the metal strips round into the desired curve. The 'flat points' must be kept right up as close as possible to the 'half rounds', in fact the points can

44

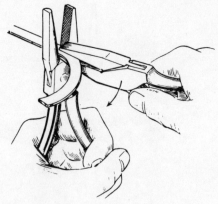

Fig. 41. (left)   Curving metal edgewise.

be actually between and touching the faces of the half rounds (Fig. 41). For most purposes, an arc with a diameter of about $1\frac{1}{4}$ in to $1\frac{1}{2}$ in (32–38 mm) (inside measurement) is a good standard to use.

Having made the arc, the metal must be annealed again and then it is ready for the bezel to be 'turned up'. This can be done with a pair of large round point pliers, or with 'half rounds'. One must judge how big to make the arc, bearing in mind that it cannot be turned up into a perfect shape at once, and after the joint has been soldered it will have to be corrected. This usually results in the bezel stretching a fraction, and an allowance must be made for this. When finished it must not show from the top when the stone is in position, and yet must be large enough for the claws, when soldered on, to fit nicely up to the edge of the stone without being pushed outwards first. The accompanying illustration (Fig. 42) will make this clear.

One may perhaps wonder why a setting should be made smaller at its base than at the top, and so perhaps at this point it would be wise to explain. Its major purpose is neatness on the finished article, and its other purposes are to emphasise the importance of the stone itself and to avoid unnecessary bulk and weight. It can be generally stated that with the normal types of ring, excluding 'cocktail' (or dress) rings and other asymmetrical types, a good guide is to imagine all the lines of the setting radiating from the centre of the circle formed by the inside of the bezel. There are many exceptions, of course,

A   B   C

Fig. 42.   (A) How the stone should fit in its setting. (B) Setting too small so that claws bend outwards. (C) Setting too large so that claws bend inwards.

Fig. 43. In the basic designs for rings, the lines radiate from an imaginary centre.
Left, single stone ring.
Right, five stone.

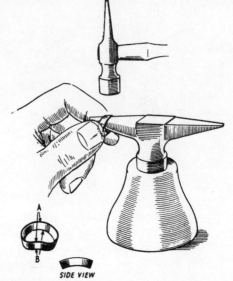

Fig. 44. (right) Tapping a bezel to shape on a sparrowhawk.

SIDE VIEW

but with the type of ring now being described, and three-stone half hoops, this can be accepted as a good guide (Fig. 43).

Having turned up the bezel and a good point made, the bezel must be soldered with the hardest solder that the metal of which it is made will stand, e.g., if 9 ct is used then hard 9 ct solder must be used, and so on. The final shaping and sizing is then done on a sparrow-hawk, a small anvil type of tool usually fixed in a wooden steady block (Fig. 44). Where necessary the bezel can also be made larger by hammering gently and evenly all round it on the sparrowhawk. While shaping up, another correction can be made. It will be noticed that the longer sides are raised upwards in the centre, this being due to the fact that the bezel is oval (if it were circular this would not be so, and top and bottom would be flat). As, however, a great deal of the necessary depth of the bezel would be lost if top and bottom were filed flat this must be corrected by tapping the longer sides of the bezel at the bottom thus stretching them just a little at the bottom only. In effect it reduces the original curve of the metal just in those two places. Then the top must be filed flat and any adjustments necessary must be made to ensure that the stone sits well on the bezel.

It is always a good plan, and helps to ensure a neater job, to file away the inner top of the bezel to make the metal thinner, and so drop the stone a little lower on to it. The outside can also be filed up at this stage and, after marking out where the claws are to be soldered, a small flat can be filed to enable each claw to be soldered securely.

Making the Claws

Next comes the making of the claws. The most satisfactory thickness is 8 gauge and the width about 4 or 5 lignes (2.5–3.2 mm) according to the number of claws to be used. This will be rolled down in a strip from square wire, and cut off into appropriate lengths, remembering always to leave sufficient length for the claws to be turned over the edge of the stone, and just that extra little fraction to allow for errors. This type of claw always looks much neater if tapered to about a half of its width towards the bottom. When soldering on the claws, always solder those at top and bottom of the oval first as these are the best guides as to whether they are accurately placed or not.

Claws can be held quite comfortably in tweezers whilst being soldered, a pair of tweezers being set aside for such purposes to avoid spoiling those used for general work. This method means soldering one claw at a time of course. There are methods of tying claws on with iron binding wire, and so doing all of them in one soldering operation. Craftsmen will develop their own pet methods of holding, but taken all round, the above-mentioned method is as good as any. An 'easier' solder than that used for soldering up the seam in the bezel can be used for the claws, but where possible it should be a medium solder rather than easy, as there is yet more soldering to be done, and there is a risk of the claws slipping.

When all the claws have been soldered on, the stone should again be tried into the setting and, if the work has been accurately done, it should fit snugly with the under facets of the stone resting on the inner top sides of the bezel, and with its edges touching the claws. The length of the claw can then be adjusted leaving about $\frac{1}{6}$ in (4 mm) of the claw above the edges or girdle of the stone. Where the base of the stone is flat, as with a cabochon cut garnet or turquoise, the top of the bezel will of course be exactly the same size as the base of the stone, and the claw must be left at an appropriate length proportionate to the height of the cabochon stone.

It can be seen that the result will be a perfectly plain claw setting, and it is no doubt fairly easy to see how a number of variations can be introduced. For instance, to give a little ornamentation and relieve the plainness, a wide saw-cut, or double saw-cut can be made in the bezel before the claws are soldered on, and effective yet simple patterns can be saw-pierced in the space between the claws (Fig. 45). The head then is ready to be soldered on to its shank.

Fig. 45. A saw cut (left) and simple designs on bezels between the claws.

Octagonal and 'Emerald Cut' Bezels

It is unnecessary to add anything about round stones, as they can be dealt with in exactly the same way throughout as described above. In fact, the shaping of the bezel and other parts is easier than for oval ones. Octagonal and rectangular stones are, however, rather different. Other odd shapes which may be met with can be dealt with in one or other of the following methods or perhaps a combination of them.

Dealing first with octagonal stones, we find that almost invariably the shape would be better described as rectangular with the corners removed or, in fact, what can broadly be referred to as 'Emerald cut'. The starting of the bezel is as for an oval one, but with the metal a gauge thicker, and instead of turning it up with large round-point pliers, it is better to use flat points. Then the four important sides can be kept straight and others will be simply rounded, instead of following the shape of the stone (Fig. 46).

Before soldering, the shape should be accurate enough for the stone to be placed on the bezel, and to give a good indication as to whether the size is correct. The same principles previously mentioned regarding size apply to all shapes. After making a good close joint, the bezel should be soldered, and then follows the correct shaping to fit the stone. This is done on the square end of the sparrowhawk (Fig. 47) and the corners should be dealt with first. By holding the bezel between thumb and finger of left hand,

Fig. 46. (above) The bezel is first made as for oval stones. Sides can be made flatter than shown.

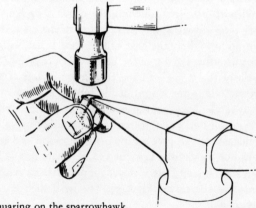

Fig. 47. Squaring on the sparrowhawk.

48

and tapping the 'small sides' or 'corner facets' with the hammer, they can be made quite sharp, and then the longer sides can be hammered as necessary to make them flat. Any stretching or adjusting for size can be done in the same manner.

It is almost certain that at the first attempt the shape will not be true and adjustments will have to be made, but nothing will remedy that except experience, and the more one handles and works with this type of setting, the greater becomes the degree of accuracy, and the quicker can a correct shape be made.

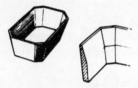

Fig. 48. The finished bezels showing how the inside is filed.

Having made the bezel as true as possible, it is ready for filing up. The top should be filed flat, then the outside filed up, starting with the four important sides and ending with the corners. It will be found here that a little more filing is required than with a simple shape and it is for this reason that the metal is a gauge thicker to begin with. After filing up the outside, it is very important to file the top of the bezel thinner (Fig. 48) and to make good, clean corners from the inside. This ensures that the stone can drop well into its setting. It should be emphasised that it is done from the *inside* and at the *top* only, as it is necessary to keep the bezel (or collet) strong and rigid while still allowing the stone to drop down, and to avoid ugly spaces between the inside of the claws and the stone as might happen if the metal was left thick at the top.

If any saw-cuts or saw-piercing are to be made on the bezel, they will have to be done at this stage, and the claws soldered on afterwards. It is usual with settings of this shape to have four claws only, one at each corner. The proportions and method of soldering on the claws is the *same* for all types and it is therefore not necessary to repeat them here.

Unique Qualities of Each Stone

It may seem at first that this method of making an octagonal bezel is very haphazard and one may wonder why a more accurate and perhaps mechanical method is not devised whereby all corners are made at the correct angle, and each side carefully measured to ensure that the bezel is correct as soon as it is turned up and soldered. There are, however, many factors which differ in each stone, for example, the depth, and the angle at which the facets on the

49

Fig. 49.   Strip for a rectangular setting.

Fig. 50.   Three corners are soldered before the fourth is completed.

base of the stone are cut, and these make it impracticable to apply any rigid rule. In addition to this, one has to remember that the time factor is important and time cannot be spent unnecessarily over such a job. Therefore, the method described is without doubt the most satisfactory. The hands soon become accustomed to shaping the metal, and using the tools to best advantage, and the eye becomes discerning and can recognise inaccuracies very quickly. All these things, of course, add up to the skill of the craftsman.

Square or rectangular settings are treated rather differently, for in these, angles of 90 degrees have to be made as opposed to angles of 45 degrees on the octagonal types and, while the small angles can be made satisfactorily by hammering on the sparrowhawk, the larger ones cannot be made sharply enough. There are two methods of doing this. In the first method one can have the strip of metal the same thickness and curved edgewise as before but about 1 ligne (0.64 mm) deeper. The end of the strip of metal is filed or chamfered off to an angle of 45 degrees and the length of the stone is measured with the dividers, not along its girdle but just below, in fact, where the top of the bezel is to reach when finished. The distance is marked off along the top edge of the strip: that is to say, the outer side of the curve, and a deep groove filed in the strip at this point, about two-thirds of the way through is most practical. This is best done with a three-square file, keeping the actual groove with its angle as near as possible to 90 degrees.

The width of the stone is measured with the dividers at the same depth below the girdle, and this is again marked off along the top edge of the strip, where another groove is filed as before. Another length as the first one, and the width repeated afterwards will give the four sides of the bezel, which is now ready to be turned up (Fig. 49). As soon as this has been done it must be soldered in all the three corners (Fig. 50). It should be reasonably accurate, but in any case it is wise to solder it before attempting to remedy inaccuracies as the corners will break through if bent about too much, and much time may be wasted in trying to repair the damage. A good joint can then be made at the fourth corner, correcting as far as possible any slight error in shaping, and this joint is then soldered to complete the rectangle. If necessary, the sides can be adjusted by hammering on the sparrowhawk.

One big fault with this method is that one must waste considerable depth in filing the top and bottom flat. Hammering on the bottom of each side on the sparrowhawk and so reducing the curvature will help to lessen this waste a little, but it cannot be entirely eliminated. That is the reason for allowing the extra 1 ligne (0.64 mm) in depth of the strip metal when making a bezel by this method. When the shape has been corrected and the size adjusted if necessary, the top is filed flat. The sides are made thinner by filing from the inside only, as before, to allow the stone to drop as far into the bezel as possible.

Another Method of Shaping Square Bezels

The second method of dealing with this shape is as follows: the strip of metal has the same proportions as for other types, varying only as necessary for the depth of the stone being mounted. This time, however, it is not curved edgewise but is kept straight (Fig. 51). The end is filed off to 45 degrees and the four sides measured off as before, the corners grooved and the collet turned up and soldered (Fig. 52). The result will be a straight-sided bezel instead of one smaller at the bottom than the top. This, of course, looks ugly and is quite wrong, but the bezel has to be altered more before claws are soldered on.

With the bezel held base upwards in a pair of flat-nosed pliers, a V-shaped section is cut with the saw from each corner, taking care that the same amount is cut from each side. This V should extend approximately three-quarters of the depth of the bezel. (In practice it will be found that only a narrow V is necessary to make a good shape (Fig. 53).)

When all four corners have been so cut, they should be filed clean with a knife-edged needle file and each side pulled in at the bottom, thus closing up the V-shaped corners and making the bezel the desired shape (Fig. 54). After soldering up the corners again, the bezel can, if necessary, be hammered on the sparrowhawk to make any adjustments of shape or size. The advantage here will be seen at once, that there is no wastage of depth in making the

Fig. 51. (above left)   Straight strip for a rectangular setting.
Fig. 52. (centre)   Corners soldered.
Fig. 53. (above right)   Corners sawn off.
Fig. 54. (left)   Corners closed and soldered.

top and bottom flat. From this point, the setting can be continued as with other shapes previously described. It is usual to put two claws on each long side of a rectangular setting and one on each short side.

When the claws have been soldered on, the stone should fit into the setting with claws straight, neither bent in or out, and with the bezel itself not seen from the top. These two points apply in all cases. A further point which should be mentioned here is that it is not necessary to file the bottom of this type of setting flat. When the shank has been soldered on, the bottom will have to be filed out to fit to the shape of the finger in any case, and a good rule is that the less one files anything the better it is, so that this can safely be left until a later stage.

Setting Big Gemstones

Quite often stones of much greater dimensions than the ones mentioned so far have to be mounted; stones of greater size usually having correspondingly greater width and depth. The amethyst is often found in fairly large crystals of good quality and is a favourite gem for a very large dress ring. The methods already described are not really suitable for such large stones. The greater value of a good quality large specimen warrants extra expenditure on the mount and, regardless of shape, it is better to use an entirely different method from those so far described. Whereas one bezel has so far been used, two or even three are used for the larger stone.

A piece of square wire of about $\frac{3}{32}$ in (2.4 mm) thick is milled down just a little to make it oblong so that its thickness is about half its width. (Remember that its width increases a little when rolled down.) From this a bezel is turned up to suit the shape of the stone, fitting below the girdle as with smaller stones. This can be done in the case of rectangular stones by cutting in the corners with a three-square file, and even with octagonal ones it makes the corners much sharper and cleaner to do so (Fig. 55). The bezel is shaped to fit correctly after soldering the corners by hammering on the sparrowhawk just as before. When the desired shape has been obtained, the inner side of the bezel is carefully filed out at the top only, making the sides very steeply angular inside, and making the top edges as thin as practicable. The bottom is left at its original thickness (Fig. 56). The outside need not be filed up at this stage.

Fig. 55. (left)   Setting for very large stones.
Fig. 56. (right)   Inside edges filed.

Fig. 57. Swaging block.

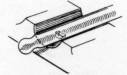

Fig. 58. Curving a bezel.

A second bezel is then turned up from similar thickness metal, but considerably smaller. The difference in size between these two can only be judged, but it should be borne in mind that the under bezel will be separated from the top bezel by sufficient depth to stop the stone from protruding through the finished setting; therefore, the depth of the stone must be considered when judging the size of the under bezel. It will be remembered that the general principles governing the angle of the sides and fitting of claws, etc, apply equally in this type. It follows, therefore, that all these points have to be borne in mind and that no specific proportions or rigid rules can be laid down.

The second bezel can be made by the same method as that adopted for the first, and then after it has been completed, it must be curved or 'swaged' to the appropriate shape for the finger-size to which the ring is to be made. This is best done by using a swaging block, which is a steel block of about 6 in by 1 in by 1 in (15.2 × 2.5 × 2.5 cm) into which a series of different sized semi-circular grooves have been cut, beginning with one of approximately 1 in (25 mm) diameter down to ⅛ in (3 mm) in diameter (Fig. 57). A series of round rods of different sizes are used with this, in fact the stem of the doming punches will suit the purpose admirably. The under bezel is placed in one of the grooves with the appropriate curve and the doming punch, used horizontally, is placed across it, and by tapping the punch with the hammer, the bezel will follow the shape of the groove (Fig. 58). The two bezels are now ready for the next stage which is to fix them the proper distance apart.

Joining the Two Bezels

Having made both top and bottom bezels as already described (Fig. 59) they are now ready to be fixed at the appropriate distance apart to complete the main framework of the setting.

The only guide to the space between them is the depth of the stone; the stone should be placed on the top bezel and the distance that it protrudes through should be measured with the dividers. From this it is quite easy to see how thick the block must be which divides the bezels. In practice, it is

Fig. 59. (left) Top and bottom bezels ready for joining.
Fig. 60. (right) Blocks which divide top and bottom bezels.

found best to have one block each end, that is to say, in the centre of the short side (Fig. 60). The block should be fairly substantial, approximately 18 to 20 gauge thick, and considerably longer than may at first glance seem necessary. It must be remembered that the top bezel is larger than the bottom, therefore the top bezel, when soldered on to the blocks (assuming that they have been soldered to the bottom one first), will extend outwards along each block much further than one might judge, and this has to be allowed for. Surplus metal of the blocks both inside and outside can easily be removed with the saw when both bezels have been soldered together.

To solder these blocks on to the underside of the top bezel or the top side of the curved under bezel (it is immaterial which) is not simple if one attempts simply to place them in their position and solder them, as they are almost certain to slide round when the solder melts, and it is even more difficult to try to push them back again.

While mentioning the point that small pieces, such as we are now dealing with, are apt to slide round when being soldered, it is interesting to know why this should happen. The tendency always is for solder, when actually liquid, to flow along the surface of the metal and when two surfaces are being soldered crosswise, the solder will try to spread in both directions along both surfaces, and in so doing will tend to draw the two surfaces parallel so that the largest possible area of both surfaces is in contact. Because of this, it is always advisable to avoid soldering in this manner.

It is not difficult to remedy the trouble. It can be done simply by making a shallow joint, gapping one piece into the other just sufficiently to hold the block steady. In the instance which I am describing, the best plan is to gap the centre of the bezel to which the block is being soldered with the edge of the gapping file, making the gap wide enough for the block to fit tightly (Fig. 61). It can then be squeezed into position and soldered without difficulty. After this, the two bezels are soldered together, care being taken to get them accurately placed, sides parallel, etc (Fig. 62). Usually it is better to tie them together with iron binding wire than to hold them in tweezers or to try to balance them on the charcoal block.

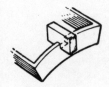

Fig. 61. (left) Block fits into rebate to stop it twisting when being soldered.
Fig. 62. (right) Soft iron wire (A) holds the parts together when soldering the top bezel.

The next step is to file up the two bezels together and make them ready to solder on the claws. This can be done as previously described with other types. It will be realised that in this setting as far as we have gone there is little more than a framework with a great deal of open space. If the work has to be kept low in cost and weight, then this is an advantage, but usually a stone of the size being dealt with will justify a little extra cost on the mount, and various designs can be used to ornament the many spaces.

Additional Decoration between the Bezels

Taking as a standard example an octagonal stone with claws placed on each side of the corner facets (Fig. 63), there are the fairly large spaces on each end between the block and claws, and the whole of the longer sides will be completely empty. There is room in each of these to put scrolls, bars or combinations of both, or various ornamental shapes (Fig. 64), to make the setting far more attractive and pleasing.

To make these shapes, fairly thin wire in strips is milled down—5 gauge is sufficient even for large work, and for finer work the thickness must be reduced accordingly, or it is difficult to make small shapes neatly. The width should be a little more than the thickness of the gold used for turning up the bezels, because some allowance must be made for filing up when the ornamentation is complete, as well as to allow for slight errors when fitting

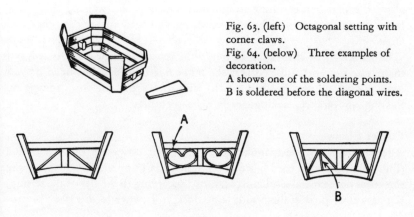

Fig. 63. (left) Octagonal setting with corner claws.
Fig. 64. (below) Three examples of decoration.
A shows one of the soldering points.
B is soldered before the diagonal wires.

Fig. 65. (left) Tapering the
ornaments speeds up the work.
Fig. 66. (right) Rectangular setting
with open corners.

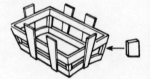

in the scrolls, etc. The shapes are turned up with fine round-pointed pliers and fitted into the spaces. A very useful hint when fitting in pieces of this kind, is to file just a little off the side which is being inserted first, at the top and bottom, making the piece very slightly wedge-shaped (Fig. 65).

In the case of rectangular settings, where the claws are placed on the sides of the collet leaving the corners open (see Fig. 66), it is always advisable to solder a block in each corner before soldering on the claws (Fig. 66), not only for strength but also for appearance. Fitting these in can best be done by taking a strip of metal, fairly thick for large stones (e.g., 16 gauge), just a fraction wider than the depth of the space at the corner, and tapering the end of the strip sufficiently to allow it to be pushed into the corner of the collet. Then a piece can be cut off the end of the strip, a little longer than is actually required, and this piece pushed into one corner to form the block or support and soldered into position.

After each corner has been dealt with in similar fashion, the surplus can be filed off both inside and outside, and any other ornamentation added as required. In practice, two corner blocks can be soldered at one time, one on either side of the original centre block, but it is hardly worth trying to solder all four corners together because after one has been placed into position, when another on the same side of the centre block is pushed in, it will probably open the space between the top and bottom bezels just a fraction and allow the first corner block to fall out, which is just wasting time. It is better to solder two and be sure of them, and then solder the other two afterwards.

Other scrolls or shapes can be put in the remaining spaces as desired, but there is no doubt that the corners should be filled. Corners left open do not look good, and the finished article will always present that 'something missing' appearance, lacking clearly defined corners.

Corner Claws

Alternatively, with rectangular settings, corner claws are often favoured (Fig. 67) and can be used whether the stone is large or small. Obviously the thickness of the metal used must be varied according to the size of the setting, but as we are now dealing with large ones, it is better to describe the pro-

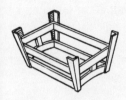

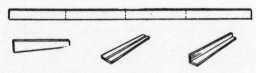

Fig. 67. Corner claws.

Fig. 68. (top)   Strip for four claws.
Fig. 69. (above left)   Claw tapered: the ends still have to be trued.
Fig. 70. (centre)   Claw grooved.
Fig. 71. (above right)   Finished claw.

cedure for making the claws as applicable in this case.

A strip of metal of 8 gauge thickness is required. The width must be sufficient for the finished claws to extend from the corner to about one-sixth of the width and length of the stone; in other words, approximately one-sixth of the length plus width. Actually there is no need to make a mathematical problem of this as one is guided mostly by good proportions, added to necessary strength, but the above will give a good indication of what can be accepted as a general standard.

Having milled down the strip of metal, the length of each claw is marked off and cut (Fig. 68). Each claw is then tapered to about half its width at the bottom (Fig. 69) and a groove filed lengthwise down its centre, preferably with a three-square needle file, and about one-half to three-quarters through its thickness (Fig. 70). Each claw can then be bent quite easily with two pairs of pliers, along the groove, to form a right-angled claw (Fig. 71). It is always wise, however, before doing this to buff along the inner surface of the claw so that it will be clean and ready for soldering on to the collet immediately after forming it into a right angle. There is no need to solder along the angle as the solder will run along there when the claw is soldered on to the collet.

When soldering on claws, one at a time is the most satisfactory way and ultimately the quickest. It is best done by holding the bezel in a pair of tweezers in the left hand, the tweezers holding the block dividing the

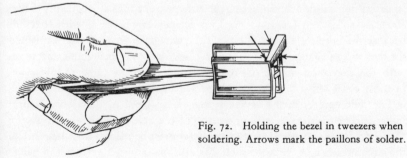

Fig. 72.   Holding the bezel in tweezers when soldering. Arrows mark the paillons of solder.

bezels. With the claw placed in position with small paillons of solder along each edge, it can be held quite steadily while the blow-pipe flame is directed on to it.

When all four corner claws have been soldered on, the stone should fit accurately just as well as when the claws are soldered on to the sides, that is to say that the girdle of the stone should touch all the claws on all sides, the sides of the base of the stone should rest on the collet and all claws should be straight, bent neither inward nor outwards (Fig. 73). The top of the claws can be then filed off until the required amount for setting is left above the stone. In the case of corner claws, not quite so much is needed as with side claws, as it is not possible to push so much metal over the stone in this

Fig. 73. Correct fitting of the stone in a claw setting.

case. That does not in any way lessen the security of the stone; in fact in many ways the corner claws are an advantage. Firstly, being angled they are less likely to be bent outwards during wear when the wearer accidentally knocks the ring against something. Secondly, the total width of the claw is in most cases more than that of side claws. A further advantage is that they tend to offer more protection to the corners of the stone itself. It is at the corners that chips most often occur.

A very wide variety of claw settings of this type have now been dealt with and it is fairly certain that, by interchanging any of the methods mentioned, almost any stone of the dress ring or fancy large type can be covered. There are other types of claw settings which will be dealt with in due course; meanwhile I shall continue to deal with larger stones to go on to the millegrain or plain edge setting.

Millegrain or Plain Edge Settings
In describing the millegrain setting of the average type of stone, that is to say, about $\frac{1}{2}$ in by $\frac{3}{8}$ in (12 × 10 mm), all shapes can be dealt with together because the bezels are made in exactly the same fashion as already explained for the various shapes, that is square, rectangular, oval, octagonal, and so on with the exception of the flat-backed stones, such as cameos, turquoise, possibly opals and a few others. These will be dealt with separately.

The difference is in the actual fitting of the bezel to the stone. With a millegrain or plain edge setting, the top of the bezel itself is used to secure the stone; it follows therefore that the bezel must be made a little larger than the circumference of the stone itself. Metal of the same gauge (that is, 9 gauge

Fig. 74. Bezel for millegrain setting.

or a little more or less according to the variety in size of the stone being mounted) is suitable, and the bezel should still be made larger at the top than the bottom by the means already described. A good guide as to the size of the bezel is that the stone's girdle should just rest on the inner edge of the top of the bezel, thus leaving the thickness of the metal showing all round the edge of the stone (Fig. 74).

Discretion must be used as to how much the sides of the setting should be tapered, bearing in mind how deep the stone is, and how deeply tapered its underside facets are. There are some exceptional cases where a stone has a very thick girdle and its side facets taper very little. Here the setting made to hold it must have almost straight sides. Generally speaking, however, the amount of taper described for claw settings is suitable in ordinary cases. The actual depth of the bezel must be governed by the depth of the stone, remembering that a stone should not protrude through the back of its setting on to the finger of its wearer.

Care must be taken to avoid the ugly plain look of a setting of this type because the very fact that the bezel is deeper than for claw settings will show that there is more metal to be ornamented than with the claw settings, and without the relief from plainness that even claws offer. Designs can be saw-pierced as mentioned before, but a very important factor is to ensure that the finished setting has sufficient strength to enable the setter to secure the stone without bending the mounting in the process.

There is no doubt that this type of setting is by no means as attractive or satisfactory, from any point of view, as the claw type, but there are, however, occasions when it is demanded.

Flat Backed Stones

When making settings for opals, cameos, large turquoises, or cabochon cut garnets which usually have flat backs, it is better to make the mount a little different from the type explained previously. The same type *could* be used but is not very satisfactory for several reasons. The first among these is that very little opportunity for relieving the plainness of the bezel is given; to do so would weaken it considerably. Secondly it makes a much longer job for the setter who will actually secure the stone in its setting, as he will have a lot more cutting away to do to fit in the stone. More about that later.

The better way to mount these stones is to build up the setting in parts,

Fig. 75. (left)   Rim bezel.   Fig. 76. (centre)   Flat bezel.   Fig. 77. (right)   Bezel
completed.

commencing by making a shallow bezel into which the stone will fit (Fig. 75).
A strip of metal approximately 5 lignes (3.2 mm) deep (varying, more or
less, according to the depth of the cabochon cut top of the stone) and 5 gauge
thick is turned up with straight sides, not tapering to the bottom or 'tucked
under', to use the familiar phrase, as before.

After the joint has been soldered with the hardest solder which the metal
in use will take, it is carefully adjusted for size and shape, on the sparrowhawk if necessary, until the stone will fit into it fairly tightly but not so
tightly that damage to the stone is likely. (Remember that we are dealing with
rather delicate stones if they are opals or cameos.) It must fit closely all round,
and with no spaces between the edge of the stone and the bezel. Actually it
should be possible to push the stone through the setting because the sides are
parallel.

The next stage is to turn up another bezel (Fig. 76). This is made from very
thin square wire, about 14 gauge, which has been rolled down to 10 gauge
one way, thus making it rectangular in section. It is curved edgewise to form
a flat rim which will fit tightly into the setting already made. Turning up
edgewise can be done by utilising the grooves in the faces of the half-round
pliers and using them in conjunction with a pair of flat points as previously
described and illustrated (Figs. 40 and 41, above). The joint of this second
bezel has to be soldered, and the bezel made perfectly flat and correctly
shaped to fit tightly into the other part.

The outer edge must be filed clean, as must also the inner surface of the
first bezel, to ensure that the solder will run cleanly. Having attended to these
two very important points, the inner bezel should be soldered into place at
the bottom of the first setting, both bottom edges being level. We now have a
shallow box into which the stone should fit comfortably (Fig. 77).

The depth of the setting can now be adjusted to leave the required depth
for securing the stone. It is not possible to give any definite rule as to what
this depth must be but it will be obvious that the height of the stone is the
deciding factor. One might say that the top of the setting must reach a
point where the stone is appreciably smaller than its base, but it must be

Fig. 78. Relationship of bezel and stone sizes.

remembered also that the edge of this setting eventually has to be pushed on to the stone, so it will be easily understood that, if the setting is left too high, this would not be possible without the edges of the setting wrinkling. The illustration (Fig. 78) will probably help to give a better indication of the required depth.

Making the Under Bezel
The first part of the setting is now complete and ready for the next stage. Here there are at least two alternatives. One is to make an under bezel of square wire (or slightly rectangular wire) a little smaller than the base of the setting and swage it to finger shape, etc (Fig. 79), in a similar manner to that described for large claw settings, proceeding as before with blocks to divide the parts and then filling in with ornamentation as desired. The other alternative is to make an under bezel by taking a strip of metal, 9 gauge thick by about 5 lignes deep (3.2 mm), and curving it edgewise, so that a tapering bezel may be bent up from it. This must be turned up so that the top is a little smaller than the base of the upper setting. When the joint in this has been soldered, and its shape corrected as necessary, the top must be filed flat in preparation for the two bezels to be soldered at the proper distance apart. In this case the space between the two need be only very little, as there is no depth of stone to be considered; the only reason that depth is required is to make the finished setting well proportioned and to stand sufficiently high from the finger to give the stone its proper importance.

We are now at the stage shown in Fig. 80, where we have the upper setting completed, the under bezel prepared and are ready to carry on to the next stage. It will be noticed, in this instance, that the height of the space

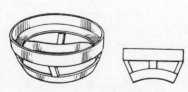

Fig. 80. Upper setting and under bezel completed.

Fig. 79. Under bezel swaged.

61

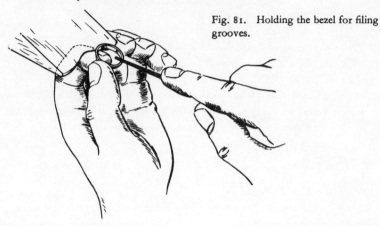

Fig. 81. Holding the bezel for filing grooves.

between these two parts will be equal at all points, because the bottom of the upper part and the top of the lower part are both flat. In the other alternative dealt with, the bottom bezel is curved to fit to the shape of the finger, thus making the depth of space between the two parts greater at the sides than at the ends. When this space is the same all round, the job of providing blocks or other supports is made considerably easier, and a very good way is as follows; cut short lengths of round wire, about 14 gauge, just a little longer than is actually required. In practice ⅛ in (3 mm) is usually suitable, and eight pieces are a good number to use. Then take the bottom bezel and make shallow depressions with the end of a round needle file, to enable these pieces of round wire to be placed in them all pointing toward the centre. The most appropriate points at which to place these is usually one top and bottom, one in the centre of each side and then one in between each of these.

It is not necessary to set about marking these out by any mechanical means. The eye is sufficient guide to their accuracy. The bezel can be held securely in the left hand between thumb and finger, against the bench pin (Fig. 81) and the top and bottom points marked lightly first, followed by those in the centre of the long sides. The other four can be marked in between, and it will be found that corrections can be made where necessary when filing the depressions (or 'grooves') a little deeper.

The depth of these need be only very little, sufficient simply to keep the small lengths of round wire in place while they are being soldered. Having done this, place the bezel on the charcoal block, and moisten the grooves where the pieces are to be soldered with just a little borax cream using a brush. Then place one piece of wire into each with the tweezers and apply a small paillon of solder to each side of each wire (Fig. 82).

Fig. 82. (left)   Wires in place ready for soldering.
Fig. 83. (right)   Bottom bezel on top, for soldering.

The normal procedure for soldering can be followed. It is best to use a *medium* solder for this, as it will not be necessary to get the parts hot enough to cause any difficulty at the later stages of manufacturing this type of ring, therefore a hard solder is not necessary. Nevertheless, there are still a considerable number of soldering operations to be done and it is better not to use an easy solder at this stage of the job.

When the small pieces of wire are soldered in place, the surplus length of each one can be cut off from the inside with the saw. The outside should not be dealt with at this stage, but left until top and bottom sections are soldered together. With a flat file gently file across the top of the eight pieces just sufficient to make them all level with each other and just a little flattened on top.

The two parts are now ready to be soldered together. To do this one can tie them together with binding wire in a manner similar to that already described (see Fig. 62, above) or in this case they can satisfactorily be placed on the charcoal block. The top bezel should be placed upside down and the bottom bezel (also upside down of course) placed correctly on top (Fig. 83). When it is in position, a small paillon of solder can be placed on either side of each of the eight dividing pieces and after carefully drying off the borax, they can be soldered in the usual manner. It should be apparent that the reason for putting these parts on the charcoal upside down is so that one can more easily see when the bottom part is correctly placed on to the top part by looking down on to it. It is much easier to place the paillons of solder in their proper places than if one attempted to do so with the two pieces the other way up. Having soldered the parts together, the surplus ends of wire can be removed with saw or file, and the outside can be filed up. The outside can then be sandpapered ready for the next part of the job which will be making and fixing the shank.

It may be noticed that the bottom of this setting or 'head', as it is called in trade terms, is still flat and no mention has been made of making it fit the shape of the finger. This is best left until after the shank has been attached when the finger shape will be filed out from underneath the head. No real purpose is served by filing it out to shape beforehand, because filing is

Fig. 84. (left)   Square divisions.
Fig. 85. (right)   Chenier divisions.

always necessary when head and shank are soldered together and there is no point in filing twice where once will do. (See Figs. 84–85.)

This type of head has been described using round wire as the means of dividing the top and bottom bezels, but there are other methods. One could use square wire (Fig. 84) or, if a greater division is needed, rectangular wire or other sections, but the favourite and the neatest method is to use chenier instead (Fig. 85). This is in fact seamless tubing and it is usual in most jewellery workshops now to purchase it already prepared from the bullion dealers who can produce the many varied thicknesses which may be asked for. In passing however, it might be mentioned that there will no doubt be times when a piece of tubing or chenier for a particular purpose will have to be made, and it is therefore very useful to be able to produce it when required. This will be described when dealing with the manufacture of other incidental items.

It is not always oval or round stones that have flat backs, and quite frequently other shapes are met with including the familiar rectangular and octagonal. These can each be dealt with by using exactly the same principles for making the shaped bezels as described for bezels of claw setting, and by using the methods described here for the actual style or type of head. In fact a sufficient range of shapes and sizes, and methods of making the settings has been described to cover all heads of this type whether millegrain or claw and, by interchanging one with the other, no difficulty in finding a suitable type should be encountered.

Other Claw Settings

Claw settings are as popular to-day for diamonds and precious stones as ever they were, and usually the type of claw setting used is quite different from the ones we have dealt with previously. The nature of the stones themselves, being very much smaller generally speaking, and much more precious, demands rather different treatment, and it is usual for platinum to be used instead of the gold which was used in settings for larger stones. The settings that can be purchased from the bullion dealers are varied in type and are very much used, to great advantage, but that does not exclude the need for hand-made settings on some occasions. It is therefore necessary that the craftsman should be able to make them when needed.

Dealing first with the settings for a single stone, whatever the design is to

64

be, the same procedure is followed in the first stages. Most frequently, these stones are round (or for practical purposes we can call them round although sometimes they are just a little 'off-shape') so manufacture can be started assuming this to be so, and square ones dealt with afterwards.

For an average sized stone (about 0.50 ct which would be roughly $\frac{3}{16}$ in (5 mm) diameter), a strip of metal 8 lignes (5 mm) wide and 8 gauge in thickness is curved edgewise in the usual manner, and from it a bezel (or 'collet' is the more usual term when dealing with this type) is made, the size being such that the stone will rest on the top and show a line of metal all round the outside. It need not be made quite perfectly as to shape, indeed one can hardly expect that it would be possible to make it so, simply by bending it up with the pliers, but the craftsman does reach a remarkable degree of accuracy with practice.

The best way to bend up a round collet from the curved strip is to hold the strip in the left hand, with the outer edge of the curve toward the body, between thumb and first finger; then with the round point pliers turn up the circle of metal approximately to size but just a little more than a circle (Fig. 86). Cut through the strip with the saw and close up the joint. The reason for bending up a little more than a full circle is that, when the collet is cut off from the strip, the end of the strip is already bent round a little to form the beginning of another collet (Fig. 87). In practice this is a very big advantage for the following reason. When starting to turn up a collet from a flat strip, the extreme end is usually not by any means easy to turn with the result that it is often straight, so that the joint in the collet is not as good as desired. If, however, this extreme end is already bent round from the previous collet, the job is much easier to do.

Fig. 86. (right)   Forming a round collet.

Fig. 87. (below)   Leaving a curve to start the second collet.

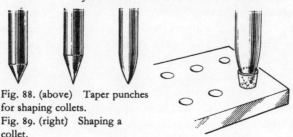

Fig. 88. (above)   Taper punches
for shaping collets.
Fig. 89. (right)   Shaping a
collet.

Fig. 90. (above)
Sides of collet and
back bezel should
be parallel to each
other.

A good tip for making a clean close joint in the collet is to close it up as far as possible with the pliers, and then saw through the joint with a medium thickness saw, and close it up again with the pliers. A good close fit is then usually made and the joint is ready for soldering. Always use the hardest possible solder for this purpose, as the collet will be subjected to many solderings before completion of the article.

After this has been done, the next thing is to correct the shape and size. It can be done either by tapping the collet round on the sparrowhawk or by using a steel punch made for the purpose, usually known as a 'collet punch'. This is quite often a home-made tool made from a piece of round section steel about 3 in (75 mm) long and $\frac{3}{8}$ in (10 mm) diameter, the end of which is tapered fairly steeply. Best made from tool steel, it must, of course, be hardened and properly tempered. A good plan is to have several of these punches each with a different taper (Fig. 88). This punch can be used to great advantage with a round hole drawplate in shaping a round collet of the type we are now making (Fig. 89).

Choose a hole in the back of the draw-plate which is a little smaller than the bottom of the collet, and place the collet over this. Put the punch inside the collet so that the end protrudes through into the hole of the draw-plate and, by gently tapping on the top of the punch with a hammer, a well shaped collet will result. This method can also be used to stretch a collet a little if necessary, but its use in this respect is limited as the joint is liable to split if one attempts to enlarge it too much. When this shaping has been done, the stone should rest on top of the inner edge of the collet, leaving a circle of metal showing all round. The top and bottom of the collet are then filed flat and the back bezel prepared.

Usually platinum is used for the setting (i.e., the collet) but the back bezel will be made in whatever metal the rest of the ring is to be made in. For instance, if the ring is to have a gold shank (which is usual), then the back bezel will be made from gold of the same quality. The bezel is made from a strip of metal 8 gauge thick for an average sized stone, and 3 lignes (2 mm) wide. After curving it edgewise in the same manner as metal for collets, a circle is bent up whose top is the same size as the bottom of the collet and, after its joint has been soldered, it can be made round and adjusted for size by using the collet punch and draw-plate in the same way as for the collet itself. When the top of the back bezel has been filed off flat, the sides of collet and back bezel should be parallel (Fig. 90), that is, they should form one continuous line when the collet is placed on the bezel. The back bezel can now be placed aside while the actual making of the claw setting continues.

Organ-pipe Claw Settings

Several patterns of claw setting are all popular, but in each the procedure is similar. Fig. 91 shows three patterns, which can be made from the collet which has been described. In all cases the bottom 'scallops' are made first, in the case of 'organ-pipe' claws with a three-square file, and in the other two cases with the saw first and afterwards trimmed up with suitable files. Often, a difficulty is how to hold the collet so that one can see clearly the part which is actually being cut or filed. A good plan here is to have a pair of pliers prepared for such work as this. The usual trade term is simple 'bent-overs' which is a descriptive name for the ends or jaws. These are made from a pair of long thin-nosed pliers, whose jaws have been well softened and the ends bent over so that the end $\frac{1}{4}$ in (6 mm) is at right angles to the rest of the jaws of the pliers (Fig. 92). The sharper the angle the better, and a close fit at the end is essential. Fig. 93 shows them in use.

Taking first the 'organ-pipe' type of claw, usually eight claws are best but in some instances where the stone is quite small, six are sufficient. The first step is to mark out with the three-square needle file the eight places which will be filed into the shape of a V and, after ensuring that they are accurately spaced, each in turn is made deeper. The filing, however, is not done with the file running parallel to the top (or bottom) of the collet, instead it is at an angle of approximately 45° to the side, so that the V-shape is being filed much larger on the outside of the collet than the inside (Fig. 94).

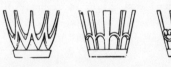
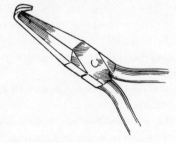

Fig. 91. (above)   Three patterns of claw setting.
Fig. 92. (right)   Modified pliers.

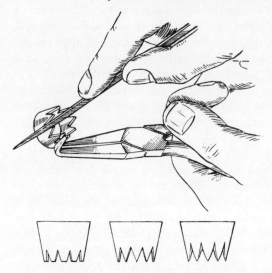

Fig. 93. (above left) Using the bent-over pliers.
Fig. 94. (above) Angle for filing V-cuts.
Fig. 95. (below left) Stages in filing 'organ pipe' claws.

When making 'organ-pipe' settings, it is a good plan to file opposing grooves, rather than those next to each other, so that one can more easily see whether they are accurately placed or not and, if necessary, make slight corrections in doing so. In other words, file two first, exactly opposite each other, then one in between each, making four, and the one in between each again. Follow in the same order when filing the V-shapes up to their final size.

Each V is filed until only a small space is left in between each, in fact *almost* to a point. The word *almost* is to be emphasised, as to file them quite to a point would most likely result in them being reduced just a little in height, owing to the human failing of being not quite perfect. In theory they should be *points*, but in practice just a tiny surface is left. When this stage has been reached, each point is rounded off on the outside; this is again done with the three-square file (Fig. 95).

The collet is next sandpapered carefully, so that it is ready to have the back bezel soldered on, but before dealing with that, a little more detail of the two other types will be appropriate because the soldering on of the back bezel is the same in each case and need only be described once.

Scallop or Arcade Claw Settings

The second type of claw, often called the 'arcade' claw, is held similarly in the 'bent-over' pliers, and with a small round needle file, eight points are marked where the arcades or scallops will be. It is advisable again to work on 'opposites'. These should be marked out so that the space left between each is fairly small but not by any means a 'point'. Now the dividers are used to mark a line round the outside of the collet to indicate where the scallops will be cut to; this should be about two-thirds of the total depth measured from the top. Let me say here that when one is more accustomed to using the saw frame, this marking with dividers is dispensed with and the eye is used to judge the depth of the scallops.

With a medium cut blade (2/o) each scallop is sawn out as neatly as possible and then trimmed with a file. The tops of these scallops are cut and filed at an angle of roughly 45° so that, in effect, the scallops are higher on the outside of the collet than they are on the inner side. The reason for this is to give a little extra strength to the claw setting and yet to enable the finished work to look neat. To get the scallops to a good shape is not quite as simple as it may at first seem. The idea is to have the line of the sides of the claws continued right through to the back bezel, each claw slightly tapering and with straight sides. (See again Fig. 91 showing three types of claw and note how these lines are drawn.) Bearing this in mind when cutting the scallops, one can visualise the shape each scallop is to be and how thick each claw must be left in between.

When all eight scallops have been cut and filed smooth with the round needle file, a very small piece of sandpaper can be used to make them smoother, care being taken not to lose the shape and sharpness. Before soldering on the back bezel, these scallops should be 'threaded'. This is a process which belongs to the polishing department and need not be described yet. The scallops are polished at this stage because it is not so easy to do them afterwards.

Scroll Claw Settings

The third type of claw, 'scroll claw' as it is usually called, is made in a very similar manner, but it is better to have only six claws instead of eight, as more space is required in between each to enable the scrolls to have a reasonable shape. The scallops are marked out as before, leaving the desired thickness of each claw in between, and then the saw is used to cut out the bottom scallops, but this time, of course, the shape is different and instead of a round point needle file being used to file up inside, the point of the three-square file is used. Alternatively, a 'safety back' file can be purchased. This is a one-sided file, a flat triangle in section, the edges of which are very sharp and capable of filing into sharp corners, although there is no danger of causing damage with the back of the file. These scallops also should be threaded before proceeding to solder them on to the back bezel.

Fig. 96. Two methods of soldering to the back bezel—by tying the two parts together with iron wire, and by first running solder round the back bezel on a charcoal block.

Soldering on the Back Bezel

Each of these three types of claw setting can be dealt with now as if they were the same. There are two ways of soldering on the back bezel, and each has its merits, but each will depend upon the individual craftsman and which method he finds most suitable:

1. The bezel can be tied on with a small piece of iron binding wire, as shown in Fig. 96, and then a small paillon of solder placed to each soldering point. The binding wire can be used to hold the setting while heating it for soldering and the usual points for soldering observed.

2. Alternatively, the back bezel can be placed on the charcoal block, and several small paillons of solder placed around the upper surface to which the scalloped collet is to be soldered. The paillons are then heated, melted and allowed to flow round that surface.

After this has been done, the collet can be placed accurately on to the back bezel, ensuring that each point is correctly aligned, and then collet and back bezel heated together until the solder again melts and so runs on to the points in contact with the bezel. Both the outside of the collet and the back bezel can then be filed up together and afterwards sandpapered. The next stage in practice is to solder on the shank but I shall be dealing with shanks in Chapter 6. It is better to continue to describe the processes concerning the top part of the claw, assuming for the present that the shank has been soldered on.

Cutting the Claws

Assuming that the shank has been made and the 'head' or setting soldered in, the ring is ready for the final stage as far as the mounter (or ring maker) is concerned. This is the cutting of the claws. To hold the ring so that it is in a good position for the craftsman to see clearly, and also to assist in keeping the ring rigid while sawing and filing, a tool known as a 'side-clamp' (or ring stick) is used. This is a boxwood handle, split into four sections with a wide saw cut to about three-quarters of its length, and with a hole of about $\frac{1}{4}$ in (6 mm) diameter through its entire length (Fig. 97). Down the centre is placed a threaded bolt with a tapered head, and a butterfly nut on its opposite end. Around the top is filed a neat shallow ridge on to which the ring will fit.

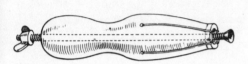

Fig. 97. (above)   The 'side-clamp'.

Fig. 98. (right)   How the 'side-clamp' is used.

When the butterfly nut is tightened, it will pull the bolt downward, causing the tapered head to force open slowly the four sections of the boxwood handle, and so grip the ring tightly. This provides the means of holding the ring firmly and securely, while still permitting manoeuvrability (Fig. 98). This is important, as it is essential that one is able to turn the ring itself round quite easily when sawing to cut the claws, and so on.

The three types of claw-setting in this group are dealt with in much the same fashion in the first stages. The ring is held in the ring stick (or side-clamp) with the head of the ring facing toward the operator. Then each division between the claws is marked with the small round needle file on one side of the ring. It will be apparent that only one side of the claw head can be dealt with without taking the ring from the ring stick and turning it over. To do this at each little stage would waste a great deal of time, and so, in practice, one side of the head is completed first and then the ring turned over to allow the other side to be completed. Having marked out where the claws will be, a medium cut saw, preferably 2/0, is used to cut down the claws and round the scallops. The bottom of the scallops are cut at an angle, as also were the scallops on the bottom of the setting, thus making the

Fig. 99. Stages in cutting arcade claws with a saw-frame.

inside much thicker than the outside. This applies only to the actual scallops, arcades, galleries or other name by which these parts separating the claws are known.

The claws themselves are the same thickness at the front (or outside) as they are on the inside. Having sawn them out, the next step is to smooth them neatly and to correct the shape as required with needle files. A very important thing in all cases is to keep strength as well as neatness, and also to keep the lines of the claws sharp and well proportioned. That is a general outline, but a few points on each particular type will be useful.

With organ-pipe claws the tendency often is to make the bottom of the claws too thin by sawing too far down. Two-thirds of the total depth is usually sufficient; this one is perhaps the easiest to do, as it only involves sawing down each side of the claw, and then cutting a normal curve to make the scallop. A round needle file will complete the scallop and finally a small piece of sandpaper can be used to make it properly smooth.

The arcade claw is a little more difficult, in that sharp corners are needed at the bottom of each saw-cut. This can soon be done quite neatly after some practice in the use of a saw-frame. The best plan is to saw down each side of the claws first and bring the saw out again; and then to cut out the scallops. Put the saw down one saw-cut again—but this time not quite to the bottom. The saw can then be turned gently inwards and a saw-cut made down to the opposite corner of the scallop, so cutting out the largest portion between the claws. The saw can then be used to cut down to the other corner. Fig. 99 will help to clarify this.

After saw-piercing as well and clearly as possible, the knife-edge needle file can be used to advantage for filing up the sides of the claws, remembering the major points already mentioned: i.e., slightly tapered claws, straight sides, etc. Use the safety back file, or end of a three square, to file up the bottom of the scallops. When completed, the arcade separating the claws should appear as a neat thin line of metal at the front (or outside) while being much thicker inside.

Following the same method described for arcade claws, the claws for the scroll type setting can be cut, although these are a little different. One has to bear in mind that sufficient space must be left for saw-piercing the scrolls after the claws have been cut; the shape has to be visualised during cutting.

Fig. 100. (above)   Partly cut
claws of a scroll setting.

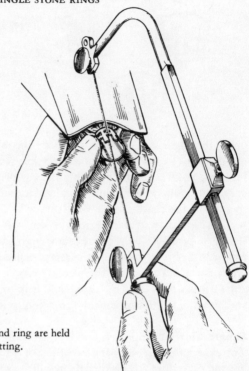

Fig. 101. (right)   How the saw and ring are held
when working on a scroll type setting.

Instead, therefore, of just a thin line of metal forming an arcade between the
claws, a distinctive shape is left with sufficient space to complete the scrolls
(Fig. 100). It is always wise in this type to mark a line with the dividers
showing the distance to which the claws will be cut, thus ensuring that each
is the same as its neighbour. The final stage with the scroll claw is the most
difficult and one which needs practice and skill in the use of the saw-frame.
It also demands good quality saw blades which can be relied upon for their
accuracy.

Drill a very small hole in each of the pieces dividing the claws as near the
centre as possible, and then remove the ring from the ring stick. Release the
bottom end of the saw from the frame and put the saw-blade through one of
the holes just drilled, fastening up the saw blade again in the frame. The ring
is now held firmly in the finger and thumb of the left hand against the bench
peg and must be moved about as necessary to enable the shape to be saw-
pierced inside the scroll (Fig. 101). It is essential that good control of ring
and saw-frame are maintained.

Several points have to be very carefully watched when doing this, one

73

Fig. 102. Three types of square setting.

being that the claws opposite to where the saw-piercing is being done are not damaged by the saw. Another very important point is to ensure that the setting is not weakened by making the saw-piercings too large, thus leaving very thin scrolls which, while looking neat, will not have sufficient strength to support the claws themselves. It must be realised that this is very small work which allows for no errors. When it is remembered that the whole setting is probably only $\frac{1}{4}$ in (6 mm) high and of a similar diameter at its top, it is easy to see why skill and experience are required to carry out this type of work. The actual saw-piercing cannot be satisfactorily described in any further detail, but Fig. 101 should help to show how the setting is held and how the saw-frame is held in relation to it.

Square Claw Settings

There can, of course, be many variations of the actual design of these settings, but the procedure for making them will remain the same. So having given three more or less standard examples, a little might usefully be added about square settings, which will sometimes be required, though not as frequently as round ones. The best method is to make the collet from metal of the same dimensions as already described, and follow out the same procedure as previously detailed for making a square bezel (i.e., measuring length of sides and filing grooves for each corner, etc). The difference lies in the making of the claws. It is usually best to have a fairly wide claw in each corner and no other claws in between (Fig. 102).

The bottom should be dealt with first, as with round claw settings, and the top left until after the shank has been soldered on. It is unnecessary to go into detail with this, because each process has been well covered in describing the making of round settings, and all the general principles apply equally here. The main points to remember are that the claws should be much wider at the top to ensure strength of the arcades (or other ornamentation) left between the claws. Several different designs can be made to form the division between claws, but again the same principles and methods will apply. Fig. 102 shows three different ideas for square settings.

5. Multiple Stone Rings

The three-stone or five-stone ring is as popular to-day as ever and it has often been said that if one can make these well, anything else will not be difficult to master. This is broadly true in that to make one well, many processes which make a good jeweller are used: the good use of saw-frame; use of the file, large and small; the observance of good proportion and general neatness: all these are exercised, as well as soldering, buffing and general handling of tools for every type of work. The standard achieved by an apprentice in making one of these can be used as a fairly good guide to his all-round capabilities. Both three-stone and five-stone settings are very similar, and it is best to describe the five-stone, as in so doing the three-stone will also be covered.

Making the Individual Collets

Beginning with a strip of metal of 8 lignes (5 mm) wide and 8 gauge in thickness for an average sized range of stones, it is curved edgewise as before and after annealing. Each collet is made to fit the stone for which it is intended. Care should be taken, however, to make a very good fit; that is to make it so that it will not need to be made larger or adjusted afterwards. Also it should be made as near to a proper round as possible. A lot will depend on how well this is done as to what the next stage will be. During one's early training, it is usual to solder the joint in each collet separately and then to adjust each for size and make them perfectly round, etc. No doubt this serves well for training, but in later practice much time can be saved if this can be dispensed with, by making each collet well to size and sufficiently round to enable them to be soldered together without further ado.

Fig. 103. Flats formed for joining collets together.

Fig. 104. How three joined collets should look from the top and from the side.

It is always good, therefore, to pay attention to these points when making round collets. It is good practice which pays dividends in time saved. In either case, having made the collets, the next step is to solder them together to form the head of the ring. It is necessary that, when together, these will form a curve which will follow the shape of the finger. The amount of that curve is important. If one is making a ring of very small finger size (for example, size J), it will have to be more curved than one for a larger size, such as Q. Neither of these is by any means exceptional. A good plan then is to make the back bezel for the head before soldering the collets together as this will be a very useful guide.

Making the Back Bezel

The back bezel is made from a strip of metal of 13 gauge, a little wider than the bottom of the centre collet of the head (the centre always being the largest in diameter). It is curved with pliers to the finger size of the ring when finished. A smooth, even curve can quite easily be obtained by making it a little smaller than needed and then gently tapping it on the triblett (the long, tapered steel tool) until it becomes the correct size. This done, the collets can be soldered together.

Soldering the Collets

Taking first the centre collet, a large flat is filed directly across the joint in it; large enough, in fact, for approximately two-thirds of the thickness of the metal to be filed away. The collet, a little smaller in size, which will be soldered next to it, is treated in the same way. These two are then held in tweezers with the flat of each together and soldered with the hardest solder which the metal will take. In doing this, the joint in each collet will be soldered as well.

The next step is to file another flat on the centre collet exactly opposite the one already used, and also a similar flat on the other middle-sized collet, again on its joint, of course (Fig. 103). This is soldered to the centre as before, making a range of three collets. At this stage there are a number of points that ought to be mentioned. Obviously, if we were making a three-stone ring, we should already have this completed, but we are making a five-stone. In either case the following points are important. Looking at the top, the three collets must be in a straight line—in other words, a line through the centre of each should be quite straight.

Looking at either end, each must be vertical (Fig. 104); and looking at its side, the curve of the bottom should approximate the curve of the back bezel. Assuming that these are correct, we can proceed with the adding of the final collets, which will again be a pair, and slightly smaller than those already used. A flat is filed on each end of the grouped three collets, as before – a flat sufficiently large to make the metal about one-third of its original thickness. Again, using the joints in the end collets, a flat is filed on each of these. Before they are soldered to the ends of the grouped three collets, however, they should be placed in position and held with tweezers while the back bezel (already made) is tried against them to see whether the curve at the bottom of the collets is approximately the same as the top of the back bezel.

If the curve is correct, then we can go ahead and solder them together to complete the first stage of the five-stone head. If, however, the curve formed by the underside of the five collets is not sufficiently accurate, adjustments

Fig. 105. Shaping the collets to the back bezel. Those on the right are not curved enough.

will have to be made before soldering. For instance, if the head is not sufficiently curved, then a little more will have to be filed off the bottom part of the flats on each collet (keeping them flat, of course), which will alter the angle at which the collets meet. On the other hand, if the curve is too great, then more will have to be filed from the top part of the flat on each collet, thus reducing the amount of curve. Fig. 105 will clarify this.

Fitting Collets and Bezel Together

Having got the curve of the collets as nearly as possible correct in relation to the back bezel, the collets can be soldered together, bearing in mind the points mentioned before with regard to keeping them all in the correct line when viewed from above as well as from the end (see Fig. 104). Any slight tendency to err in this matter is exaggerated in a five-stone ring and the finished ring looks very wrong indeed. These points having been dealt with and the five collets soldered correctly together, the next step is to make the bottom of them fit exactly on to the back bezel by filing with a half-round file until the curve is even and the back bezel, when placed against it, touches all along without gaps or spaces. This is very important.

Fig. 106.   Different radii for top and bottom curves.

It will be realised that the bottom of each collet, when it was made, was flat. So, when the five were soldered together, they became a series of five flats forming an approximate curve similar to the back bezel. Now, after filing the bottom of the collets, there should be a true curve with no flats at any point.

A good fit having been ensured, the next step is to file the top of the collets also into an even curve. This, however, should not be quite parallel to the bottom of the collets. It is in fact an arc of a larger diameter than one which would result in top and bottom being parallel. In practice, a little more is filed off from the centre than from the ends, making the end collets a little higher (or 'deeper') than the centre one (Fig. 106).

The purpose of this is to give the end diamonds, when set in the finished ring, a little more prominence than would be the case if the curve were greater. To describe it a little more easily, we make the top of the ring a little flatter so that, when viewed from above, the end stones will not be too far below the centre one. Care must be taken not to over-emphasise this difference in depth of the collets, otherwise the finished ring will look badly proportioned and clumsy. A check should be made at this stage to see that the diamonds fit correctly to each setting. There should be an edge of metal showing round the outside of the stones when each is placed on its setting, while in between each stone a smaller amount is shown.

Clawing the Head

Now we come to the job of clawing the head, starting as we did with the single stone settings at the bottom, and leaving the top until after the shank

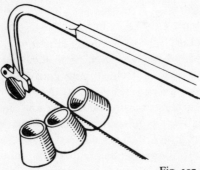

Fig. 107.   Saw out between the back of the collets to one-third of the total depth.

78

has been soldered on. Broadly speaking, the same main principles apply with this type of ring as those already dealt with, and the types of claws which can be made are similar in style; e.g., organ-pipe, scroll and arcade, the only major difference being in the placing of the claws. To avoid unnecessary repetition, each type can be dealt with, describing only the processes which apply to the three- and five-stone ring as distinct from the single stone. Figs. 108, 109 and 110 show the three types of claw heads completed.

The Organ-pipe Claw

Taking first the organ-pipe claw; before starting to file the V-shapes on the outside, some of the metal must be cut away from in between the collets at the back only (see Fig. 107). This is done by putting the saw-blade through one collet and securing it in the saw-frame again and then, by sawing at an angle, cutting away the in-between section of the collets, taking care to do so at the back only. The saw can be held at a fairly steep angle for this. Assuming that the saw has been put through the centre collet first, both sides can be sawn out before removing the saw-blade.

The saw-blade is then placed through the next collet, and the same process repeated. This will result in the removal of the in-between sections of the collets at the bottom only, to about one-third of the depth of the collets. The reason for doing this will be more apparent when one looks at the diagram of this type of setting when finished (Fig. 108). It will be noticed that a V-shape has to be filed where the collets are joined, which would be very difficult without the removal first of the metal from the inside. This may sound very difficult and complicated but in practice it is not so.

From there we carry on to making the V-shapes on the outside of the head. Usually, for an average sized head, one V to the centre of each collet and one in between each is usual. The 'bent-over' pliers can again be used to hold it.

The Arcade Claw

The arcade type of claw is rather different and it is not necessary to cut away

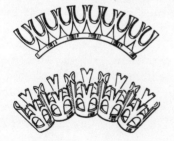

Fig. 108. (above left)   Organ pipe claws.
Fig. 109. (above)   Scroll claws.
Fig. 110. (below left)   Arcade claws.

79

the in-between sections. In fact they *must* remain and form an essential part of the claws (Fig. 110). It is wise to mark out where the scallops will be cut, preferably with the round needle-file, before actually starting to saw them out. Taking as an example an average sized head, it is mostly sufficient to have one claw in the centre of each collet, and a moment's reflection will show that this means two scallops to each claw. The same general points which apply to single-stone claws of this type, with regard to the shape of scallops and so on, apply here also. Once again the arcades (or division between the claws) must be left thicker on the inside than outside.

The Scroll Claw

Little need be added regarding the scroll type, because all points have already been covered. The same number of claws are appropriate as for the arcade type, and the cutting is exactly the same as for a single collet. The stage we have now reached is where the bottom of the claw head has been completed and is ready for soldering on to the back bezel.

As with the single-stone ring, the cutting of the claws at the top is left until last, when the shank has been soldered on, and the ring is in fact more or less complete. The best method of soldering the collets to the back bezel is to use a little binding wire to hold them together and, after cutting up very small paillons of solder, place one to each contact point with bezel and claw and proceed to heat and melt the solder in the usual manner. This, of course, will apply regardless of the type of claw. After ensuring that each point is soldered, the back bezel must be filed to correspond to the shape of the collets.

Shaping the Back Bezel

Up to this point the back bezel has been a parallel-sided strip of metal, curved to the shape of the finger, but otherwise bearing no resemblance to the shape of the five collets. Now, with the aid of a saw and a file, it is made to follow the outline of the collets so that, when viewed from underneath, it resembles five circles joined together. As with the single stone, the general appearance from the side view will be that the outside of collets and back bezel form one continuous line.

To file up the back bezel, the bent-over pliers are very useful and, in this instance, the head is held in such a manner that the top of the settings are facing toward the body, the back bezel then being held against the bench peg in the manner shown in Fig. 111. There is no necessity to sandpaper this at the moment, as it can quite well be left until the final stage of manufacture has been reached, when all sandpapering can be done together. The next

Fig. 111.   How the back bezel
can be filed.

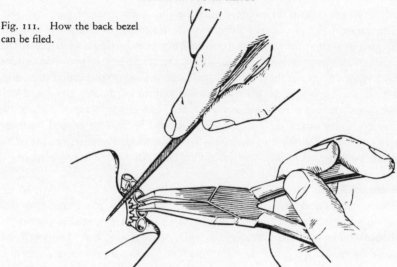

step is to drill a hole in the centre of each of the circles which now make up
the back bezel, after which each hole is enlarged carefully with the saw,
leaving what appears to be a back bezel to each of the five collets. When this
stage has been reached, the shank will be made and soldered on to the head,
but I shall again assume for the present that this has already been done and
that the ring is ready for the claws to be saw-pierced.

Saw-piercing the Claws

There is a greater difference between the top claws on a multi-stone head and
those on a single-stone head, than is the case with the bottom scallops. Taking
first the organ-pipe style, the ring is held on the ring stick (or side-clamp)
for this process, and again the saw is used for the cutting out, preparatory to
the final smoothing with the file. The chief difference lies in the shape of the
spaces between the claws. Whereas, in the single stone, the straight-sided
claws are left as in Fig. 100; with the three- or five-stone ring (especially
if one has, as is usual, one claw on each side of the head to each stone),
the claws are left much wider at the top. The in-between sections or joined
sections of the collets ('ear pieces' as they are usually called) are left wider
at the top, too. The sides of the claws are not made straight but are slightly
curved, and each of the claws is 'split' at the top to form two claws as may
be seen in Fig. 111. This split is only a shallow one and is best done with
a three-square file. It should be exaggerated a little on the outside to make it
look larger than it is.

The arcade type of claw differs less from the single stone of the same type. The major difference is that the claws on the three- or five-stone ring are divided or split at the top, and so, to enable this to be done, each one is left a little wider proportionately than it is in the single-stone type. The arcades or divisions between the claws are again left thicker on the inside than they are on the outside, thus giving neatness and strength. All claws and 'in-betweens' or 'ear pieces' are straight-sided and wider at the top than the bottom. Once again the finished effect should be that of several tapering claws held together by an arcade. Lastly, with the scroll collet, little need be added with regard to detail as this differs but little from the single stone.

Point to Watch

Briefly mentioning the important points, one should remember that this type of claw is more suitable for larger stones so that the detail of the scrolls should not be too small. A slightly wider space is required in between the claws to enable the scroll to be saw-pierced, and, when cutting down the claws, it must be remembered that the distinctive shape needed for the claws must be left.

As with the single-stone collet, it is usually found best to leave the actual drilling and saw-piercing of the scrolls to the last of all, that is to say after the ring has been completed and the claws cut down as described.

Many variations in the actual detail of the three- or five-stone can be made, and a number of different styles can be adopted.

On the larger stone settings more claws can be put to avoid very wide spaces (and, of course, wider claws, too). Different shapes can also be fashioned between the claws instead of scrolls, but sufficient has been written to show how each is made and, regardless of the particular variations adopted, the methods and processes covered will enable any type to be understood and made.

Cluster Rings

Designs which can safely be placed under the heading of cluster type rings would be almost impossible to enumerate, as one could go on making variations to existing and time-honoured patterns almost indefinitely. Indeed, it would not be to any great advantage for the purpose of practical description to attempt to do so. It is sufficient to take a standard style, and describe its making, and leave the fairly obvious variations to be dealt with when they actually demand attention. Methods of dealing with the under part of the setting need more description than the top itself. Nevertheless, we must begin with the top, or setting for the stones.

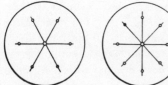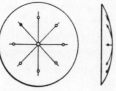

Fig. 112. The cluster marked out and domed.

Often cluster rings are made to a particular size and style and the stones which will be set in it are selected afterwards. But there are many occasions also where the mounter is given the stones to work to, and possibly a design also. In the former case, the job is no doubt a little less exacting, but for the purpose of the practical method of manufacture, it is better that we should assume that we have the stones. Assume also that the style required is the simplest of all clusters, the nine-stone, or seven-stone round top.

Measuring up the Circle

A useful tip is to place the stones (usually diamonds) on a small piece of Plasticine exactly as they would be in the ring. This enables us to measure the diameter of the piece of metal required to start off with. With the dividers, measure from the centre of the cluster of stones to beyond the outer edge of one of the stones to give a radius for the circle, which can be marked on to the metal. If the cluster is to be about $\frac{1}{2}$ in (12 mm) across (diameter) the dividers should be opened up to approximately $\frac{1}{16}$ in (1.5 mm) beyond the stones, thus making the circle on the metal $\frac{1}{8}$ in (3 mm) greater in diameter than the actual arrangement of stones on the Plasticine. For a cluster of this size, which is a fairly good average, the metal should be 12 gauge in thickness. It is usually platinum, but not necessarily so. Palladium is often used instead where it is considered suitable.

Doming the Circle

Having marked out the circle on the piece of sheet metal as economically as possible, avoiding waste as far as it is practicable to do so, saw round it and anneal it. Annealing is always wise, because it is probable that the metal has been milled down and not annealed afterwards; thus it is best to make sure. The next step is to dome the circle in the doming die with a punch of a suitable size to make an even-domed surface, not very high, but sufficient to ensure a well-shaped setting. Fig. 112 shows approximately the amount of dome required, and also the most suitable shape.

The correct shape can be achieved only by choosing the most suitable part of the doming block and most suitable punches to use. It can here be laid down as a firm and unbreakable rule that any shaped cluster *must* be domed. It is not sufficient only to curve it on long shapes, but more about that later. Doming is the only way to effect a good job and, if this is not done, the finished ring will *always* have a 'sunk in the middle' appearance.

The drilling for the stones has to be done next. Starting with the centre, the other six or eight stones, as the case may be, are marked off with a scriber (simply a pointed steel, round in section, suitable for scratching lightly on the surface of metal). There is no need for mathematical precision in doing this. The eye is the best guide. Mark one line straight across the diameter, another diameter crossing at right angles, and subdivide these to give eight points radiating from the centre. In the case of six outside stones, it is not at all difficult to guess where the appropriate lines should be, having marked one diameter. Then, after making sufficient allowance for the size of the centre stone, make a mark on each line where the centre of each of the other stones will be. These are the points for drilling, which is the next job to be done.

Drilling the Holes for the Stones

Enlarging the holes to the appropriate size must be done mainly by the use of a saw-frame, always starting with the centre hole. It is 'opened out', or enlarged, evenly all round, parallel to the edge. A very important thing *always* is that the hole must be smaller at the back than it is at the front, the reason for this being that a 'bearing' or support has to be left for the stone (which will be finally adjusted and set by the setter at a later stage, after the mounter has finished his part). If the holes were made with their sides vertical or parallel, the stone would probably drop through. The top of the hole should be made sufficiently large for the stone to rest on its upper edge only, and not for the stone to drop right in.

When the hole for the centre stone has been completed, those for the outer stones should each be treated in a similar manner. The best plan is to deal with opposites; that is, to do any hole first, and then follow this by dealing with the one directly opposite. This ensures that the finished cluster has its stones correctly placed around the centre with equal spacing. After the first two holes have been enlarged sufficiently, the next two directly between them

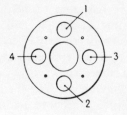

Fig. 113. Order of drilling.

should be done, and finally the remaining four (Fig. 113). Each of these holes must be smaller at the back than the front, as previously described. This is an invaluable rule regardless of pattern or type of work being done.

It is difficult to give a guide as to the amount of space which is left between the centre stone and the surrounding ones. It must be governed to a considerable extent by the actual size of the stones. The ideal is to have but very little space between any of them, just enough in fact for strength and to enable the setter to secure the stone.

After the holes have been sawn out as far as practicable, they can be smoothed on their inner surfaces by the use of a 'fraise', which is similar in appearance to a counter-sinking bit used by a carpenter or engineer. There are numerous types and sizes and various shapes; Fig. 114 shows an average range.

Fig. 114. 'Fraises' or rotary files.

The outer edge of the cluster top is now scalloped with a three-square file to follow the shape of the stones, leaving a rim of metal around each. This rim of metal should be approximately 0.04 in (1 mm) for an average sized cluster, and correspondingly less on smaller ones. In scalloping this edge, the angle should be kept at approximately 90° to the surface and should not be vertical. The reason for this will be more apparent when the later stage of adding the under bezel is described.

Raising the Centre Stone
Frequently the top or 'setting' of the cluster is left in the form which it has now reached, but sometimes it is desired to have the centre stone raised a little from the others by means of a claw setting or by a slightly raised mille-grain setting. In either case, if this is desired it must be done next, before proceeding to make the under bezel or 'gallery', as it is called. If the centre setting is to be raised millegrain, it is simply a matter of making a very shallow rim (very thin square wire of 0.04 in (1 mm) or less is most suitable) to fit the stone in the manner already described and leaving a thin edge of metal showing all round the edge of the stone.

This small bezel will usually be made in platinum, as will the cluster top itself. After it has been correctly joined and made quite round, and a good fit for the stone ensured, it is filed flat and clean on one side and soldered directly on to the top of the cluster. It should be mentioned here that the maker will be

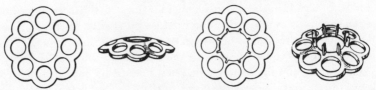

Fig. 115.   One form of cluster top.

aware, before he commences the job, whether the centre stone is to be raised, and in what manner, and so will make slight allowances when working on the cluster top. For instance, he would not make the hole for the centre stone quite so large as he would if the stone were to be set directly into the cluster without being raised. He may perhaps choose to solder on this raised setting *before* he opens up the holes for the surrounding stones, but the effect is the same, and a jeweller will, of course, have a wider choice of methods as he gains experience.

If the centre stone is to be set in claws, it is always better to reach the stage described above before putting in the claws. These are made by drawing down, in the square draw-plate, a strip of platinum wire to approximately 0.04 in (1 mm) or even slightly less if the centre stone is comparatively small. It is then flattened in the flat mills to the thickness of a No. 7 saw-blade. (Saw-blades of this size are used only for special purposes, as in this particular instance, as they are too thick, by far, for normal usage.)

Taking the cluster, insert the No. 7 saw-blade into the saw-frame, passing the blade through the centre hole, and then make a series of saw-cuts between each of the outside stones, each radiating from the centre, just sufficiently far to accommodate the now rectangular wire. Then cutting off short lengths ($\frac{1}{8}$ in (3mm) is usually ample) and after removing the saw-blade, insert one piece of wire into each saw cut. It should be sufficiently tight to stay in place. The wires should be placed in such a manner that they slope outwards just a little toward the top, making a slightly tapered claw setting. A small paillon of solder to each one then fixes them permanently, and the top can be levelled off with a file and the cluster top is ready for the next stage. When soldering in the claws, it is wise to use the hardest solder which the metals in use will take.

Fig. 115 shows a cluster top with some of the claws in position, and the slots for the remainder. When all claws have been soldered in, the stone should rest on top of them in just the same way as other claw settings.

The Basket Back

Backs for clusters of the round, oval, or similar shaped types can be made in

Fig. 116. The
'basket back'
cluster.

Fig. 117. Patterns for cluster tops.

various styles, but probably three distinctive types will be sufficient to cover them for all practical purposes. Firstly, there is the 'basket back' type, shown in Fig. 116, which gives a side view of a finished cluster head with a basket back. This is made from a piece of gold of the same quality as that which the shank, etc, will be made from, starting with a piece slightly larger than the cluster top, of 9 gauge for an average sized ring. Firstly, it must be domed by the same methods as used for doming the top, but this time a rather greater amount of doming is preferable, and a good even dome gives a better final shape than a shallow, flattish dome.

When this has been done, the diameter has to be reduced, if this proves necessary, to correspond exactly to the size of the top. The edges should also be scalloped so that, when the top and bottom are held together, the scallops of each are in contact. These points of contact will, in due course, be soldered; but before soldering, an appropriate design is marked on the back for saw-piercing. Simplicity is the key-note and it is usually found that the simplest type of pattern which does not involve any complicated saw-piercing will also look most effective.

The style of the design can be varied in many ways, but a small selection of quite well used and very effective ones will suffice for the purpose of this practical description (Fig. 117). As one gains skill with the saw-frame, the need for filing up the shaped piercings will be reduced, and usually saw-piercing alone is sufficient. It will be remembered that these piercings are quite small, and little room is left for filing up. Indeed it should hardly be necessary.

After the back has been thus completed, it should be filed very gently across the top of the scallops, just sufficiently to make a small flat where each will meet the corresponding scallop of the top part. This should be treated in a similar manner and, when both parts are placed together, close contact should be made. A piece of binding wire or pair of tweezers will hold the halves together whilst each point of contact is soldered. Only a small paillon of solder should be used so that there is no risk of solder spreading too far and probably running to places where it will be extremely difficult to remove.

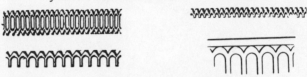

Fig. 118.   Machine-made gallery.

The Gallery Back

The second type of back for clusters is often called a 'gallery' and one can purchase numerous styles of gallery wires from the bullion dealers. This is made as a strip, and simply formed into the appropriate shapes as needed. Fig. 118 shows typical examples of machine-made gallery. The use of this needs little or no description. It may, however, not be possible or suitable to use one of the machine-made type, and an individually fashioned one may be preferred. Where this is so, a gold bezel is made approximately 5/32 in (4 mm) deep from 9 gauge metal, and with its sides tapering steeply in precisely the same manner as similar bezels which have been described. Its top should be large enough to come to the inner edge of the scallops of the top portion (or setting). After it has been correctly joined and shaped to make a proper fit, the top should be filed quite flat and the bezel is then ready to be fashioned into the type of gallery required.

The fashioning of a cluster gallery, after the bezel has been made as previously described, depends upon the design to be followed. Usually this will be fairly simple, and will be somewhat similar in appearance to a claw setting.

The best method is to mark a line with the dividers about two-thirds of the distance from the top, and saw completely through this line, thus making two separate bezels. The lower portion will now become a back bezel for the gallery which we are about to make, and can be laid aside for the moment. This leaves us with a fairly shallow bezel into which to work the design. The usual type will simply consist of filing scallops into the bottom of this piece and then soldering on the piece that was cut off previously. When this has been done, the top of the bezel can be scalloped to follow the same pattern and then the completed gallery is ready to be soldered on to the cluster top.

The actual filing of scallops has already been described in detail and therefore it is unnecessary to do so again, because the only difference is in the

Fig. 119 and 120.   Making two types of cluster gallery.

style and proportions, while the actual method remains the same. Figs 119 and 120 show stage by stage the making of two different designs of gallery wire. One or two points should be borne in mind. The shallow back bezel, which is sawn from the original bezel, must be sufficiently deep to permit the shape of the finger to be filed out of it from underneath when the shank, etc, have been added. The bottom scallops should be filed first and then the back bezel soldered on again before the top scallops are made; otherwise the gallery, being very weak to handle, is liable to be pulled out of shape.

The 'Chenier' Gallery Back

The third and last type of under bezel for clusters of the ordinary round or oval type is usually referred to as a 'chenier' gallery. Chenier (a narrow tube) is the means by which the back bezel and cluster top are separated (Fig. 121).

For this type a fairly shallow bezel of approximately $\frac{1}{16}$ in (1.5 mm) high and 11 gauge in thickness is made, tapering steeply toward the bottom as before. Its top, however, should be smaller than the diameter of the cluster top, and the only guide to its actual size is to bear in mind that, when the cheniers have been soldered between bottom and top, an imaginary straight line projected from the side of the back bezel should join the side of the cluster top.

After this has been correctly shaped and the top filed flat, the next step will be to divide the surface of the top into eight (assuming that there are eight outside stones, but six if there are six stones). Again this can be done by eye and not necessarily with any mathematical precision.

It is best to use a small round needle-file and file a very small groove at each of the eight points, just sufficient to enable the cheniers to be placed, one in each, for the purpose of soldering. Short pieces of chenier about $\frac{1}{16}$ in (1.5 mm) are then cut and, preferably on the charcoal block, each one is soldered in position with one end of each overhanging the outer rim of the bezel by as much as practicable. This is to ensure that, when the cluster top is soldered on, the cheniers will be touching the appropriate outer edge where the soldering will be done. Before soldering top and bottom together, it is

Fig. 121.   Cluster with chenier gallery. The last illustration shows a circle of ten stones.

advisable to remove any surplus length of chenier from the inside of the bezel as it is much more convenient to do so at this stage than afterwards.

After very lightly filing across the top of the cheniers to ensure that they are quite flat and clean for soldering, top and bottom are tied together with iron bending wire and positioned so that one chenier is in the centre of each of the outer holes in the top part. Each contacting point is then soldered, giving the result shown in Fig. 121, which shows various stages cf making this type of back bezel.

After the top and bottom have been soldered together as described, the outside of the back bezel has to be filed up and scalloped in exactly the same way as the top, care being taken to avoid filing away the metal which is left for the actual setting on the cluster top. From this step follows the making of the shank.

Other Shapes for Cluster Rings

So far we have dealt with the ordinary shape and style of round clusters and it needs little imagination to see that other similar shapes and slight variations in pattern will be dealt with in similar manner. Cushion shapes and square or round clusters with centre stones are quite common, and these present no greater difficulty when one has followed out the general principles outlined here. Obviously the numbers of claws and positioning of them when the centre stone is square or oblong, will be subject to variation. It is sometimes more satisfactory to use four claws only, but they must be very much wider ones in such a case. Whatever the variations, the methods remain the same.

There are, however, fancy types of clusters, or rather fancy rings of quite different shapes, which one might put in this category. These will be treated rather differently. Fig. 122 shows a few of the limitless number of shapes which are often met with. The number of stones which are set in them (and the size of the stones) also varies very greatly.

In these days, when demand is for a ring which looks much more than it

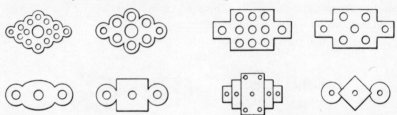

Fig. 122. Some of the many shapes upon which the design of cluster rings may be based.

Fig. 123. An 'illusion' type of setting, showing the steps in construction.

really is, it is quite usual to have very few, very small stones, and leave it for the setter's skill to make up for the lack of gemstone. Right or wrong, this type of jewellery forms an important part of the jeweller's work and so has to be dealt with. For all rings of this type, the top shape is cut out first, just a fraction larger than its finished size is to be, thus allowing for filing up and finally turning up the shape. Next it has to be domed.

It must be stressed again that doming is essential; it is not sufficient to curve it (or 'swage' it, to use the trade term) to fit the appropriate curve of the finger, nothing less than doming is good enough. This is also necessary with fairly long shapes, they should be curved to follow the shape of the finger in addition to being domed. By using the doming die in the usual manner, this curve will naturally be formed, and the process is actually much easier than it may sound. The next step is to drill out the holes for the stones and enlarge them as before, according to the size required, finally fraising the holes to smooth their sides. Following this, a back bezel has to be made the same shape as the top but a little smaller (Fig. 123).

The best plan here is to cut the piece of gold from which it will be made to follow approximately the outline of the top but without the detailed shape. Nine-gauge is sufficiently thick for most purposes. This must then be swaged to the finger size required, after which two pieces of chenier may be cut long enough to be soldered on to the underside of the top in the most appropriate place for the design. A slight groove filed across will keep the cheniers in place while they are being soldered. Usually it will be found convenient to place them with equal space between them and from each end; in other words roughly dividing the length of the head into three. When these have been soldered, the back bezel is placed on to these cheniers and held in position either by a strand of binding wire or simply placed on to the charcoal block, and then soldered together.

The back bezel is next filed up to follow the shape of the top, bearing in mind the usual principles, that is to say that the back should be slightly smaller than the front and the ends should be at such an angle that they follow a line radiating from the centre of the ring as shown in Fig. 124. The result will be a rather solid-looking and very straight-foward type of head, and it should be improved now by drilling holes in the back corresponding to those in the front. These can be opened out with the saw-frame either to follow a pattern or they may simply be enlarged and left round. Care must be exer-

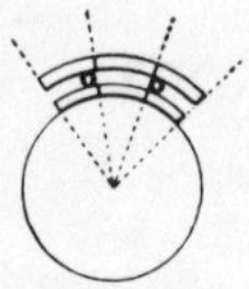

Fig. 124. Proportions of the cluster shown in Fig. 123.

Fig. 125. (opposite) Stages in making a claw cluster.

cised in doing this to avoid damaging the holes in the cluster top which have already been made to their proper size.

The head is now ready for the shank to be made and soldered on. This is, of course, the simplest type of cluster head, and is often referred to as a 'plate' type.

There are countless variations of these, but they need not be specially mentioned, as sufficient has been written to cover the general principles which will apply to practically any style of cluster.

The Coronet or Claw Cluster

There is, however, one very notable exception, and this is the coronet cluster, or claw cluster, which is so different that it warrants description in detail. Usually, the mounter has the stones to work for this, and they are placed on to a piece of Plasticine or white wax for convenience. They should be placed as close together as it is reasonable, allowing only sufficient metal between each to enable the setter to secure the stones, and to give the head sufficient strength.

In principle, the less metal that is left showing in the finished ring, the better the appearance, but one has to be careful with this setting not to carry the principle too far, thus sacrificing the strength of the finished ring. Having set out the arrangement of stones, which we will assume to be an average size of approximately $\frac{3}{8}$ in (10 mm) up to $\frac{1}{2}$ in (12 mm) in diameter, the first step is to mill down a strip of metal (which in most cases is platinum but need not necessarily be so) of 14 to 15 gauge (not less) and a fraction more than $\frac{1}{8}$ in (3 mm) wide. This is curved edgewise to form an arc whose diameter would be about $\frac{3}{4}$ in (20 mm). Then from this a circle is bent up in a manner similar to the methods used for making a collet. This will result in a steeply tapered shallow collet. The top should have a diameter of $\frac{1}{16}$ in (1.5 mm) greater than the diameter of the outside of the stones arranged on the wax or Plasticine. After the joint has been soldered with the hardest solder possible, the shape is corrected either on the sparrowhawk or with punches.

It should, perhaps, be mentioned here that I am assuming this to be a round top cluster. It may be oval or 'cushion' shaped, but that is quite immaterial as far as the method and general principles are concerned, and so these slight

variations can be ignored for descriptive purposes. When the shape and size are correct, the inside top edge can be filed to approximately half its thickness, but at the *top* only, in the manner indicated in Fig. 125.

The cluster top has to be made next, but cutting out a circle of platinum from 10 gauge sheet, just a little larger than the diameter of the inside of the top of the bezel just described. This is domed to a smooth, even shape, as with the usual cluster tops. Then the edges are filed, and the shape and size adjusted so that it fits correctly into the top of the bezel, and in such a manner that the top of the bezel itself is level with the top surface of the domed circle just made. Another important point is that the angle at which the edge is filed must be such that no gap is left between it and the inner side of the bezel. The illustration showing a sectional view of the cluster at this stage (Fig. 125) will help to clarify this point.

At this stage the bezel is placed on a charcoal block and the top placed in position; using the hardest possible solder the two parts are soldered together. A minimum of filing is now done in the preparation for the next stage. It is sufficient only to remove surplus solder, if any, and to make the top surface of bezel and cluster top appear as one. The bottom of the bezel can also be filed flat and parallel to the top edge, but it is not necessary at this stage to file up the outside of the bezel.

Drilling the holes and enlarging them for the stones is the next job. Starting again with the centre hole, it is enlarged to accommodate the centre stone, bearing in mind whether this stone is to be set in raised claws or raised millegrain, or set directly into the surface. Almost invariably the centre stone is raised in claws, in which case the centre hole will be left just a little smaller than would otherwise be required. From there the outside stones are dealt with in the same manner as with ordinary clusters. If the centre stone is to be raised in claws, now is the time to make the claws and insert them in between each of the outer stones, gapping them in with the saw, and so forth.

Scalloping the Cluster

When this has been completed, the outside is filed up in scallops, following the shape of the outside stones. One will probably see now the reason for the

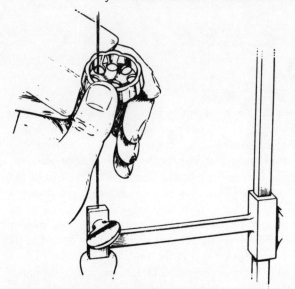

Fig. 126. Sawing scallops inside the bezel of the cluster.

original bezel being so thick (14–15 gauge). If it were not so, it would not be possible to scallop in the outside without filing right through the metal, and it must have sufficient strength left after being scalloped to keep the head strong and able to stand up to reasonable wear. It should also be noted that the whole of the outside is scalloped, from front to back, and not just front only. When these scallops have been completed, the outside can then be sandpapered to a smooth finish before continuing.

Looking now at the bottom of the head so far made, it will be seen that the inside of the bezel is not scalloped, and so does not correspond to the outside. A good plan is to bring the saw-frame into use to alter this. By placing the saw through the outer halo in the setting (each in turn) with the cluster head held upside-down to enable the work to be watched carefully, the bottom of the bezel can be scalloped on the inside also (Fig. 126). See again the illustration showing stages of making this type of setting in Fig. 125.

The last stage can be done by using the small round-point needle-file instead of the saw-frame, but it is always an advantage to make good use of the latter whenever possible.

Before beginning to shape the claws, it is best to make the under bezel. This is made in a similar manner to the back bezel for a single claw setting, but from thicker metal. Using metal (gold in most cases) of 12 gauge by $\frac{3}{16}$ in (5 mm) wide, the bezel is made with tapered sides, sufficiently large for the top outer edge to extend to the bottom outer edge of the cluster head,

Fig. 127. (above) Proportions of claw
cluster to under-bezel.

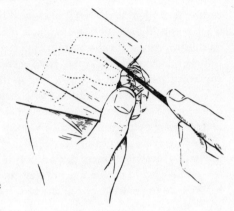

Fig. 128. (right) Holding the cluster
for filing. The fingers shown dotted are
under the bench pin.

in effect so that the sides of both will form a continuous line, except that the
back bezel will not be scalloped (Fig. 127). The depth of this back bezel
($\frac{3}{16}$ in, 5 mm) may seem rather great, but it must be remembered that, at a
later stage, the shape of the finger will have to be filed out of it.

When this has been completed, its joint soldered, etc, and corrected for
shape and size, the next step will be to form the claws on the head. As
with other claws the bottom is done first. The back bezel can be placed aside
for a while. Usually the style of claw used for the coronet-cluster is the 'organ-
pipe' type. In fact, although other styles are used on odd occasions, one might
say that this is the only really suitable style, and the only one we need to be
concerned with.

Scalloping the Base of the Cluster
Continuing with the making of a coronet cluster, we now have the head
ready for scalloping, the back bezel made in readiness for when it will be
required and from there we can proceed to scallop the bottom part of the
claws. An important question here is how best to hold the head for this
operation. Most workers can hold it quite satisfactorily in the left hand, resting
it against the bench pin, in the manner shown in Fig. 128. The right hand
will, of course, hold the three-square needle-file, and while the work is held
in this fashion, it can clearly be seen just where and how far the filing is going.

Some jewellers prefer to use another means of holding it. A good one is to
have a piece of hard wood $\frac{1}{4}$ in (6 mm) or so in diameter to which has been
melted some shellac or setter's cement. The head can be warmed and placed
upside-down into this cement while the latter is still warm. After cooling,
any surplus cement can be removed from the sides. This will provide a
rigid means of holding the head while scalloping it. It will be noticed, of

course, that whereas the head when held in the hand has its side uppermost, when it is held on a stick as described, it can be held either way, that is with its side uppermost, or the bottom uppermost according to individual choice. Whichever method is selected, from there the next step is in effect the same, so we can assume that it is now held in the hand as first described.

With the three-square file, cut a V-shape immediately below each of the holes for the stones and one in between each of these. This means, of course, that there are twice the number of V-shapes as there are stones in the cluster. These V-shapes are cut in a very similar manner to that for the claw settings previously described, i.e., having only a point in between each. The file should be used in such a manner that the V is larger on the outside of the head than on the inside, and finally each 'point' should be rounded off on the outer side.

Fig. 129 shows several stages in this operation. It is most important that none of the points is reduced in height while filing them as they must be soldered to the back bezel and therefore must all be equal in height. This then is the next stage. The back bezel can either be tied on with binding wire and thus held in position while all the points are soldered, each with a small paillon of solder. Alternatively, solder can be 'flooded' round the surface of the back bezel first and then the back bezel placed in position on the claw head (on a charcoal block) while the solder is again heated sufficiently to join points and back bezel.

Of the two methods, the former is better and usually cleaner, as in this case one may use very small paillons of solder, just sufficient in fact to attach the point, whereas in the latter there is always the danger that too much solder will run to one point, and so the neatness of the finished article will be impaired.

Cutting the Claws

The shank is now made and soldered on, but this part will be dealt with shortly as a separate process, and so for the present we will assume that this has been done (see Chapter 6). Cutting the claws is the final operation as far as the mounter is concerned, and is carried out in a very similar manner to the cutting of claws in the other types of claw head. Once again the ring stick is used to hold the ring rigidly during this process. Each scallop is made with the saw at such an angle that the outside is larger than the inside. In fact, the jeweller has no alternative but to do this, as the cluster top (or

Fig. 129.   Stages in filing the V-cuts.

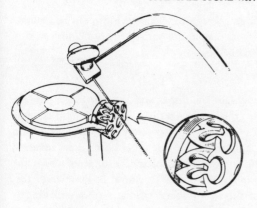

Fig. 130. (left)   How the
scallops are made.
Fig. 131. (above)   The scraper.

setting surface) makes it quite impossible to do otherwise. The 'in-betweens'
or 'ear-pieces' as they are often called (that is to say the parts of the outside
setting edge between the stones), are left as wide as practicable to give more
security to the stones when set. Fig. 130 shows an enlarged view of these
scallops.

Practice at cutting claws with the saw will lead to the stage where very little
needs to be done afterwards; the claws themselves can be smoothed and made
even, where necessary, with a knife-edged needle-file. The bottom of the
scallops can be finished off firstly with a round point needle-file and finally
scraped with a scraper.

The scraper is a very useful addition to one's tools and simply is an old
three-square needle-file broken off a little from the end and then ground down
to a steeply tapered three-cornered point with the corners kept very sharp
(Fig. 131). The corners are the important part and it is these which are used
to scrape the inner side of small curves such as found at the bottom of
scallops. At this stage, the ring goes from the mounter to the polisher for its
preliminary polishing and then on to the setter.

Most general types of rings have now been described and practically any
ring can be placed in one of those types. One exception, however, is the
fancy asymmetrical large ring usually referred to as the cocktail (or dress)
ring. The designs of these are impossible to enumerate, in fact, each one is
usually an individual article and is not produced in quantity or repeated more
than a very limited number of times. Thereby lies its character and attraction.

Such rings, however, do not (as far as making is concerned) follow in the
same general principles as the more usual type of ring, namely head made
first and then shank and shoulders, with 'shank' being one of the fairly
regular types of design. In fact, the shank of a dress ring is more often

'built in', as it were, to the general design of the ring. More can be detailed about those, but having now reached a point where ordinary shanks can well be dealt with, I shall proceed with them.

Making the Shank

The shank is a band which encircles the finger and the 'shoulders' are the parts which join immediately to the head or setting. The very simplest type of shank is made from half-round wire approximately 0.085 in by 0.065 in (2 × 1.7 mm) bent into a circle, with the flat side innermost, to the required finger size. Allowance is made for the width of the head, after which the shoulders are hammered to form a spear-point. This must be done very carefully and without wastage of metal. In other words, without making it necessary to do much filing to remove any hammer marks or marks from a rough hammering block. The best way to do this is to get a hammer with a smooth face and a smooth-surfaced 'flat-iron' (steady block or other name by which a solid block of steel for hammering on may be known).

After annealing the ends of the shank, hold the ends (one at a time must be dealt with) at a slight angle to the surface of the block and also hold the hammer with its face at a slight angle so that hammering makes the end of the shank into a wedge shape, with a point on the outside and a thick part on the inside of the ring. Fig. 132 will help to clarify this. After completing the hammering, the shoulders must again be annealed and the shank corrected for size and roundness.

A half-size should always be allowed in making the shank, for later correction and finishing. For example, if a ring is to be made to finish at size M, the shank should be made as L½ and kept as round as possible through all its stages. Thus, when the head has been soldered in and the ring is ready for its final tapping round and filing, it will finish at its required size. Returning now to the tapped-up shank, the next job is to file the ends of the shank to the correct angle to fit the head, which can then be soldered in.

Soldering Head and Shank Together

The actual soldering is easy enough but holding the head in position on the shank is another matter. Three ways might be mentioned:
(1) Tie it in with binding wire;
(2) Hold between lightly sprung tweezers; or
(3) Make a very small step at the bottom of the back bezel, and fit the shank into this, sprung very lightly so that it remains in position without further means of holding it (Fig. 133).

An important point with the shoulders of this type of shank is that one

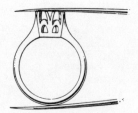

Fig. 132. (above) Shank
hammered to shape.

Fig. 133. Three ways of
holding the cluster for
soldering.

must avoid getting them too thin and weak. The skill lies in making the shoulders high enough and thick enough at the same time.

A few points which apply to this and indeed all kinds of shanks in relation to the heads might be mentioned here, and afterwards not repeated as it should be understood that they always apply!

When soldering the head into the shank, an imaginary line through the centre of the head must point directly to the centre of the shank (Fig. 134). Looking from the side of the ring, an imaginary line across the top of the ring must be at right angles to the line of the shank, and the shank itself must be flat. When looked at from above, a line drawn through the centre of the head should continue through the centre of the shank on both sides of the head. These are perhaps fairly obvious points, but are very common faults.

Making a Heavier Shank

It may be necessary to make a shank of this style but with heavier and stronger shoulders than would result from using the above method. For this one must start with a piece of gold, square in section, about 24 gauge in thickness and $1\frac{1}{2}$ in (35 mm) long for an average sized head and for a ring of average finger size. Then a rather difficult milling operation follows, which needs great care.

Unscrew the square mills so that the square wire being used can be placed with its centre in between the mills. Screw down the adjusting screw on top of the mills so that it will reduce the thickness of the square wire. Then, by very careful manipulation of the handle of the mills, steadily roll out the wire in the centre only, leaving about $\frac{1}{4}$ in (6 mm) at each end of the original thickness (see Fig. 135). Only a little difference in thickness can be achieved each time, and then the adjusting screw of the mills must be raised again so that the wire can be taken out, turned over, and put into the next groove of

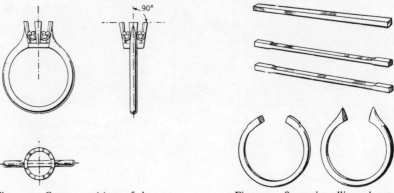

Fig. 134.   Correct positions of cluster in the shank.

Fig. 135.   Stages in rolling a heavy shank.

the mills for further reducing the centre part only. This is not by any means easy, and is a method only used when it is not practicable to use any other.

The centre is reduced to about 19 gauge square and, after annealing, the thinner part is hammered on the swaging block to make it half round, after which it is bent round to form the shank. We now have very heavy square shoulders which can be hammered to the appropriate shape and filed as necessary to fit the head.

There are several difficulties met with in making a shank of this type. A very real one is how to judge the final length. It will be realised that in milling the centre thinner, the length is considerably increased and the amount of this increase can only be judged by experience. The length of the head of the ring and the finger size of the finished article all have to be borne in mind. However, there are some occasions when this method has to be used, and therefore it is worth mentioning. There was a time when more or less all shanks were fashioned in this way.

6. Special Shank and Dress Rings

A further step from the tapped-up shoulder shank, which has been dealt with, is the 'split-up' type, which is made in a similar fashion. Using the half-round wire, as before, the ends are hammered a little to give a slightly spear-point appearance, but not so much as with the tap-up shank; this will, of course, leave the shoulders thicker.

Taking a very fine saw-blade (6/o is the best type), a saw cut is made $\frac{1}{4}$ in (6 mm) along each of the shoulders, keeping carefully to the centre. After annealing them, the upper part can be carefully lifted a little with a penknife in the fine saw cut to make the shoulder higher. Then a pair of pliers can be used to improve the shape of this lifted-up part to form a slight curve, as illustrated in Fig. 136. This is not a very strong shoulder at this stage; a good plan is to solder a small piece of chenier into each of the openings thus left. This improves the appearance as well as adding strength. A lot will depend upon the thickness of the wire from which the shank is made as to whether it is possible to use this method, or even the tapped-up shoulder.

The tendency to-day is for very light shanks of a fairly flat D shape section, and with these it is practically impossible to make a satisfactory job of this type. The following type of shoulder is much to be preferred in such cases. Most bullion dealers have a fairly wide range of stamped-out shoulders to offer to manufacturers while many ring makers stamp out their own (Fig. 137). Either way, such shoulders can be used to very great advantage where speed of manufacture and lightness in weight are important considerations. They might be divided roughly into two types:

    (1) Those which are not particularly wide; and

    (2) Those which are wide enough to render it necessary to divide the ends

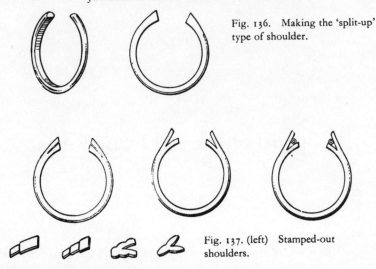

Fig. 136. Making the 'split-up' type of shoulder.

Fig. 137. (left) Stamped-out shoulders.

of the shank widthwise and open them to make them up to the width of the top of the shoulders.

Narrow-shouldered Shanks

Taking the first type: before the shank is soldered to the head, it is necessary to place the shank on the triblett and hammer the ends of the shank a little thinner. This will make them wider, just sufficiently wide in fact to equal the width of the shoulder to be used. When this has been done and the shank kept as round as possible and correctly to finger size throughout, the head can be soldered in by using either of the three methods already described (see Chapter 5).

Now comes the soldering of the shoulder pieces themselves, but before doing this the shank must have a step filed into each shoulder to provide a proper support and resting place for them. The position of the step will depend upon the length of the shoulders, and must be filed at such a place as will make the shoulder rest against the side of the head of the ring at an appropriate height. Each shoulder can then be soldered in position. However a point is worth mentioning here about the solders used. Usually the shank itself will be of yellow gold, while the shoulder pieces will be of white gold or palladium. It is a good plan to use a good medium flow silver solder at the top of the shoulder where it joins the head, and a medium, or easy, flow gold solder where it joins the shank. There is not much soldering to be done to the ring after this stage and therefore a hard solder is neither neces-

Fig. 138.   Stages in making a ring with stamped-out shoulders.

sary nor wise. The colour of the solders used is always worth considering nonetheless.

After both shoulders have been soldered on, a piece of chenier can be cut out for each and placed into the space between shoulder and shank, so that it is touching both. A small paillon of fairly easy silver solder should be used to solder it in position (Fig. 138).

Wide-shouldered Shanks

The next step can be left for the present while mention is made of the type of shoulder which is too wide for the shank to be used in this way. With this, the shank is tapped on the shoulders (on the triblett as before) and then using again a very fine saw-blade it is cut down as far as necessary to enable the shank to be opened width-wise to the full width of the shoulder being used (Fig. 139). It may also be necessary in addition to opening it, to shape it in such a manner as will simulate the shape of the shoulder itself. It cannot be made a perfect shape, of course, and will need to be filed afterwards. Not very much thickness is available for filing into the shoulder shape and so care has to be used to ensure that the shape is at least similar in outline.

This done, the shank can be soldered to the head. Again there must be a step filed in the shoulder part of the shank to accommodate the other end of the shoulder to be soldered on. As before, the shoulders, when placed in position, must have the top part resting against the head at an appropriate

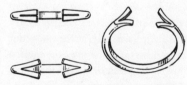

Fig. 139.   A shank split another way.

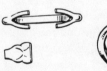

Fig. 140.   Final stages in making the wider shouldered ring.

height. When soldered, a length of chenier can be used to strengthen and improve the shoulders as already described (Fig. 140).

Correcting Shape and Filing Up

In both types now the procedure is the same. Firstly, the inside of the ring must be filed with the half-round hand file to remove surplus solder, if any, and to bring the back of the head of the ring to an appropriate curve with the shank. After that, the ring can be placed on the triblett again and gently tapped with the hammer to make it perfectly round and to correct finger size. When this has been done, a check should be made to ensure that the ring is true with regard to the points described as being necessary in all rings, i.e., geometrically correct as to alignment of head and shank, etc. It is quite easy during the stage of making a ring round on the triblett to lose this proper alignment.

When these points are satisfactorily ensured, the final stage of filing up the ring can begin. It is well to begin with the sides of the shoulders and shank. There will be very little filing to be done on the back of the shank as its thickness is already as near as possible to the required weight; and the only purpose in filing it at all is to remove any hammer and other marks that may have resulted during the work. The shoulders themselves, if of the stamped variety, will need only sufficient filing to remove the burrs from stamping, but the part of the shank which is underneath the shoulders will have to be filed to follow exactly the shape of the shoulder pieces. During this procedure the ends of the pieces of chenier will also be filed off to be level with the shoulders. Any surplus solder which may have run on to the ring is also filed off and the ring is then sandpapered to the required finish.

Other Points to Remember

A few further points worthy of note, with regard to the relative position of heads and shanks, might well be mentioned here. When soldering the head into the shank, it is necessary to arrange it symmetrically in relation to the number of claws. For example, a single-stone claw ring could have a claw to the centre of the shank or the space between two claws to the centre of shank (Fig. 141). The choice of the most suitable depends upon the type of shoulder to be used. If the shoulder finishes in a point, then it will be necessary to have a claw for this point to be soldered to. Alternatively, if the shoulder finishes up fairly wide at the top, then it is much better to have two claws to which to solder. In the case of a round cluster ring, there is not the same necessity to decide because the shoulders will have to be made to fit to the cluster edge anyway, but it is usual, and certainly it looks better in most

Fig. 141. Arrangement of heads in relation to shanks.

cases, to have a stone 'top and bottom' as it is usually termed. That is to say, to have one stone on each side of the ring, which if joined by an imaginary line would make a right-angle to the shank itself.

Shoulders Set with Diamonds

If the ring is to have diamonds in the shoulders, the method is very similar to those described. It may be done with the type of shank which has been rolled in the centre to leave heavy shoulders. In which case, a thin layer of platinum is soldered to the top of the shoulder before the head is soldered in. Then, in the final stages, small holes are drilled to take the diamonds.

The more usual method at present, to save time and weight of metal, is as follows: the shank is made from half-round wire and the ends hammered just a little wider before soldering in the head as already described. The shoulder pieces are then made of platinum, 12-gauge in thickness and a little wider than the shank itself. After cutting off the appropriate lengths for each shoulder, a step is filed into the shank at the position where it will support the platinum pieces at an appropriate height up the side of the head, as shown in Fig. 142. When soldered in position, a piece of chenier can be soldered in each for strength. When filing up, the shoulders are then left their full width at the top by the head and tapered off to the width of the shank. Right at the top, it is usual to file the shoulders to a very steeply tapered point, after which they are ready to be drilled.

Drilling is a rather difficult operation and has to be done with utmost care to avoid the drill from going astray and not finishing in the centre of the shank underneath the shoulders. A good plan is to drill the top hole in each shoulder (that is the one nearest to the head) through the shoulder piece only, and the other two holes through both shoulder piece and shank. This is where the greatest care is needed, as a slight error in angle is sufficient to make the drill break through the sides of the shank.

Fig. 142. Shoulders for setting diamonds.

Cross-over Shanks

Cross-over shanks are still very popular indeed, with three-stone and five-stone rings, as well as with two-stone rings. One can find a very wide variation in the patterns of the shoulders in either of these, just as can be found with half-loops ('straight' rings). The methods of making these, however, do not vary much, and for the purpose of practical description can be treated alike.

Firstly, it should be mentioned that the good old-style method of making the shank from square wire, as described above, is very useful on the odd occasions where heavier shoulders are needed for diamonds or other reasons, especially when the shank is made of one metal only, such as platinum. In that case, no other metal is soldered on to the shoulders to add thickness. This involves considerable judgment and practice to get the correct length and also involves a fairly high wastage of metal in filing, because a little extra in all dimensions must be allowed for correction and shaping afterwards. However, for the present we can assume that the shank has been milled in the centre and bent roughly to form the finger shape. We can leave it there until the first stages of the more usual method have been described, because from there the method of bending the cross-over will be the same for both types.

Preparing the Shank and Shoulder Pieces

Using half-round wire of the thickness mentioned previously for shanks (approx. 0.08 × 0.06 in, 2 × 1.5 mm) a little more than a complete circle is bent up at the correct finger size with sufficient overlap to permit the cross-over shank to be fashioned, and for the shoulder ends to be soldered in the proper place on the head. This is usually between two settings, as in Fig. 143. The required allowance can only be decided upon by considering the type of head, e.g. three-stone, five-stone, etc. The next step is to straighten out the back of the shank and so part the shoulders (Fig. 142). This is simply to facilitate handling whilst soldering on the shoulder pieces. White gold or palladium is mostly used for shoulders, and the metal should be wider than the shank, and approximately 12 gauge in thickness.

Taking up the shank, a step is filed in it and the top surface of the shoulder part is filed flat for the length which is to be thickened with white gold. The shoulder strip must then be cut off to the proper length and bent to fit exactly to the curve of the shank. A good tip here is to bend up a length of 3 or 4 in (7.5–10 cm) of white gold strip rather than do each piece separately. In doing this, a more even curve is thus ensured. The inside curve of the white gold must be made clean by sandpapering to make sure that the solder

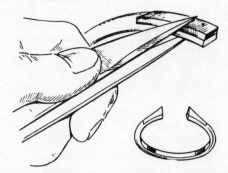

Fig. 143. (above)   Preparing the shank
for shoulder piece.
Fig. 144. (right)   Soldering the
shoulders.

can run and, after brushing borax on the surfaces to be soldered, they can best be held together in position by tweezers, then soldered with the hardest possible solder that the metals will stand (Fig. 144).

Forming the Shape

Having soldered on the white gold strip, we can now continue to form the shape required for the cross-over. In many patterns, particularly those with the plain type of cross-over shoulders, it is better to hammer the ends only, to make them a little thinner and a little deeper. Whenever the pattern permits, it is wiser to do this, otherwise the shoulders look too low in proportion to the height of the head when the ring is finished.

The next step is to make the shank round again, with the shoulders crossing each other by the appropriate amount. It is most important to ensure that these cross over the correct way, namely that, looking downwards from the top of the shank, the right-hand portion is uppermost. The illustration (Fig. 145) will make the meaning quite clear. The reason for cross-over rings always having their shoulders crossing in this and not in the opposite direction is not easily discernible.

When starting to bend the cross-over shoulders, it will be found most convenient to hold the shank very securely with a pair of flat-nosed pliers at the point where it is wished to commence the bend. This first bend can then be made with a strong pair of half-round pliers. This is done to both shoulders with the result shown in the illustration (Fig. 146). The ends of

Fig. 145.   Forming the crossover.   Fig. 146.   Ends bent to fit claws.

Fig. 147.   Head soldered to cross-over. Arrows show the four soldering points.

each shoulder can now be bent round with strong round-nosed pliers to the appropriate curve. A very important point here is to keep the shank round throughout this process, constantly correcting it as necessary, as it is very difficult to correct a badly-shaped cross-over ring after the head has been soldered in.

The shank should be so shaped that, in the case of a three-stone or five-stone ring, the shoulders are in contact with the head at two points each side (Fig. 147). When the head has been fitted correctly, ready for soldering in, the inner side of the shoulders should be filed up and sandpapered quite smooth. The head itself should also be finished off by sandpapering and, if it is a claw head, then the claws should also be cut and the whole head completely finished. It is a good plan to have the head and inside of the shoulders polished before soldering together. This results in a much better finish to the completed ring.

A Useful Tool for Claw Cutting

A point which arises here is how to hold a claw head without a shank whilst cutting the claws. A simple, but very useful, addition to one's equipment can be made for this job, and should always be kept close to hand. It consists of a circle of metal wire of approximately size M with a piece cut out roughly the size of an average three-stone head. The ends are hammered flat and a hole drilled in either end. Into each hole, a very short peg, about ⅛ in (3 mm) long, is soldered. The gadget is now ready for use (Fig. 148). One peg is placed in each end hole of the head to be scalloped and the whole is then placed in the ring stick which is tightened up, thus holding the head firmly (Fig. 149).

Fig. 148.   Fixture for holding head.

Fig. 149.   Head in position on tool.

Fig. 150. Alignment of head on shank.

Soldering in the Head

Continuing now with the shank after polishing, it is ready to have the head soldered in, and this is the next step. If the shank is one of the fancy types, where the outside of the shoulders has to be filed up to form one of the variety of patterns possible, it may be necessary to make some variation in the way the shank is shaped, but the principle is the same in all cases.

After the head has been soldered in, the general principles for filing up and finishing are much the same as for half-hoop rings. That is to file out the surplus solder, etc, from inside the ring under the head, and then make the ring perfectly round on the triblett. Begin by filing the shoulders into the proper pattern, and continue on to the back of the shank.

There are several points to be observed with regard to the accuracy of the general lines of a cross-over ring. Looking from the top of the ring down on to it, the shank should be shaped the same amount on each side of the head. The parts of the shank on either side of the head before the cross-over pattern commences should be in a continuous line with each other (Fig. 150).

From the end view of the ring, an imaginary line drawn across the top of the head should be at right angles to the vertical line of the shank. Practice is needed to make a well-shaped and well-proportioned cross-over ring. Little needs to be added to the above description in the case of cross-over rings with diamond shoulders.

Shanks with Sharp Angles

A slight variation of method is required when a shank which has a sharp angle as part of its design, has to be made (Fig. 151). A good sharp corner cannot be achieved simply by bending; instead, the shank has to be filed in the appropriate place to form the sharp angle. Measuring as accurately as possible the amount required for actually crossing over and also for the section beyond the angle, a V-shaped groove is filed in the shank with a three-square needle-file, as far as is practicable, after which the ends of the shank are bent round and solder is flushed into the groove (Fig. 152).

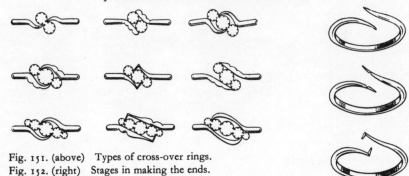

Fig. 151. (above)   Types of cross-over rings.
Fig. 152. (right)   Stages in making the ends.

This method can be used both when the shank is made of one metal only, or when the shoulders are fronted with a white metal. A good plan with this type is to file up the shoulders and remove surplus solder, etc, and then sandpaper the top and inside of the shoulders before soldering in the head.

An easier flowing solder must be used for soldering in the head than was used for soldering up the groove at the angle of the shoulder. This will avoid remelting the solder at this point.

Drilling the Shoulders

Quite often fancy scalloped shoulders, as well as plain shoulder shapes, are drilled and set with diamonds. Drilling is an operation which needs the greatest possible care as it is almost always necessary to use a very small diameter drill. The thickness of metal, too, which has to be drilled is usually considerable. It is therefore obvious that the drill must be kept perfectly upright to avoid any breaking through the sides of the shank. Care must also be exercised to keep both the ring and drill absolutely steady to avoid breaking the drill in the hole.

At this point, it might be useful to mention one or two methods which are worth trying, in the event of such a mishap. Assuming that the drill has broken off flush with the top of the hole, it will be necessary to anneal the ring very thoroughly and allow it to cool as slowly as possible. This will soften the drill, as well as slightly loosening it by the expansion and contraction of both drill and ring. It is quite useless to try to hasten the cooling by quenching in water as this only rehardens the drill.

Sometimes the drill breaks off when it is almost through the shoulder; if so, there is sometimes the impression formed by the drill on the inside of the ring just at the actual breaking-through point. If this is so, then the job is easy. With a small pointed punch, such as a scriber, the drill can be knocked back from inside the ring and the hole completed at the same time. One is not usually so lucky, however. More often no trace of the place where the drill will come through is visible.

Two methods are now available. In the first one, get another drill, the same diameter as the hole, and drill the old drill out, then continue drilling through the shoulder as before. This sounds easy but in practice it does not work out quite so simply: drill steel is tough, even when softened, and it takes a lot of drilling with a good drill, sharpened repeatedly, to remove it in this manner.

The second method of removal is to estimate the spot on the inside of the ring where the drill hole will break through, and then start drilling from that point towards the top of the shoulder. It is almost certain that the drill will not meet the opposite end of the hole exactly, but usually it is sufficiently accurate for the hole to be continued and the broken drill pushed out through the top of the hole.

'Goldware' Rings

Sufficient has now been written about cross-over rings to cover more or less every type to be met with and, in fact, the only type of rings left are the 'goldware' rings (e.g. wedding rings, signet rings, and variations of both), and the individualistic type of fancy dress ring or cocktail ring which cannot be said to follow any special type. With regard to wedding rings and signets, a little can be added which may be of practical value to conclude the description of ring work. Before that, cocktail and fancy rings can be dealt with as far as it is practical to do so.

The symmetrical type of ornate ring known, generally, as the cocktail, or semi-cocktail, ring is usually an individual piece of workmanship, following no orthodox pattern or style but being, instead, just 'extra ordinary'. The more unusual its lines, the better it seems to fit its purpose. To discuss its beauty or otherwise is not part of the intended work of this book, and no doubt opinions will vary very greatly on this point.

One can imagine, however, how infinitely greater is the scope of the designer when working on this type of ring; how much greater, also, is the opportunity of the workman who carries out the design. For however carefully the former may do his work, the craftsman must have in mind the moulding of the ring, its relief and its incidental ornamentation such as the gallery, etc. One can realise, also, just how difficult it is to describe the making of this type of ring. It is only possible to take one more or less average specimen and, from the stages in producing it, to describe what may be applied as general principles.

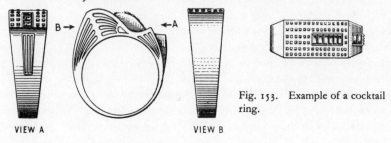

VIEW A   VIEW B

Fig. 153.   Example of a cocktail ring.

Starting Point for a Cocktail or Fancy Dress Ring

It is fairly certain that the beginning of this ring will be either from an array of stones set out upon a waxed tin or from a carefully prepared sketch card. It does not matter very much which is used, because in either case the essential dimensions are obtained. What one has not got, is the full amount of relief, or 'side view', and the height from the finger in its various places. Right from the start, one must picture this and visualise the finished article so that, as soon as the first piece of metal is cut and shaped, a clear picture of its position and relation to the rest of the ring can be visualised, and so with each progressive piece.

The first parts to be made will be those into which stones will be set. Usually there are several pieces, and each will have to be cut and shaped before any holes are cut for diamonds or other stones. Assume now that the ring in the diagram is the one we are making. (This is, in fact, a drawing of an actual ring made by the author, Fig. 153.) The first piece made in this instance is the platinum setting for the diamonds; this is fairly straightforward as far as its size goes, having the diamonds to work from. An allowance has to be made for the actual bending. Fairly thick platinum, 13 gauge, is needed to give sufficient strength, bearing in mind that the diamonds are set closely together and little metal is therefore left for support. This piece is shaped only and, in the initial stages, no holes are drilled for the diamonds (Fig. 154).

Making the Side Pieces

The next step is to make the yellow 18 ct gold sides which form the settings for the square sapphires. This is done by taking two flat pieces of 9 gauge metal cut to the appropriate shape and separated, or held apart to the width required by the sapphires, by soldering three or four struts of metal in between. These should not extend quite to the outside of the curved edge, as they might obstruct the setting of the sapphires at a later stage. It might be noted that, in this type of setting, no metal shows at all in-between the sapphires as they actually touch. This and the outer edge holds them in place.

This is a particular style of setting which the setter has to learn. As far as the mounter is concerned, the correct width has to be made in accordance with the stones to permit the setter to do his part. This means, in effect, placing the two setting edges at such a distance apart that the stones, when placed in position, rest on the edges, but do not drop through, and leave a thin edge of metal showing at each side (Fig. 155).

Having made this part, then, the first piece must be cut out in its centre to allow this section to fit in tightly. This is done simply by drilling and saw-piercing. There are two main reasons why this should be so fitted in and not simply soldered on top:

1. It would be extremely difficult to place it in position and solder it accurately without it moving out of place;

2. It would not, if so soldered, allow light to come through from the back of the stones, and it would also trap particles of dust and rouge, etc from polishing, underneath the stones.

Having fitted this piece as described, it must be placed aside and not, at this stage, be soldered in position (Fig. 156).

Fig. 154. (left) Platinum setting cut and shaped.
Fig. 155. (right) The mount.

Fig. 156. Parts shown in Fig. 154 and Fig. 155 in position for soldering together.

This is a *very important* point with this type of ring. It will be noticed that it is made of two metals, platinum and 18 ct gold, and it will also be remembered that platinum has a much higher melting point and will, therefore, stand much harder solders than gold of any quality. If this gold section were soldered into the first part at this stage, it would mean that, from then on only comparatively easy-flowing solders could be used throughout. These would be totally unsuitable for the many platinum joints and would also show up badly in the finished ring. It follows then that this gold piece, and the other gold piece yet to be made, must be left as late as possible before soldering in position.

Drilling the Holes for the Diamonds

Returning now to the first piece made, we can now mark out the places for drilling for the diamonds and then proceed to drill these and saw-pierce out the holes as required. It is quite a sound policy to drill all the holes with a fairly small drill. However care must be taken, when saw-piercing them out to the size needed for the stones, to do them in an order which will ensure that they can be so enlarged. In this instance, the centre line of holes must be enlarged first, and then the outside lines afterwards. If it were done in the other way (outside lines first), it may be found that there is insufficient room to open out the centre ones as large as is required.

After each has been sawn out and fraised, the backs of the holes can be saw-pierced to form a neat but simple pattern. This may perhaps seem unnecessary, but it does help to make the finished ring a little better; people do look inside a ring when examining it, and it looks so much better to see a neatly finished article with clean back settings than to see ragged ones which result from the saw-piercing, etc. Again, an article of this value is worthy of the little extra time spent on achieving a good finish. A very simple but neat pattern is shown in Fig. 157 for saw-pierced back settings.

Building the Framework

We follow now by building up a framework for the ring, and making two circles of square wire in platinum, quite thin (10 gauge is sufficient), to the required finger size, allowing about a half size for actually finishing the job. These two rims or circles will be soldered with the hardest possible solder and will require very careful handling. On to the side of one of these, a small piece of wire is soldered which represents the width of the back of the ring. This can be done with easy-flowing solder because, at a later stage, this piece will be removed. It is, in fact, only to serve as a temporary support that we use it at all. The other circle is then soldered to the other end of this 'strut'. This is not as difficult as it may sound; it can be done fairly easily by holding it in place with tweezers while heating it for soldering (Fig. 158).

After adjusting the width of the top to correspond exactly with the width of the setting section already made, this can be soldered very carefully in place, again using a very hard solder and using tweezers or binding wire as the means of holding in position. When both rims have been soldered to the underside of the top, we have the start of the structure of the ring, as yet very weak, but nevertheless something on which to build (Fig. 159).

Fig. 157. (left) A new pattern for saw-pierced back settings.

Fig. 158. Soldering circles and strut together.

Fig. 159.   Part Fig. 154 soldered into position. *The slot has been omitted to simplify the drawings.*

Fig. 160.   Setting supports soldered in position.

Placing the Supports and Outer Band

Two supports for the ends of the setting are now placed in position and soldered (Fig. 160). The angle for these should be carefully considered as it will affect the general lines of the ring very considerably. If they are made to radiate from the centre of the circle, they are usually quite well placed.

The complete outer band comes next. This is extremely difficult and no amount of detailed description would alter that fact. Experience and practical craftsmanship are the prime factors in fitting this piece correctly – and it is essential to get it right. Time and patience are the most important requirements. It is made from a piece of platinum sheet of 8 gauge, the length being measured, as far as is practicable, with the aid of a piece of binding wire. It must be saw-pierced to the required shape, allowing sufficient for filing up and fitting, but at the same time unnecessary wastage of metal should be avoided. This piece is then bent round to form the proper shape and to touch in the proper places.

Nothing more can be said which will make this easier. When a good fit has been made, the small strut of metal which was soldered at the back to keep the two rims apart can be removed, after the solder has been melted, by pulling it out with tweezers. The rims are now supported and held in position by the top part. The outer band is now soldered all round the back of the rims and to the top settings, using hard solder (Fig. 161).

After this has been done, it is as well to remove any surplus metal from the sides of the ring and to check for roundness and general accuracy, before proceeding with the next part.

The second gold setting is the next portion to be made and fitted. Again cut from sheet gold two sides of the required shape, and separate them with short bars to the same width as the previous piece of sapphire setting. This must be fitted into the ring by first marking its position on the outer band, drilling, and then saw-piercing a shaped hole into which it will fit tightly. This must be done very carefully to provide a good close fit, and so avoid any gaps which would have to be filled with solder (Fig. 162).

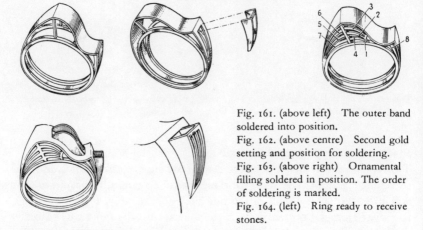

Fig. 161. (above left)   The outer band soldered into position.
Fig. 162. (above centre)   Second gold setting and position for soldering.
Fig. 163. (above right)   Ornamental filling soldered in position. The order of soldering is marked.
Fig. 164. (left)   Ring ready to receive stones.

Making the Final Ornaments

This piece too is now put aside as there is still more platinum soldering to be done before we finally come to the gold. It is clear now that we have the general shape and style of the ring made, and only the filling in with ornamentation remains to be done. This is left, to a very great extent, to the maker of the ring who will himself build in what seems appropriate, and what will also avoid ugly open spaces, as well as providing strength where needed.

The various strips and pieces in this particular ring are done from either side, separately, and do not go right through the ring (Fig. 163). Generally speaking, they are made from square wire, 10 gauge thick (the same as that used for the two rims of the framework), each shaped and soldered individually. The platinum pieces must be soldered in first, before the two gold settings and any additional gold ornamentations are added (Fig. 164).

The illustration shows the order in which the various strips are fitted more clearly than any written description. However the above description of this particular ring will serve to show how a ring of this type is formed, and the infinite varieties of shape and design can be built up, broadly speaking, in a similar manner.

7. Eternity, Wedding and Signet Rings

Eternity rings take several forms and are set with either square coloured stones—emeralds, rubies or sapphires—or the more usual round stones— diamonds—or a combination of the two set alternately. An example of this would be three diamonds, then three square stones, then again three diamonds, and so on right round the ring (Fig. 165).

Despite the fact that bullion dealers are able to offer an excellent range of machine-made eternity rings in various widths, suitable for a varied number of stones, nevertheless, it is still necessary to make rings by hand in specific cases.

Take the diamond eternity ring with round stones first. It must be realised that the number of stones used is governed by their size and the finger size of the ring. The number can also be varied according to whether they are set close together or slightly apart. It is the general principle to get them as close together as reasonably possible while maintaining the strength of the ring.

Preparing the Band
Platinum is usually the metal used and the ring is started by rolling out a piece of square wire to approximately one and two-thirds the width of one of the diamonds, and then rolling it in the flat mills to 22 gauge (usual for an average ring, but this can be varied a little either way according to size of stones). The rolled-out metal is then bent up to form a band of the appropriate finger size, with allowance of one size for final correction and shaping, and soldered with the hardest possible solder.

After removing surplus solder from the joint, the ring is rounded correctly

Fig. 165. Two shapes of stones in an eternity ring.

on the triblett, and filed up as necessary to the correct width, with sides perfectly flat and the outside of the ring just gently smoothed. That is fairly easy and no further detailed description of that stage is necessary.

The next stages call for accuracy and skill in working, particularly with the saw frame. The first thing that must be done is to space out the ring to decide the number of stones. A great help here is to have a series of home-made marking out plates, suitable for a variety of odd and even number of divisions. These plates are made, quite simply, from pieces of flat plate which have a number of circles all marked out deeply, with the aid of a pair of dividers, upon each. The circles are concentric and fairly close together.

Radiating from the centre of the circles are a number of lines, equally spaced around the circumferences of the circles. The plates can be divided into from six to thirteen divisions, and these will be found adequate for most purposes. It is quite easy to sub-divide each division if a greater number is required. An average eternity ring has between 20 and 24 stones. Fig. 166 shows two examples of dividing plates.

Marking Out and Drilling the Ring

Marking out a ring from the plates is quite simple. Hold the ring tightly in place on the plate so that its outer edge is on one of the circles, or at least parallel to it. With a scriber, make a light mark on the ring against each of the radial lines; this divides the ring into the required number of divisions.

Having marked out the ring, the next thing to do is to drill a hole in the centre of each division. It will be found best to use a small drill first, opening out the hole afterwards with a larger drill. To use a large drill initially is more likely to result in inaccuracies. Apart from that, the larger drill generates more heat with consequent 'binding' up with the ring metal. The size of the diamonds must determine the size of the holes, bearing in mind that they must be appreciably smaller than the stones, so that the setter, when doing his work, can enlarge the top of the holes to create a 'bearing' for the stones; but more about that later.

No definite rule can be laid down regarding the actual size of the holes relative to the stones, this being decided in the light of experience. The main point is that they should be as large as practicable, consistent with strength of the ring and the size of the diamonds.

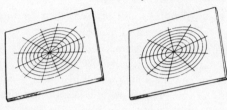

Fig. 166. Two dividing plates.

Saw-piercing the Back Holes

When all holes have been drilled, the inner side of the ring should be gently filed to remove the burrs thrown up by the drill. Now follows the operation requiring the greater skill. This is to saw-pierce the 'back holes' or inside of the drill holes (Fig. 167). The general practice is to cut them into squares, but this can be varied and a number of fairly simple patterns followed (Fig. 168).

Great care has to be exercised when saw-piercing to avoid cutting the sides of the ring and the tops of the holes. The pattern that is cut must be at the back of the holes only, the tops of the holes being left round.

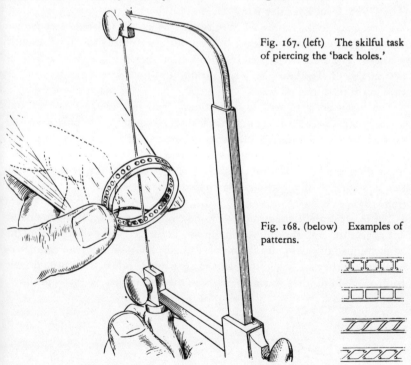

Fig. 167. (left)   The skilful task of piercing the 'back holes.'

Fig. 168. (below)   Examples of patterns.

One may wonder why this is done when it cannot be seen when the ring is being worn. Actually there are two main reasons; one is neatness – the finished ring being subject to examination inside and out by a prospective customer – the other, no less important, is the avoidance of any unnecessary weight in the finished ring. When one considers the price of platinum, it will be realised that to remove even half of one gram of metal will make a noticeable difference to the cost of the ring.

Alternate Stone Eternity Rings

The next type of eternity ring, very similar in manufacture, is that where three or four diamonds and an equal number of square coloured stones are set alternately. The only real difference here is that, when the ring has been drilled, the outsides of the holes which will be set with square stones are saw-pierced and made square, leaving very little between the square stones on top (outside) of the ring. The inside will have sufficient strength left and will, in fact, be similar to the inside of the ring previously described.

The Calibré Set Eternity Ring

We next come to the calibré set eternity ring, which has square or rectangular stones. These are usually coloured stones, but sometimes baguette diamonds are used. The stones touch each other and no metal whatsoever shows in between them. The best plan when making this type is to build it up rather than cut it from one piece.

The first step is to roll down platinum strip to 7 gauge thickness and $\frac{3}{16}$ in (5 mm) wide; roll enough metal to bend up into two circles for the outside rims of the ring. This flat strip is then curved edgewise, by the same method as that used for bending collet strip, to form two flat circles, the inner diameter being slightly smaller than the required finger size. A half size is sufficient, if the circles are shaped as accurately as they should be (Fig. 169).

The joints of these rims must be a good close fit before soldering, to avoid any chance of them showing when the ring is finished and polished. It might be mentioned in passing that solders are usually a little softer than the metals upon which they are being used, and so are liable to polish out a little from a badly made joint, thus leaving a mark on the finished article that will show.

 Fig. 169.

On an eternity ring such as we are dealing with, especially if the sides are left plain and not engraved, this would look very bad indeed.

When the two rims have been made and corrected for shape and also made quite flat they must be held apart by 'struts' or divisions. The distance between the two side rims should be such that, when the stones are resting in position across the two rims, half the thickness of the rims should be visible.

The number of stones to be used is not so very important from the mounter's point of view; indeed it is unusual to find stones, touching each other as these must all round the ring, that will fit exactly. Invariably one or two stones have to be cut to fit closely and complete the circle.

It is very important that sufficient strength and support is assured by the soldering in of a sufficient number of 'struts' without adding unnecessarily to the weight of the ring; the cost of the platinum must be borne in mind.

Making the 'Struts'

The best method of making these 'struts' is to roll out a piece of platinum of the required width and 7 gauge in thickness, then cut it into a number of short lengths as required. Then solder four such pieces on to one of the sides, equidistant from each other. These should be soldered on in such a manner as to reach a little beyond the inner diameter of the side and not quite reach the outer diameter (Fig. 170).

When this soldering has been completed, check for accuracy and distance by which the two sides will be separated by them, to ensure that this is correct for the stones. The other side can then be held in position with binding wire while being soldered to the 'struts'.

Having now the main framework of the ring (Fig. 171), other 'struts' are added (Fig. 172). These will fit tightly enough to stay in position for soldering. It is wise to follow an orderly method of adding the 'struts', to make sure that they are properly placed at equal distances around the ring. A total of sixteen divisions in the ring is an easy and convenient number, and usually sufficient.

When all have been placed and soldered, there remains but the final cleaning up. Start this by filing off the surplus ends of the 'struts' protruding through the inside of the ring. After checking the finger size, and that the

Fig. 170.

Fig. 171.

Fig. 172.

ring is truly round, the inside can be sandpapered ready for polishing. The flat sides of the ring need only very gentle filing, and sandpapering will complete the job.

The Swivel or Triple Eternity Ring

The last type of eternity ring is the 'swivel' or 'triple' eternity ring. This comprises a complete calibré set eternity ring, set with square or rectangular stones, one half of which are of one colour. The stones in the opposite half of the ring are of a different colour. Combinations of stones are chosen from sapphires, rubies, or emeralds—any two of which may be used.

To this ring two semi-circles of diamonds are hinged (Fig. 173). The purpose of this ring is to give the wearer the choice of displaying a band of sapphires, flanked on either side with a band of diamonds, or, by swivelling the two outer half-rings to the opposite side, giving a centre band of different coloured stones. By this means the wearer can choose the band most appropriate to the colour of the dress being worn.

Making the Outer Half-rings

It is unnecessary to describe again the making of the centre band, so we will assume that the ring has been completed to this stage. We now continue with the two outer half-rings. These are a little thinner, in both width and thickness, than the main ring, and are not quite parallel-sided semi-circles. In fact, they taper down towards both ends.

Commence with a piece of square platinum wire and roll it down until the width and thickness are approximately three-quarters of the width and thickness of the centre band. The metal so milled must be longer than required for the two half-bands; the reason for the extra material will be seen shortly.

The next step is to bend up the two half-circles to exactly the same finger size as the centre band, allowing, on each half, $\frac{1}{8}$ in (3 mm) more material than a half circle. When cut, each half is filed very carefully so that it is flat and slightly tapered towards the ends.

It is very important that the sides should be kept flat otherwise, when the joints are made, these outer sections will not fit correctly against the centre part, the result being a very unpresentable and badly finished ring. Following

Fig. 173.   Swivel or triple eternity ring.

 Fig. 174. Completed ring with hinge pieces shown dotted.

 Fig. 175. Hinge shown filed to correct proportion and shape.

their being filed to shape, the two halves should be very carefully sand-papered, and finally smoothed with fine emery paper.

The next operation has to be done with extreme care and patience, accuracy being the key-note; we mean, of course, the joints. Putting aside the outer halves for a while we take up the centre band, and on the side mark two points which are exactly opposite to each other. In other words we divide the ring, literally, into two semi-circles by an imaginary line passing through the centre of the circle.

Taking four small pieces of platinum, 10 gauge in thickness, solder one on each side of the ring across each of the four centre lines, as shown completed in Fig. 174. Each block should be directly opposite its pair and each pair diametrically opposite. It is unnecessary to file these hinge pieces to shape at this stage; the most important thing is the accuracy of their positions.

Returning to the two half-circles, the ends of each of these are filed to half-circles to permit them to swivel freely on their hinges. Into each end is cut a gap to permit the 10 gauge blocks in the centre band to fit smoothly and tightly. These gaps must be cut a little at a time, to avoid the possibility of too deep cutting and consequent unsightly gaps in the finished hinges.

When the two half-circles have been fitted correctly and are satisfactory in all positions, the small hinge blocks, on the centre band, can be filed to shape and correct size. Fig. 175 illustrates the correct size and proportion of the hinges.

Fitting the Hinged Sections

It is important to note that the two hinged sections, when placed in position, should be exactly the same finger size as the centre band. Therefore, if the ring is placed on a triblett, both the centre band and the outer halves will rest upon it. It will be noticed that the outer edge of the hinged sections will be parallel to, but not level with, the outer edge (top surface) of the centre band, the reason being, of course, that the outer halves are thinner than the centre (Fig. 176).

Finally the hinges must be drilled with a very fine drill, and the holes for the diamonds drilled in the outer halves. The hinges are not riveted until the

Fig. 176. Half-ring shown in relation to centre band.

ring has been set and partly polished. The ring is, in fact, left in three pieces for convenience until it has reached its final stage of finishing.

Mass Production of Wedding Rings

The making of wedding and signet rings, and similar types of work, is dependent more upon methods of quantity production than individual skill. Although skill is required in making them, the approach is different from gemstone rings.

The processes involved and description of the work are not too detailed, but a little general information will not be amiss. Taking wedding rings first, one might say the most important thing is to reduce actual work and handling of them to the minimum: the less handling involved the better.

As these are sold by weight, it follows that to obtain from the bullion dealers—or to draw down for oneself, whichever is applicable—wire of the exact shape and thickness required is the first requisite. The sectional shape varies from rectangular, to half round, or what is called flat D shape. Whichever it is, no allowance has to be made for wastage of weight in finishing— there must not be any.

When the wire has been drawn to the shape and size required, it is marked off, with a pair of dividers, or other suitable means, into lengths of $2\frac{1}{4}$ in (6 cm), which is the average length needed for a ring. These should not be cut off but sent to the Assay Office, in lengths of about 6 ft (1.83 m), for hallmarking.

This is, of course, essential for all work of this kind. After being assayed, and satisfying the examiners that it is up to the required standard, i.e., 22 carat, 18 carat, 14 carat, or 9 carat, the Assay Office will stamp the appropriate hallmarks on each of the lengths marked off.

Following this, the best plan is to coil up the lengths of wire, rather after the fashion of a coil spring, by winding it around a mandrel. To cut rings off then is quite a simple matter. Avoiding the hallmark, they are sawn off as needed (Fig. 177). The result of cutting off one of these rings will be a circle slightly twisted, as can be seen in Fig. 178.

Proceeding from there the ring should be annealed to make it quite soft, and then the joints closed together to fit correctly. A saw-cut through the closed-up joint will ensure a good clean job that can be closed up again

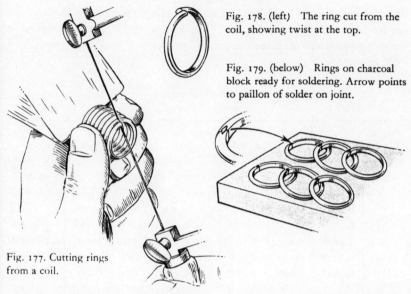

Fig. 178. (left)   The ring cut from the coil, showing twist at the top.

Fig. 179. (below)   Rings on charcoal block ready for soldering. Arrow points to paillon of solder on joint.

Fig. 177. Cutting rings from a coil.

ready for soldering. To solder, the normal rules for hard soldering should be followed, which means using the hardest solder possible.

It is worth bearing in mind that these rings are usually made in quantity rather than just odd ones, so it is useful to be able to solder as many as possible without too much waste of heat. A number can be placed on a charcoal block, if arranged as shown in Fig. 179, each with its joint in the same position relative to its neighbour, that is at the top. The borax can then be painted on the joints and a paillon of solder placed upon each. When the borax has dried, the whole row of rings can be soldered quite quickly because, as one is being heated to soldering temperature, the next one to it is also being heated. In this way, two dozen or more rings may be soldered at one time.

After soldering, the rings are dropped into the pickle while still hot—not red hot, only black. After rinsing and drying, they are ready for the next operation before polishing. First remove the surplus solder from both inside and outside the joint, and tap the ring gently with a hide mallet on a triblett to ensure that it is quite round and to the correct finger size. If a slight bulge or distortion on the outside of the ring shows where the hallmark has been stamped, this should be carefully filed off, and that should be all the filing that is necessary.

All that remains to be done now is to sandpaper and remove file marks and any other incidental blemishes inside and outside of the ring. A table of usual weights and relative thicknesses in different metals is shown here for guidance. Weights may vary slightly against those shown in the table because rings made for larger or smaller fingers will use a little more, or a little less metal.

Table of Weights

Finished weight		22 ct		18 ct	
dwt.	g	in	mm	in	mm
3	0.1944	0.120 × 0.074	3.0 × 2.2	0.130 × 0.085	3.3 × 2.2
2½	0.1620	0.106 × 0.070	2.9 × 2.0	0.115 × 0.078	2.9 × 2.0
2	0.1296	0.094 × 0.065	2.5 × 1.8	0.100 × 0.070	2.5 × 1.8
1½	0.0972	0.082 × 0.060	2.2 × 1.6	0.085 × 0.065	2.2 × 1.6
1	0.0648	0.070 × 0.055	1.8 × 1.5	0.074 × 0.060	1.8 × 1.5

Finished weight		9 ct	
dwt.	g	in	mm
3	0.1944	0.145 × 0.094	3.7 × 2.4
2½	0.1620	0.130 × 0.087	3.3 × 2.2
2	0.1296	0.115 × 0.078	2.9 × 2.0
1½	0.0972	0.100 × 0.069	2.5 × 1.8
1	0.0648	0.085 × 0.063	2.2 × 1.6

Measurements are the approximate proportions (width × height) required for various weights of D shaped wedding rings.

The Faceted Wedding Ring

One very popular and typical pattern might be chosen to be dealt with in a little more detail—the faceted wedding ring. This is made from the half-round section wedding ring, as already described (Fig. 180). From there a dividing plate is used to mark out equal divisions on the outside of the ring:

Fig. 180. (left)   Half-round section wedding ring.   Fig. 182.   The completed
Fig. 181. (right)   First row of flats filed on ring.   ring.

12 is the most practical number for average finger size; but for sizes larger than P, 14 is advisable; and for sizes smaller than J, 10 is sufficient.

Upon each of the sections so marked off, a flat is filed with its table at 90° to the side of the ring (Fig. 181). This is important, as the facets will not be correctly shaped if this point is neglected. When all twelve flats have been filed, the position of the ring against the bench peg is altered, so that another set of facets can be filed at the junctions of the top facets, and at an angle of 45° to the side of the ring. A third set is filed on the opposite side.

The result will be a series of diamond-shaped facets on the top of the ring, and a row of half-diamond facets on either side (Fig. 182). The pattern is quite simple but very effective if the facets are filed accurately. The facets are lapped, following filing, to achieve a good result. Any attempt at polishing by any other means cannot possibly maintain the required sharpness.

Variety of Fancy Wedding Rings

The wedding rings already described are the basic and simple types. An enormous quantity of fancy patterns is produced but this is not a book on design and the basic skills described can be used to produce any other design. Bullion dealers supply basic wedding ring blanks of required width, finger size, and flat or D shape for manufacturers to use and create their own patterns and finishes.

Many patterns are produced with the very useful diamond milling machine which is very good when used by a trained operator. Very brief details are as follows. Specially shaped industrial diamonds are built into cutting tools, with various angles and various widths, so that when cuts are made on rings (and other articles) they can be of various depths or widths to create the required pattern. The tools are set into a rotating holder or fly cutter which is electrically driven. The item to be cut is set into a holder which can be moved to bring the item into contact with the diamond cutter. It is not helpful to proceed with any further details because a person who is concentrating upon hand-made jewellery craftsmanship would not be also involved in purchasing and using a diamond milling machine.

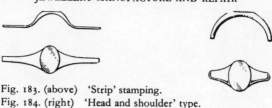

Fig. 183. (above)   'Strip' stamping.
Fig. 184. (right)   'Head and shoulder' type.

Signet Rings

We now come to signet rings. As with wedding rings, the variety of patterns is endless but, as far as manufacturing goes, they can all be considered as one. A very important point is their weight, as once again this is the governing factor in their selling price. It follows, also, that the less waste by filing, etc, that there is, the more effectively can the cost of manufacture be kept down. A very important matter, therefore, is the thickness of metal used for making the stamping.

Manufacturers and stampers will know the thickness required for the various patterns which will produce the necessary finished weight in the ring. There are two types of stampings, namely 'strip' (Fig. 183), which are complete full-length stampings; and 'head and shoulder' (Fig. 184), which leave the shank (back of the ring) to be made from half-round wire and then added to the stamping.

Having got the strip stampings, the first thing to do is to send them for hallmarking. It is most important that this be done before any other work is undertaken. Having been hallmarked and passed by the Assay Office, the stampings are then annealed to fit them for bending. Each is bent round to form a complete circle of approximately the right finger size (making considerable allowances for final hammering and correction), and a good joint made at the back ready for soldering.

These rings can be soldered in quantity, by standing close together and table downwards on a charcoal block (Fig. 185). Upwards of a dozen can be handled in this manner each time. When soldering, the hardest possible solder should be used.

The other type of stamping—the one where the shank is added separately—must also be sent for hallmarking, and in addition, the wire which will be used for the shank must also go. The method of manufacture from this stage is quite easy to follow. It might be said that the most important features, when dealing with these rings, are the methods whereby a large quantity may be made at one time and quickly. Time spent in manufacture is one item by which final cost is assessed. Therefore no time can be wasted if prices are to be competitive.

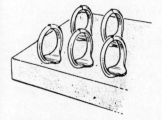

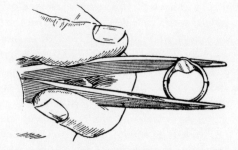

Fig. 185. (above) 'Strip' stampings shaped and ready for soldering.

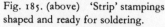

Fig. 186. The two parts of a 'head and shoulder' ring ready for soldering.

The preparation and soldering of this type of ring takes a little longer than does the strip-stamping type. The length of wire to be used for shanks is coiled around a mandrel, and then cut into sections approximating to half a ring each. Each half ring must be hallmarked. The ends of the half-circles, and the ends of the stampings are filed flat to enable good joints to be made. The half rings and stampings are then soldered together.

A fairly large pair of tweezers, between which the ring is placed, is probably the best method of holding the two halves together (Fig. 186). Binding wire could be used, but this would be a much longer and more expensive process. Following soldering, the methods for finishing both types of rings are the same, and need but little description.

The surplus solder is filed away from the inside of the ring and the ring is then rounded on the triblett using a hide or wooden mallet. The use of a hammer is best avoided because the result would be marks on the ring that would need filing off. This would also result in loss of weight. The less filing that has to be done, the better; therefore fewer marks mean less filing.

When all the rings have been made round and are of the correct size, all that remains is to file the rings on the sides of the shanks and the shoulders. This operation is really a truing and smoothing one, and very little metal should be removed. It is most important that the two shoulders of the ring match up. All surplus solder should be finally removed, and the top of the signet filed flat, ready for lapping (i.e. polishing).

All that remains is to sandpaper, to finish and remove any small burrs, etc. Step shoulder rings, and similar patterns, need a little more attention but detailed instructions are not necessary for them.

Stone-set Signet Rings

It is also appropriate to mention stone-set signet rings for men and women; this applies as well to the stamped signets already dealt with. Stamping for these will have the centre table stamped open to take the stone to be set by a trained setter. It is very important that the thickness of gold from which the stampings are made, is sufficient to accommodate the stones. It is therefore much thicker than a plain gold-topped signet. Several shapes of stones can be dealt with by the same shaped stampings; for example, oval, square, oblong and cushion-shaped have for many years been dealt with by stamping specialists. When the rings have been sent to the Assay Office for hallmarking, the means by which the work is done is basically the same as dealing with ordinary unset signets. It is necessary, however, to ensure that the shape of the setting is not distorted during the work, otherwise setting the stone would not be possible. Another important point concerning stone-set signets is that, instead of stamping, they can be cast as one-piece complete rings with much more varied and complicated types of patterns with designed shoulders, etc, which could not be stamped because of the more complicated pattern. The details of casting and setting are dealt with and described in Chapters 10 and 11.

8. Brooches

Brooches are less in favour to-day than was the case many years ago, and styles have certainly changed. The demand then was for very ornate yet still fairly cheap brooches, whereas now the taste in gold brooches is more subdued. Perhaps inexpensive artificial jewellery suits the purpose better when an ornate article is required.

This leaves the worker in gold and gem jewellery with either:

1. Very expensive diamond clip brooches, double clips, or sets comprised of brooch and ear clips; or

2. The neat but fairly plain cameo brooches and similar articles of jewellery which are much less expensive.

These latter still hold a considerable place in the fashions of to-day. Bar brooches are not very much in demand nowadays.

This explanation is just incidental to the practical work of jewellery manufacture but does serve to indicate that a great deal of the old style of craftsmanship and excellent workmanship of 50 to 100 years ago—where a small brooch containing very small stones, beading and scroll work demanding expert skill was a regular product—is no longer fashionable. Consequently methods of manufacture have changed.

Making a Cameo Brooch

It is very difficult to choose an example of what might be called a typical brooch. We might start by making a cameo brooch, and then proceed to a diamond brooch, which may have several different types of fittings. From there we might turn to the various fittings for a double-clip brooch adding, where possible, guiding principles for all types.

Fig. 187. Cameo brooch with burnished edge and twisted wire beading.
Fig. 188. Bezel bent round to form an oval and soldered.
Fig. 189. Double curve of cameo to which bezel has to be set.

The gold cameo brooch most popular to-day is the neat burnished edge setting with a 'twisted' wire beading surround, and nothing more (Fig. 187). There are variations, but it will be sufficient to describe the making of one particular type.

The first operation is to roll down a strip of gold to $\frac{3}{16}$ in (5 mm) wide and 6 gauge in thickness. We are assuming that the cameo is an average-sized one, oval, and about $1\frac{3}{4}$ in by $1\frac{1}{4}$ in (4.5×3.2 cm). It is understood that the proportions of the metal vary according to the size of the cameo. Thinner metal than 6 gauge would be easier for setting, but would be more difficult to work, therefore a happy medium must be struck which most nearly satisfies both needs.

The strip of metal is annealed, and bent round to fit the outside of the cameo. This is difficult to do exactly, bearing in mind that the cameo must eventually fit into this bezel tightly and accurately. In fact, it is much better to make the bezel just a fraction too small, then completing with a good joint and soldering with the hardest possible solder. The bezel must then be adjusted in shape and size to accommodate the cameo. The bezel is shown in Fig. 188 before being shaped. This has to be bent so that it fits closely round the edge of the double-curved cameo, as shown in Fig. 189.

This operation is best done by hammering lightly, with the bezel on the triblett, and also by using pliers to correct the shape, until a perfect fit has been achieved (Fig. 190).

It should be said here that cameos are seldom flat. That is to say, when placed on a flat table, the back of the cameo does not touch the table all round; mostly it is found that top and bottom of the oval are the places which are above the flat plane (Fig. 191). This is because cameos are cut from a shell which is similar in shape to a cockle, but very much larger. This, however, creates another difficulty, especially if the cameo is very far from flat, as the edge of the bezel or setting, just made, has to follow this shape.

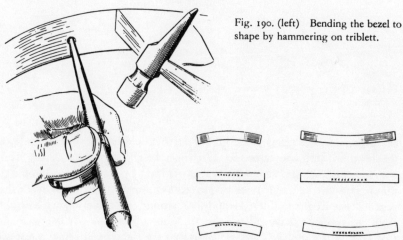

Fig. 190. (left)   Bending the bezel to shape by hammering on triblett.

Fig. 191. (top left)   Looking longitudinally along a cameo.   Fig. 192.(top right)
Looking at it laterally with eyes at the same level.   Fig. 193. (below)   The crosses
mark the spots where the bezel must be stretched.

Here again the triblett can be used to make adjustments. By hammering
one edge of the bezel, it can be stretched into a curve, approximating to the
curve of the cameo edge. A little more detail here will perhaps be useful, as
it is a technique which may well be used for other purposes.

Looking longitudinally along a cameo placed on a flat surface, with eyes
at surface level, the cameo would seem to curve as Fig. 191, and looking at
it laterally, with eyes at the same level, it would appear as Fig. 192. The
setting which we are making must obviously follow the same shape. Having
made an oval bezel, we must shape it to accommodate the cameo. This can
be done by placing it on the triblett, or a large sparrowhawk, and stretching,
by hammering, the edges where it is necessary to form a curve. If it is done,
as in this instance, so that the top edges are stretched at the two ends of the
oval, and the bottom edges are stretched at the two sides of the oval, then
the desired effect will be achieved (Fig. 193).

With smaller cameos this work, which is quite difficult to perform accurately, can be avoided by making a bezel sufficiently deep to allow for the
shape to be filed out from the flat bezel. To do this for a fairly large cameo
would require an exceptionally deep bezel, and would be very wasteful in
metal.

Fitting Supports for the Cameo

Having mastered the shape and fitted the bezel to the cameo correctly, we

Fig. 194. Cameo supports shown soldered in.

Fig. 195. Fitting the strengthening bar.

can proceed to the next operation. Supports should be put on the inside of the bezel to keep the cameo at its correct height within the bezel. This operation is fairly simple, and is best carried out by cutting four lengths of thin square wire, 14 gauge thick by ⅜ in (9.5 mm) long, curved to fit inside the bezel. These are then soldered equidistant around the inside, at such a height from the top that they will support the cameo (Fig. 194). It is important that each of the supports are so placed that the cameo will actually rest on all of them. If this is not achieved, there is a possibility of the cameo being broken during setting, or when being worn.

It is almost certain that the bezel will warp when the supports are soldered in, due to the uneven expansion that takes place during soldering, and this must be corrected where necessary. This will not be very difficult as the bezel did fit originally and will probably need only a little correction at various points in the curve.

A strengthening bar, which also provides a base for the catch and pin, has now to be made and added. This is made from a piece of strip, 12 gauge thick by ⅛ in (3 mm) wide. The position of this piece is important. It should be above the half-way line across the brooch, that is to say across the *width* of the oval, not the length (Fig. 195). It is generally understood that most cameos are cut so that they are worn with the oval in a vertical position. There are exceptions and the bar is then fitted accordingly.

The reason for fitting the bar above the centre line is to avoid any possibility of the brooch falling forward when being worn. When fitting the bar, it is best to cut two slots in the edge of the bezel, into which the bar will fit tightly. So tightly, in fact, that it has to be squeezed into position with pliers. This will stop any tendency to warping by the bezel during soldering. The bar must be soldered at both ends, any excess length of bar being filed off flush to the sides of the bezel after soldering.

The cameo should again be tried for fit and the bezel then smoothed all round with a file. During this operation, the setting edge should be filed thinner to provide a better working edge for the setter when he comes to set the cameo. This edge must not be so thin that it would buckle during the setting operation. As a guide to actual thickness necessary, it might be said that this should be approximately 2 gauge. This filing operation applies only to the top of the setting edge. The outside of the bezel should then be sandpapered before beginning any ornamentation. Cameos are often completed at this stage without any additions other than the catches and pins. A larger number have an addition of a neat twisted wire border (Fig. 196).

Twisted Wire Decorations

There are two types of twisted wire decoration. There are variations, but they are fairly obvious and need little explanation. The first type is made by taking two pieces of round wire of equal lengths, about $1\frac{1}{4}$ times as long as necessary to go round the outside of the bezel. These two pieces of wire are twisted together by holding the two ends in a vice, and the opposite two ends in a hand vice; the wires are then twisted while being held taut and until a sufficiently close twist has been obtained. The thickness of each wire for this operation can vary between 6 to 12 gauge, according to the weight and thickness desired in the finished article.

Fig. 196.   Completed cameo bezel with twisted wire decoration.

The other type is made from a strip of rectangular wire approximately 8 gauge in thickness by 16 gauge in width. This strip must be annealed evenly along its whole length to enable an even twist to be obtained. The annealing is *very* important and a few minutes longer spent on this operation will be well repaid in the finished job. Uneven annealing will result in an uneven twist—the wire twisting more in the softer places. The actual twisting is done, as before, with the two vices. After further annealing, the procedure adopted for both types is the same.

A border is formed from the twisted wire to fit very tightly around the outside of the bezel. It is better to make this border slightly smaller than the bezel. The wire should then be cut so that the twist, when the border is soldered, follows on correctly without an obvious joint showing afterwards. Soldering should be accomplished with very little solder being used. The shape of the border is then corrected as necessary.

To complete the fitting of the border to the bezel, the border can be sandpapered on the inside to enlarge it slightly until it fits tightly on the bezel. The border can now be soldered on to the bezel by the use of an easier-flowing solder than has been used throughout the manufacture to this stage. When soldering, heat should be applied at a point opposite the joint in the border; this prevents the joint from becoming unsoldered and the border from springing off the bezel. A paillon of solder should be placed at points around the border and each one should be melted in turn. In this way the risk of the joint becoming unsoldered will be avoided.

Very little further cleaning and sandpapering is required. The brooch should be pickled in acid to clean it thoroughly. Special attention should be paid to smoothing and cleaning the bar at the back in readiness for the pin and safety catch to be soldered in position.

This a job that can be left for a while as the method to be used applies equally to all types of brooches. It is better, therefore, that we should leave this and continue making brooches, dealing with their fittings afterwards.

Bar Brooches

A type of bar brooch which a jeweller may be called upon to make is the claw-set five- or seven-stone brooch with an overall length of $2\frac{1}{4}$ in (5.7 cm). The stones are set close together in the centre of the bar; the remainder of the length—either end—consists of a square, or possibly a triangular, section bar.

One of the main considerations with such a brooch is strength: this must be found in the metal from which it is made and in the soldered joints. It should always be borne in mind that, no matter how well the joints are made, they remain a point of weakness in a finished article. The metal itself is important and must be chosen with cost being kept in mind while still maintaining strength. A bar made in platinum would need to be fairly substantial to overcome the softness of the material. A brooch made of this material would be very heavy and consequently very costly. It is, therefore, better to use 18 ct white gold for the bar when heavy expenditure in metal is out of the question.

Again, it would be useless to make the bar from soft 9 ct white gold unless it were made very thick and this would be clumsy. If 9 ct is the quality white gold to be used, then a hard alloy must be chosen. This choice of metal would apply also to the pin; this must be strong enough to withstand fairly rough usage from the subsequent owner. It naturally follows that the metal used must be chosen with considerable care, with similar care being taken with the soldered joints throughout the whole cycle of manufacture.

Making a Bar Brooch

The job must be started by making the setting for the stones. Alternatively, this may be chosen from the wide range of individual settings available from the bullion dealers and specialists in such items. It is unnecessary here to

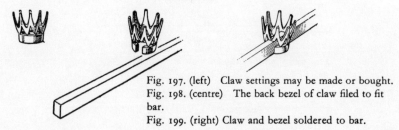

Fig. 197. (left)   Claw settings may be made or bought.
Fig. 198. (centre)   The back bezel of claw filed to fit bar.
Fig. 199. (right) Claw and bezel soldered to bar.

add to what has already been said about the manufacture of settings; these were described adequately in Chapter 5. Assuming then that we have made or purchased claw settings of the type shown in Fig. 197, we proceed to make a back bezel for each individual setting.

These bezels, however, are not in quite the same proportions as those used previously in ring work. For brooches, it is preferable to use square wire of approximately 12 gauge. The back bezels are soldered to the points of the settings as before.

The bar itself now has to be made and, wherever possible, this should be in one piece. An average bar might be ⅛ in (3 mm) deep by 18 gauge thick. The bar is soldered to the setting in such a manner that, when looking at the brooch from on top of the stones, the narrowest side is seen. This serves two purposes; for while strength is maintained, the brooch is also neat in appearance.

Before soldering the claw and bezel to the bar, starting with the centre setting which is usually the largest, a gap is carefully saw-pierced through the back bezel and part of the claw as necessary. This is to allow the bar to be placed into it at such a depth that the bottom of the back bezel will rest level with the back of the bar (Fig. 198). The fit must be good and firm. After ensuring that the setting is placed in the centre of the bar, it must be cleanly and carefully soldered with the hardest possible solder (Fig. 199). This solder should have a slightly lower melting point than that used for soldering the claw to the bezel.

A gap is next saw-pierced into the two settings that will be soldered either side of the centre setting and fitted in exactly the same way as described previously. When soldering these two claws on to the bar, they should be touching the top of the centre setting. Further pairs of settings can be treated in the same way. When in position, the tops of each of the settings should be soldered together where they meet, using a small paillon of solder (Fig. 200). This will add strength to the bar. When soldering of the settings has been completed, the brooch is ready to be filed up to remove the surplus solder, filed flat along the back of the bar, and generally cleaned up to a fine finish.

Fig. 200. Settings shown soldered to bar.

Fig. 201. Bar cut away after soldering.

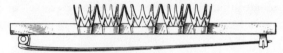

Fig. 202. The finished brooch.

One important operation now remains to be done, that is to remove, by saw-piercing, those parts of the brooch which run through the back of each setting (Fig. 201). This will take a little from the general strength of the brooch, but it should, nevertheless, leave sufficient strength for its purpose. The main purpose of removing these sections of the bar is to allow more light to circulate through the stones from the back. It also makes for general neatness and eliminates dust and powder traps.

After sandpapering, the brooch is ready for the pin, joint, and safety catch to be fitted. A variation that could be introduced into the brooch, would be for the settings to be spaced equidistant along the bar, instead of touching and being confined to the centre as in this instance. From the practical point of view, the latter method would not make any difference when manufacturing (Fig. 202).

Diamond-set Fancy Brooches

A third, and quite different, type of brooch is the larger, diamond-set fancy brooch. This must always be individually designed and made, with character of its own. It should not be repeated (Fig. 203). Here again it would be impossible to follow up the variety of designs that occur with this type. It will be sufficient for our needs to follow through the methods of making one such piece (Fig. 204).

The illustrations will probably be more easily understood than would a written description, so each piece in the construction of this work is shown numbered according to the order in which it has to be made. Begin with the two larger pieces marked with the *No 1*. These are cut out of 12 gauge sheet metal (for this brooch it should be assumed that the metal being used

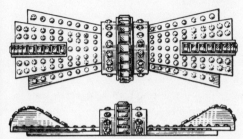

Fig. 203. A completed diamond-set fancy brooch with character and style of its own.

is platinum) and are cut to form an exact pair, with a little extra length at the narrower end. Apart from this, the pieces are cut and filed up to their exact size.

The section *No 2* follows, again being made of 12 gauge metal, and cut this time with an extra $\frac{1}{32}$ in (0.8 mm) allowed on the width to permit the first pieces to be soldered under the edges. *No 3* now follows, made from the same gauge metal, and it is cut and bent round to form an arc. This should not be a semi-circle, as this would be too high, but a good even curve in the form of a flattened semi-circle.

Side pieces, *No 4*, are cut from slightly thinner-gauge metal, 8 gauge would be sufficient, and soldered on to the outside of *No 3*. It is better here to have the soldered joints where they are least likely to show. As will be seen in this

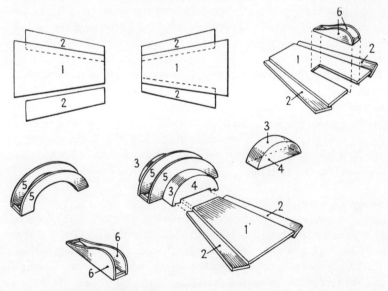

Fig. 204. Parts of the brooch are shown numbered and in the positions they will assume.

instance, the top of this section will be cut up into grains, to secure the stones, which will hide the soldered joints. If these pieces were to be soldered *inside* the curve, there is a possibility of a faint line showing when the brooch is finally polished and finished. That establishes one principle, i.e., put soldered joints where they are least likely to show.

The part marked *No 5* comes next. This is a setting for baguettes or square-cut stones, similar in principle to the type mentioned previously, consisting of sides only, with no metal between the stones. This piece is made from 12 gauge strip, a little less than ⅛ in (3 mm) wide, and curved edgewise to fit closely round the surface of the part marked *No 3*. *No 5* is made of two exactly similar pieces and soldered, the stones' width apart, appropriate for the particular stones being used. When soldering these smaller parts together, the hardest possible solder should be used. It is only when a piece has to be soldered to another piece that has already been soldered that a lower melting-point solder is used.

Returning to the first two pieces made, these should be very carefully and accurately fitted into the base of *No 4*, where they are soldered. A very substantial part of the main brooch has now been completed; it only remains to make the baguette settings for the ends of the brooch, *No 6*.

It is wiser here to work on both end sections together to ensure that they are correctly matched. These pieces are made with sides only joined at either end but with the appropriate stone width separating the two. These pieces will each be fitted into *No 1* by saw-piercing out a section of the brooch to the appropriate size to permit a tight fit. The pieces should then be soldered into place.

Having made and soldered all the pieces together, the next operation is to drill and saw-pierce out the holes for all the diamonds. No detailed explanation is necessary here concerning this operation as it has all been adequately covered before. All the general rules should be applied: stones as close together as is practicable; holes larger at the top than at the bottom; and when these have been opened up, the back of the holes can be opened up into a neat and effective pattern.

Making a Gallery for the Brooch

A gallery has now to be made, to follow the outside shape of the brooch. In such a piece as this there are two methods that may be employed. The first, and by far the easier one, is to take a large sheet of 10 or 12 gauge metal. On to this is marked the exact outline of the brooch—do this by marking round the brooch with a scriber—and then cutting out the correct shape and size, filing it to the exact proportions of the brooch, and then saw-piercing out the centre to leave only a parallel edge. The great objection to this method is, of course, the large amount of metal involved, although the piece from the centre can most likely be put to good use on another job.

The second method for making the gallery is to get a length of rectangular wire, of approximately 15 gauge by 10 gauge and, slowly and accurately, corner by corner follow round the edge of the brooch, forming each corner in the usual way by filing a V-shape slot into the wire, bending it round and soldering the joint thus formed.

The last method is no doubt a very much longer way, and requires a lot more careful handling. The advantage in it rests solely in the saving of material—either way the result is the same. From now onwards the procedure for completing the brooch is similar.

In a few appropriate places on the rim that has just been made, a length of chenier is soldered to form supports. These supports will divide the rim and the brooch; and, at this stage, the brooch top and gallery edging can be soldered together.

The patterns that could be used to decorate the remainder of the space are numberless, and it is here that the individual craftsman can choose a decoration that goes well with the pattern and style of the brooch. Neat scrolls, blocks at various corners, and diagonals here and there will soon form a very neat pattern, adding considerably to the appearance of the brooch. These items are made and fitted individually from very thin strips of metal. Their making will be similar to those described for rings.

The final stage has now almost been reached as the edges are filed and sand-papered to remove the surplus solder and other blemishes, and finally smoothed with emery paper ready for the preliminary polishing. All that now remains is to fit the catch and joint, or clip fittings as required, but these will be dealt with separately.

Double Clip Brooches

The double clip brooch is, in principle, one brooch which can be detached from a frame as two separate clips; each of which can be worn as an individual article or as an identical pair. It is not essential that they should be identical, indeed some excellent effects can be achieved by two quite different clips with the same theme of design.

Broadly speaking the only difference in manufacture from an ordinary brooch is in the fittings on to which the brooches or clips will fasten. This is definitely true of the identical pair of clips which together form a symmetrical brooch. The best way to make it is as one brooch using the same principles already described, and then, at the appropriate stage, cutting it into two and proceeding separately with the fittings and attachments for each one. To go into further detail would only repeat a lot of what has been said in previous chapters. It would be better, therefore, to continue with one other type of brooch, and then to describe the various types of brooch fittings including those for double clips.

Asymmetrical Spray Brooches

The other type of clip is one which can be used equally well for a single item or for a double clip, and is the asymmetrical 'spray' type representing either a floral spray, or a design which has a theme of lines or shapes not attempting to simulate any natural form. Fig. 205 shows a spray brooch made in platinum and diamonds; with this goes a matching set of ear clips. Shown in Fig. 206 is the outline of a type of brooch, depending upon lines for its shape, as a theme upon which a design could be built.

When using the floral spray brooch as an example, all the general principles of manufacture apply; but it also introduces one particular method of dealing with parts which might involve some difficulty in setting, because of their shape or overlapping other parts. These are parts which are usually referred to as· 'brought on', a cumbersome expression meaning parts which are placed into position after the work has been set and polished. This applies to the flowers where it would obviously be impossible to set diamonds if the stamens were permanently fixed in position during the manufacture.

The brooch as a whole is one example where 'relief' and depth are important. This, of course, depends upon the maker: a work of this type can look very flat and lifeless if its shape is not accompanied by sufficient 'depth'. It is important to have a clear impression, right from the beginning, of what the finished work should look like from all angles.

Fig. 205. A spray brooch made in platinum and diamonds.

Fig. 206.   The outline of a brooch depending upon lines for its shape.

Plan for Manufacture

The actual making can be followed through fairly easily without too much detailed description. The first part will be the stem, made strong enough to provide a firm base for the whole brooch. It will need to be about 24 gauge in thickness, as a lot of its strength will be taken away by the holes for the baguette diamonds to be set along it. A good plan is to have a small tin box into which Plasticine has been pressed to form a thin layer over the inside. Upon this can be placed the parts of the brooch as they are made, so that the whole article can be steadily built up, while the mounter is able to see in front of him the parts placed in their relative positions.

The stem being completed, the leaves are then cut out and built around it. The flowers can be made in separate parts and none of them need be soldered together until the maker is quite satisfied that proportions and shapes are correct, each piece in relation to the others.

Reference to Fig. 207 will show the appropriate parts of the flowers and the means by which they are attached to the main stem. The petals of the flowers should be saw-pierced from 14 gauge sheet metal, generous allowance being made for doming, as this will reduce the diameter by approximately one quarter in such an instance as this, where deep doming is required.

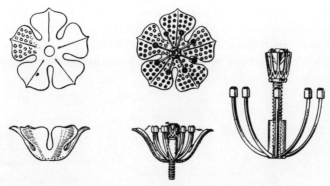

Fig. 207.   Various parts of the flowers showing means by which they are attached to the main stem.

By careful and patient use of doming tools, lead-cake and doming block, the shape required is steadily formed, and the outside filed up to its correct size and shape. The centre claw setting is made according to the size of the diamond to be set, and this needs no further explanation, having been dealt with previously. To the back of this setting is soldered a length of stout screw-threaded wire of the same metal. (Taps and dies for making the screws are available from tool suppliers.)

Making the Stamens

The next part to be made is the stamens, each set with a diamond. Start by drawing down platinum tube to the size needed for the settings, saw off the appropriate number of short lengths and place aside. Next, draw down round wire to the thickness needed for the actual stamens, bearing in mind that these must be reasonably strong while retaining neatness. Finally a small collar into which the threaded stem will tightly fit is made from 14 gauge metal. Having got the necessary materials together, the rather difficult task of making the stamens is begun. This calls for extreme care and neatness.

As will be seen from Fig. 208 the stamens are each approximately a quarter of a circle and it is better to deal with them in opposite pairs. In other words, if a length of wire is bent round to a semi-circle and one of the short lengths of tube soldered on to each end we have, in fact, two stamens already formed. This is repeated until four pairs are made, each matching the others for length and amount of curve. They are then ready to be joined together to form the circle of diamond settings representing the complete set of stamens for the flower centre.

The next operation is to take the small collar and file into it, on opposite sides, a groove in which the wire forming the stamens will fit fairly tightly, Fig. 209. This is then soldered into position with very hard solder, and the next pair, at right-angles to the first, are fitted in a similar manner. From thereon to the third and fourth pairs, after which the centre of the collar is saw-pierced free from the wires which now almost completely fill it. It is

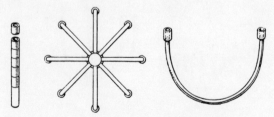

Fig. 208. How the stamens are bent and soldered.

Fig. 209. Soldering the stamen to the centre collar.

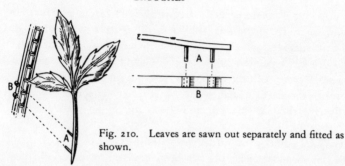

Fig. 210.   Leaves are sawn out separately and fitted as shown.

then threaded to accommodate the stem of the centre setting of the flower (Fig. 208).

This is not easy to follow from a written description, but reference to Fig. 208 should clarify it. It is a very difficult piece of work and one which serves, as far as this text is concerned, only to illustrate a method of putting together complex parts, rather than to present a design to be followed.

Making the Leaves

When making the leaves, these should be made separately, each leaf being cut individually from 12 or 13 gauge metal. It is then domed and shaped to resemble the natural product, and made to take its place in the complete spray of leaves.

The stem is made from 'knife-edged' wire, as light as possible consistent with strength, remembering the softness of platinum. Each leaf is sawn out to fit on to the stem as shown in Fig. 210, and not simply soldered on to the end of the stem wire. By fitting the leaf in this way, a double purpose is served: firstly it adds strength, and secondly it gives the very natural appearance of a vein running into the leaf.

Where the shorter stems of the side leaves in each group join the major stem, another joint should be made, preferably by using one piece of 'knife-edged' wire to go across the main stem and so serve two leaves. A slotted joint is made where they cross, the joint then being soldered with a very hard solder. This method will eliminate any possibility of weakness at these places. When making leaves, the aim should be to make them appear as natural as possible, therefore 'depth' must also be considered.

All of these parts, having been completed and made to fit on to the main stem or wherever is appropriate, are placed aside until all work is completed. After setting and polishing, they can be assembled together and a very small paillon of easy-flowing silver solder flushed into the threads of the screws which will secure them.

In other cases where parts overlap to such an extent that it would be impossible to set the diamonds, similar methods have to be adopted. For example, the small leaf which is attached to the main stem almost at the bottom, has to be fixed separately after the main stem has been set. This is done by fixing small pieces of tube at the side of the stem and corresponding pegs at the back of the leaves which enables the leaf to be attached and soldered with easy-flowing silver solder. Fig. 210 shows this in detail.

Safety Catch, Ball Joint and Pin Fastenings

Work on brooches generally has been covered by other chapters so far, and so we can pass on to the fittings appropriate to various kinds of brooches. The usual type fitted to bar brooches, cameo brooches and others is the safety catch, ball joint and pin as shown in Fig. 211. The safety catch and joints can, of course, be purchased from bullion dealers and makers of jewellers' findings, but it is useful to be able to make these if necessary.

For the trigger safety catch, a piece of wire is milled down to 24 gauge square, annealed, and then $\frac{1}{4}$ in (6 mm) of its end is hammered on the edge of a flat die until it spreads out and is approximately 10 gauge in thickness, as shown in Fig. 212. Annealed again, it is curved around with a pair of small round-point pliers, then filed up carefully and the end cut off, if necessary, to leave an opening sufficient only to accommodate the end of the pin (Fig. 213).

The next operation is to saw across the back of the curve, cutting right through the metal. The saw-blade is then inserted through the hole so formed and the cut continued to about $\frac{1}{16}$ in (1.5 mm) down the stem, as shown in Fig. 214. This saw cut should be made with a thick saw-blade (about a No. 7) which will leave a fairly wide gap for the trigger. Next the holes for the rivet which will hold the trigger in place are drilled (Fig. 215), after which the main part of the catch is cut off from the original piece of square wire (Fig. 216). A small semi-circle is now cut (or filed), with a small step at its one corner, from a piece of flat metal the thickness of a saw cut. Into this is placed

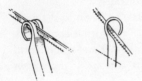

Fig. 211. (above left)   The safety catch, ball joint and pin as fitted to brooches generally.

Fig. 212. (above centre)   Starting the manufacture of the trigger safety catch.

Fig. 213. (above right)   Forming the end.

Fig. 214. (left)   Sawing across the back of the curve. Note direction of sawing.

Fig. 215. (left)   Drilling the rivet holes for the trigger.
Fig. 216. (right)   The two sides of the catch sawn off from the bar.

Fig. 217. (left)   Marking out the trigger.
Fig. 218. (right)   The trigger and the sides pegged together.

the catch, as shown in Fig. 217, and the hole drilled in it is used as a guide to enable it to be continued through the sheet from which will be cut the trigger. A small peg is now pushed through the hole (it must be a tight fit) and cut off, leaving a very small piece projecting each side. Saw-pierce the trigger from the piece of sheet metal by following round the shape of the catch except at the top, where a small circular knob is left as a means of operating the trigger, Fig. 218. The whole is then filed up but no attempt should be made to adjust it or make it work until it has been soldered into its final position on the brooch. It will be fairly obvious that, before soldering, the peg should be removed and the trigger taken out to avoid the whole being soldered together.

The joint is made from a strip of 9 gauge metal, $\frac{1}{8}$ in (3 mm) wide. After annealing, a piece is cut off the end $\frac{1}{8}$ in (3 mm) long, making $\frac{1}{8}$ in (3 mm) square, Fig. 219. This will form the centre part of the hinge. The end of the strip is now folded over, book fashion, with the square folded in between and squeezed tightly. The 'book' is then cut off from the end of the strip, Fig. 220. File the joint to finish it, first rounding off the corners on the 'open' end of the 'book', and then, with a small three-square file, nick in deeply on either side to give the appearance of a complete circle with a small piece attached. The back of this is hollowed out slightly with a small half-round file and the whole joint smoothed and sandpapered. The centre piece can now be pushed out and the joint itself is ready for soldering, Fig. 221.

The piece which has been pushed out from the joint is soldered on to the end of the round wire (17 gauge) which will make the pin. It is better to drill these separately, thus ensuring that the holes are centrally placed. Fig. 222

Fig. 219. (left)   The start of the hinge.
Fig. 220. (right)   The 'book' formed and cut from the strip.

Fig. 221. (left)   The hinge shaped with centre-piece pushed out.
Fig. 222. (right)   The hinge soldered to the brooch.

Fig. 223. The 'pin' clip shown open and closed. This type of clip allows the brooch to be pinned anywhere on the dress.

shows the completed joints. After these fittings have been soldered on to the brooch, the final work of adjusting and making them work is carried out.

One point is important. The opening of the safety catch should face *downwards* when the brooch is worn. The reason for this is that, should the safety catch come unfastened while the brooch is being worn, there is less likelihood of the pin coming out of the catch completely.

Fastenings for Clip Brooches

There are two principal types of fittings for clip brooches with, as usual, many variations, but they can nevertheless be dealt with as two main types: the 'pin' clip or the 'flat back' clip. The pin type (Fig. 223) can be worn anywhere on the dress because the pins can be pushed through the dress in the same way as an ordinary brooch pin, whereas the flat-backed type is limited to the edge of a dress. In the first type there are two main variations in the method used for making the actual spring and it will help if both are described separately.

Making a Pin Clip

Assuming that the whole of the clip front has been completed so far as the mounts are concerned, that is to say, made but not set or polished; a fairly thick and shallow 'wall' is made to stand on the back at the top of the clip. This should be of 16 gauge, $\frac{1}{8}$ in (3 mm) high by $\frac{1}{2}$ in (12 mm) long. This is soldered at the back, choosing the position carefully with regard to the design but, for all practical purposes, as near to the top edge as possible.

The points which must be considered are:

1. Whether this piece will show through any saw-piercings when viewed from the front;

2. Whether it can be soldered securely and strongly; and,

3. In the case of a double clip, how it will suit the overall arrangement of the double clip fitting.

The top edge of this wall is then filed with a small round needle-file to accommodate a piece of tube which will make the hinge. A small piece of suitable tube one-half of the total length of the wall is then cut off and soldered, centrally, in the groove filed in the wall. This will be the centre section of the hinge for the clip back. One more portion remains now to be soldered on before starting the actual back and that is the piece which will cause the back to spring. Upon the care and accuracy with which this is done will depend the efficiency of the spring back.

What is now required is a piece of 14 gauge square wire as long as the piece of tube. Next a flat surface is filed on the tube at an angle of approximately 40° to the back of the clip, so that when the small section of square wire is soldered on to it, it will be sloping backwards; Fig. 224 will make this much clearer. The piece of wire is then filed into what one can only describe as a 'wedge' shape, leaning backwards from the centre part of the hinge. The ends are filed off to the level of the tube. This part can now be left aside while the clip back is made. A piece of 8 gauge, hard 18 ct white gold is required as wide as the wall which was made and soldered on to the clip, and approximately the same length. Using the small round needle-file, a groove is filed along two parallel sides of this piece, as close as possible to the edges; in fact, one could say *on* the edges. These will form a seating on to which the pins will be soldered.

The pins are made from 0.045 in (1.2 mm) round wire, preferably hard 18 ct white gold, but at least the hardest obtainable of the 9 ct alloys. Soft golds would be quite useless. These are made as long as possible, but not to overhang the end of the brooch. They need not be of the same length as each other; this will be decided by the pattern of the clip. For instance, if the clip is asymmetrical in design, then the pins might be unequal in length. Each will be filed to a point, but not a long, slowly-tapering point; rather better to make a fairly short sharp taper as this is much stronger. These pins are then soldered into the recesses filed in the flat piece of sheet. Across the bottom end, the other tube for the hinge will be soldered but, before doing that, two saw-cuts must be made. These are set apart to the same distance as the length of the centre hinge piece, and sawn to approximately half-way along the piece of square metal (obviously in the same direction as the pins). This will leave a small section of metal, called a 'tongue', which is bent downwards out of the way for a while.

Now the grooves which will accommodate the hinge tubes are filed in the back plate, but *not* right at the edge. A space of $\frac{1}{16}$ in (1.5 mm) is left at the end so that the tongue will be left overhanging. The purpose of this will be seen shortly. Next a piece of tube long enough to go right across the width of the back is cut and soldered into the groove (still in one piece). The centre piece which is now crossing the tongue is saw-pierced out, leaving two pieces to complete the hinge. Reference to Fig. 224 will show this more clearly in various stages.

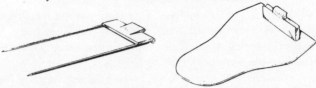

Fig. 224. The pins and hinge apart showing method of manufacture. Note how the clip back (upper figure) is grooved to seat the pins.

A general filing and sandpapering now completes the work apart from actually making the pin clip work correctly. This is done by bending the tongue back to its original level and gently hammering it flat. Being of hard metal, it will retain its springy nature. The back is then placed in position and pressed down to enable a piece of round wire to be pushed through the joint. At this stage it is not riveted into position, but only used temporarily to adjust where necessary. The final burnishing over of the ends of the rivet is left until the setting and polishing have been completed. At this stage it should be found that the back will spring open, or closed, from a position approximately 45° from the clip, as the tongue rides over the block on the top of the centre piece of the hinge.

A More Complicated Pin Clip

Another method of making a spring back with two pins is far more complicated but probably neater when finished. The illustration will prove more useful in showing how this is done than descriptive work, but stage-by-stage description will help to clarify points which might not otherwise be clear. The first step is to make a box without a top, $\frac{1}{2}$ in (12 mm) long by $\frac{1}{16}$ in (1.5 mm) in depth and $\frac{1}{16}$ in (1.5 mm) in height. This is made from 8 gauge hard metal and is soldered on to the clip in a position similar to the wall in the other type, and with the top or open side uppermost. Both sides of this box are then saw-pierced and filed to the shape shown in Fig. 225, and along the top of the box two pieces of tube which will form the outer sides of the hinge are soldered. These need only be quite short, $\frac{1}{32}$ in (0.8 mm) long will be sufficient.

Next a small but very hard piece of 6 gauge 18 ct white gold, preferably a piece which has been milled down but not afterwards annealed, is cut to fit into the box, supported by the steps in the sides of the box. This is, in fact, a loose piece which forms the spring, and is held in position only by the steps in the box and centre part of the hinged back. The next stage is to make the pins, and these will be as described earlier. This time, however, the piece of sheet metal on to which they are soldered needs to be considerably shorter, $\frac{1}{4}$ in (6 mm) is enough. The width, of course, will be only what is needed to

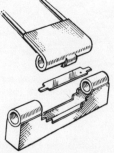

Fig. 225.   An alternative method of hinging the pins to the brooch.

fit between the two ends of the hinge already soldered on to the box. Along the back edge·the centre piece of tube for the hinge will now be soldered and made to fit tightly into the appropriate place. On the centre of this tube is soldered a narrow band or 'collar' which must be filed thinner at its ends, leaving the thicker part approximately 45° from the back. This will be the part which rides over the spring and so makes the clip spring open, and closed.

One main advantage with this method is that the spring, being a separate piece which has nothing soldered to it, can be left quite hard and so remain tougher than the tongue in the other method. The latter does lose some of its efficiency as a spring as a result of being heated when the pins are soldered on. That is one more reason why 18 ct hard white gold must be used for this purpose because, even after soldering, it does still retain a great deal of its hardness. By careful hammering in the appropriate places, it can be made springlike again. This would be quite impossible to the same extent with other alloys.

Returning to the second method of making the spring-pin type of clip back: all that now remains is to put the back into place. After the small spring has been put into position, and after pressing it down, a rivet is pushed through the hinge joint and the effectiveness of the spring tested. It will no doubt need some adjustment to make it work with the correct amount of spring in the correct direction. As before, it should spring closed from approximately 45° and spring open if the angle is enlarged. Filing the collar which was soldered on to the centre piece of the hinge is all that is necessary for adjustment. This must be done with extreme care, and any amount of explanation would not make it possible to complete a spring back of this type successfully. Practical experience and skill are indispensable. When the working is satisfactory, the rivet is withdrawn and the small spring put carefully away until the whole piece of work has been set and polished and is ready for its final assembly.

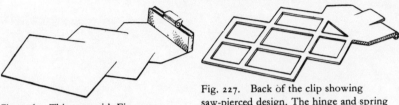

Fig. 226.   This part with Fig. 227 shows the 'flat back' clip.

Fig. 227.   Back of the clip showing saw-pierced design. The hinge and spring of this clip are similar to Fig. 223.

Making a 'Flat Back' Clip

The third type of spring back (Figs. 226 and 227) which is also often used for double clips, as are the two types described above, works on a similar principle but is probably the easier one to make. The beginning is the same. A small wall is made and soldered on to the back of the main part of the clip, but longer than before. This time it stretches practically the whole width of the clip and again should be positioned as near as possible to the top. The top edge of the wall is grooved with the small round needle file to accommodate the tube which forms the hinge. A length of tube, one-half of the total length, is soldered centrally into it, and again as before a block is soldered leaning backwards on top of this piece of tube.

The clip back is made from 8 gauge sheet metal of the hardest appropriate alloy. It is cut out to follow fairly closely to the general outline of the clip front, but a little smaller. It is not absolutely necessary to keep strictly to the outline; one should be guided by the practicability of the shape in question, and how to deviate from it, when necessary to avoid awkward corners. Into this shape is saw-pierced a tongue, as before, but it will in this instance be much bigger. This is an advantage for the efficiency of the spring. The two end pieces of tube are then soldered into position, as before a little away from the end. This is to allow the tongue to project a little, and after soldering, the surplus is filed away to the level of the tube.

At this stage the clip can be tested to try the spring, and any adjustments made. The final part is to saw-pierce a design on the back, Fig. 227, which will generally make the whole job lighter, neater and more pleasing to look at. Again it is left to the maker to choose a pattern that will suit the design of clip and which will not take away the strength that is so necessary around the tongue. All that remains is the sandpapering and final adjusting.

Fittings for Double Clip Brooches

The two clips which fit on to a frame to form tne double clip, whether they are asymmetrical, or an evenly-balanced pair, will both have the same type of spring-clip back, and it depends to a great extent upon what type of backs

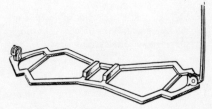

Fig. 228. Frame for flat back clips with thickening bar shown soldered in position.

these are, as to which type of frame will be most suitable for them. The principles which apply in all cases are that the clips must be easily detached and replaced and, when attached to the frame, must be held quite firmly without rocking or moving about. It is fairly obvious that, after many years of wear, they will fit less snugly than is required of a new and properly made set. Another important point, which applies only to the symmetrical pair, is that they should be interchangeable, that is to say, no left or right. Whichever one is picked up first may be placed into either position on the frame; a common fault with many brooches is that this is not so.

Frames for Flat Back Clips
The first type of clips, which have backs made from sheet metal and have a shape similar to but slightly smaller than the fronts, will fit most satisfactorily into a fairly substantial sheet-metal frame (12 gauge is suitable). This is made from a sheet of metal large enough for the whole outline of the two clips, when placed in position, to be marked out and then saw-pierced. Into the centre of this is cut one accurately-placed slot, through which the clip back can be slid in such a manner that they can be closed and the two clips will then stay closely together. One cannot give a detailed description of how to do this, because it depends entirely upon the construction and design of the two clips and these will vary so widely that to choose one would be impossible. Suffice it to say that, with 'identical pairs', the line where they meet will be made by the top of the clips. This is not always so but, when designing or making a pair of clips with this end in view, one must bear in mind the practical side of its manufacture.

Having made what is in effect a piece of metal of similar outline to the two clips (tops together) with a hole for the clip backs, we can proceed to make a more ornamental pattern by saw-piercing out much of the surplus metal and leaving instead a neat design. This can follow practically any theme but simplicity is by far the best guide, having in mind that a certain amount of strength is required.

One very important point must now be dealt with in relation to the fitting of the two clips. It will be observed that the thickness of the frame would not

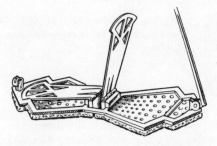

Fig. 229. Flat back clips in position in the frame with one side open, showing the purpose of thickening bar.

be sufficient to keep the clips from moving up and down; in other words, the thickness of the metal of the frame is not equal to the space in between the clip back and front. Fig. 228 will make this much clearer. To overcome this, a thickening bar is soldered on to the frame on each side of the opening wherein the clips are placed. This should be filed carefully to permit both clips to fasten securely and rigidly on the frame (Fig. 229). All that remains now is for the joint, safety catch and pin to be made and fitted on to the frame.

Frames for Pin Clips

The other type of frame particularly useful for the type of clips which have 'box' fittings and pins instead of flat backs, is made from substantial rectangular wire of approximately $\frac{1}{16}$ in by $\frac{1}{32}$ in (1.5 × 0.8 mm). This probably sounds far from substantial, but in jewellery it is so, in proportion to the thicknesses which are more frequently in use. From this rectangular wire, a small frame is made which will accommodate the backs of the two clips in much the same way as the backs were accommodated in the previous instance (Fig. 230).

The usual means of making such shapes will, of course, be used, and no detailed description will be necessary. This small frame will be made with the wire edgewise, so that it will give extra strength in the direction most needed i.e., lengthwise along the brooch. The depth of this box will be sufficient to occupy the whole of the space between clip backs and clip front, and therefore no addition should be necessary for that purpose. It may in fact be found

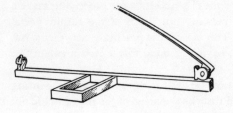

Fig. 230. Frame for pin back clips. Thickness of the frame serves as its own thickening bars.

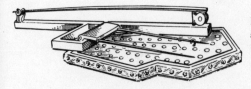

Fig. 231.   Pin back clip in position showing small hook soldered on to back of brooch for safety.

necessary to reduce it a little. The next step is to add a bar made from the same rectangular wire, still edgewise, which will coincide with the length of two clips placed together and whose ends will fit snugly into some part of the ends of the clips. There can be no set rule for doing this; it must depend entirely upon the design of the clips, and it can be emphasised that the bar does not need to be straight, but can in fact be shaped in a convenient way to suit the two brooches attached.

When in place, the two clips should again fit very firmly. On to the back of this bar, the usual type of catch joint and pin will be fitted. A useful addition, as a safety measure for the two clips when in position on the frame, is to solder a small hook on to the back of the clips into which one of the pins on each can be hooked. This also serves when the clips are used separately, and forms an extra measure of safety (Fig. 231).

9. Earrings, Necklaces and Bracelets

Clip earrings generally are similar in style to ordinary dress-clips but smaller in size. One important difference is that a 'pair' does not convey the same meaning as with a pair of dress-clips. With clip earrings, they must be 'opposites' but with the same design. To express this more clearly, one could say that, if a drawing were made of the design and a tracing taken, the tracing would have to be turned over to be used as the drawing for the second clip. The making will follow the usual principles of manufacture in every respect, and the backs will broadly follow the style of dress-clips.

One important point, however, is that the clips must be hinged from the *bottom* instead of the top, and the overall design of the clips must follow a style which will be suitable for the ear-lobes, and for the clips to be thus hinged (Fig. 232).

It is not essential that they should be clips; equally popular are screw fittings and peg fittings with small spring clips for pierced ears. Fig. 233 will show the types in question.

Very little more need be added to the description of the making of the clips because, from the practical point of view, they are exactly as before. There are one or two points, however, regarding the actual clip back which should be borne in mind. The most important one is that the space between the clip front and back must be appropriate for the thickness of an ear-lobe; this is, broadly speaking, $\frac{1}{16}$ in (1.5 mm). The next point to be remembered is that the comfort of the wearer must be thought of. For instance, a very strong vicious spring would be hardly acceptable for several hours' wear, and so a firm, but yet not too strong, spring is needed.

The third important consideration is size and shape of the clip back, it

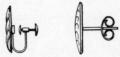

Fig. 232.   Three views of an ear clip.

Fig. 233.   Earring with screw fitting, left, and peg fitting, right.

being remembered that this must go behind the ear-lobe, which limits the size. Its shape must be such that it will hold firmly in position without discomfort to the wearer. For this reason, it is quite often the case that the overall shape of the back has to be made quite different to the front.

Turning now to screw fittings and fittings for pierced ears, one might say at once that it is not worth while for the maker to make these himself; particularly this is true with screws. There are manufacturers of jewellers' 'findings' (the name by which these sundries are generally known), who specialise in them and so manufacture such items in quantity, thereby making them at very much lower cost than it is possible otherwise. In this particular instance then, it is without doubt wise and economical to purchase such fittings ready made. If for any special reason, one *has* to make these fittings they are not by any means difficult and a brief description is all that is necessary.

Screw Fittings

Take a piece of round gold wire of 16-gauge and $1\frac{1}{4}$ in (3.2 cm) long, on to the end of which is soldered a short length of tube with fairly thick walls through which a similar thickness of wire would not quite go. This need be only $\frac{1}{8}$ in (3 mm) long. Using taps and a screw plate of the appropriate thickness (obtainable from jewellers' tool-merchants), a thread is made inside the short length of tube, and a piece of wire is made to screw into it. This is cut off to $\frac{5}{16}$ in (8 mm) length, its end filed flat and one end soldered to the centre of a $\frac{3}{16}$ in (4.7 mm) disc, the edges of which are filed into very small scallops to enable them to be turned more easily.

The length of screw is now put through the threaded tube and on to its opposite end a small domed cap of $\frac{3}{32}$ in (2.4 mm) is soldered. This forms the grip on the ear-lobe when in use. The fitting is now ready to be soldered to the main part of the work in hand, after which it is wiser to leave it straight until preliminary polishing and setting have been completed, as both of these operations are facilitated by the wires being straight. They are easily bent to the correct shape afterwards.

Wire or Peg Fittings for Pierced Ears

Wires for pierced ears are even easier, as they consist of a straight round wire $\frac{1}{2}$ in (12 mm) long, 12 gauge in thickness, soldered to the back of the ear-stud. They would, of course, be pushed into a small hole drilled for that purpose before being soldered, to give sufficient strength.

The clip itself is made from gold strip, 5 gauge in thickness, $\frac{1}{8}$ in (3 mm) wide, which has not been annealed and is therefore still springy. The strip needs to be about $\frac{3}{4}$ in (20 mm) long; each end is bent round to form a small circle and then a small hole through which the 12 gauge wire will pass is drilled in the centre of the strip. To prevent the clips from coming off too easily, a very small ridge is filed near the end of the wire, into which the two circles of the clip fit.

Making a Pendant

Broadly speaking, pendants are supported by a chain around the neck of the wearer, and fastened at the back with a bolt ring or snap. Of these articles the most important, from the manufacturing jeweller's point of view, is the pendant, because the chain and bolt ring are items of specialised manufacture and are uneconomical for the general mounter to make for himself. Chain is purchased by the foot from the chain maker, and bolt rings from the 'findings' specialist. We can, therefore, leave these items and go ahead with the pendant.

Again it is better that we should only describe differences in general principles of manufacture which have not previously been covered in detail. The designs are innumerable, and we will choose one fairly easy general type of design as shown in Fig. 234 for our purpose. A very important point is that the pendant must hang correctly when worn and so show its design to the best advantage. It must also rest correctly and comfortably upon the wearer and not twist or turn over when its wearer moves about normally. The control of these points rests chiefly upon the joints in the pendant itself and upon the amount of free movement each joint will

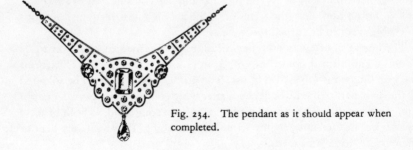

Fig. 234. The pendant as it should appear when completed.

allow in any direction. Also the distribution of weight will have some bearing upon its hanging correctly but this will depend more upon the designer than the maker.

Assuming that a design similar to that shown in Fig. 234 is to be carried out, here is described very briefly the actual processes of manufacture, with emphasis on the manufacturing principles that have not yet arisen.

The whole pendant should be kept as thin as possible consistent with the depth of the stones to be set therein, and any 'relief' or modelling put into it should be considered carefully with the distribution of weight in mind. If a large coloured stone, such as an aquamarine, which is cut quite deeply—left 'thick'—is the centre piece, sufficient depth is necessary in the mounting to prevent the stone coming through the back. If this were to happen, it would prevent the whole pendant from resting correctly when worn. Nevertheless the surrounding part, or parts, of the pendant must be kept shallow—as thin as is practicable—to avoid ugliness and general clumsiness.

It is in this type of work that the skill of the mounter combines with that of the designer to effect an overall loveliness in the piece being made. It is skill which is gained partly by experience and is partly a natural attribute that will make a necklet look good, and give prominence and importance to the appropriate part of the design or the particularly valuable centre stones around which the design is built. The maker must have in mind exactly how it will look right from the earliest stages: its balance, its moulding and its practicability in wear.

The positioning of joints will be of the greatest importance, and the amount of movement in either direction allowed by each joint will also have a bearing on how the finished work will hang in wear. Usually not many joints are required, but no set rule can be laid down for this. The parts will be saw-pierced from metal of approximately 11 gauge and a neat shallow gallery of thin square wire added. This part of the work needs no further detailed description, and the type of joints can be dealt with.

Tube Joints

Take Fig. 234 as an example. The joints most suitable would be tube joints, allowing movement in one direction only—in the same way as a hinge. This is done by filing, with a small round needle-file, a depression along both of the edges to be joined, each one being filed so that the tube to be used will rest one half of its thickness into it. Into one of these, exactly in the centre, will be soldered a length of tube of one-third the total width of the joint. Into the opposite section of the joint will be soldered two pieces of similar length, one to each end, leaving sufficient space between them for the first

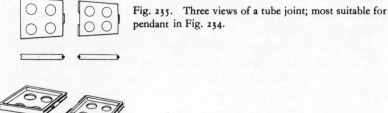

Fig. 235.   Three views of a tube joint; most suitable for pendant in Fig. 234.

piece of tube to fit tightly. This type of joint would keep the pendant in its appropriate shape while allowing sufficient movement in the one direction to keep it lying neatly against the wearer (Fig. 235).

Part Gallery Joint

Another method of joining sections together where a little more movement is required in more than one direction is to place the gallery along two sides only of each section, those two sides being the parallel ones which follow along the pendant, the gallery between the sections being omitted. On the inside of the gallery at one end only, and on both sides of each joint, a short piece of gold or platinum is soldered and left projecting by approximately $\frac{1}{8}$ in (3 mm). This need not be more than 8 gauge in thickness, and as wide only as the gallery. The two pieces can now be placed inside the gallery of the next section and should allow both pieces to fit closely together.

The next operation is to drill a small hole through the sides of the gallery and each corresponding projection. The holes in the projections can now be elongated sufficiently to allow the required amount of movement in a lengthwise direction. Only a very slight elongation of the hole is necessary to permit considerable movement, and care must be taken to avoid overdoing this or the finished work will permit far too much movement and lose its shape in wear.

That deals with the movement lengthwise, but it may also be desirable to allow a limited movement in one or both of the opposite directions. This can be done by filing off the corners of the small joint pieces as much as necessary; again it should be emphasised that care must be taken to avoid allowing too much movement or the necklet may become too 'floppy'. Fig. 236 will show these steps stage by stage.

Round Wire Pegs

The actual fixing of the round wire peg which will secure the jointed parts can be done by either of two methods:

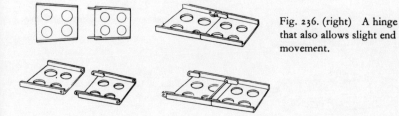

Fig. 236. (right)   A hinge
that also allows slight end
movement.

(1) A peg can be pushed through both sides of the joint and, leaving it right across, the ends of the peg soldered very carefully to the outside of the gallery. This needs extreme care to avoid soldering up the whole joint; or

(2) To go a stage further for neatness after the ends of the pegs have been so soldered, each peg can be snipped in the centre with the point of the shears, and each half of the peg bent round until it reaches the inside of the gallery to which it is carefully soldered.

It may not be necessary to use the whole length of the pegs for this but they can, of course, be shortened as is suitable.

Ring Hinge Joints

The only other type of joint which may at times be useful for necklets is made quite simply by soldering two rings made of thin, round wire on to one section of the pendant, and two similar rings facing the opposite direction, similarly spaced, which can be opened. After being placed through the first two rings, they can be closed up and carefully soldered. This type of joint is not a very satisfactory one for most purposes but does nevertheless have its uses where a very flexible and widely spaced joint is suitable (Fig. 237).

Fancy Gem-set Snaps

One other important point is that valuable pendants with the amount of work involved in such pieces as described above are not always fastened by a bolt ring. Sometimes a fancy diamond-set snap is used. These are usually made by hand as individual items and designed as far as practicable to suit the pendant itself, although the similarity must be very limited with such a small

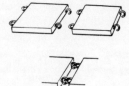

Fig. 237.   The simplest form of hinge, which allows
movement in all directions.

Fig. 238.   Gemset and engraved pendant snap.

Fig. 239.   Snap, with top removed, showing square wire pieces and tongue in position.

item. Usually, the length of the snap is kept down to between $\frac{1}{2}$ in and $\frac{3}{4}$ in (12–20 mm) long (Fig. 238).

To make such a snap, one must bear in mind that stones set in it must not protrude through the back of the setting, or they will obstruct the tongue of the snap from going into position. As only small and shallow stones are used, this is not a very serious problem. Should there be any larger stones, they will be set in raised collets to supply the necessary depth. Ten gauge metal will be used for the top and, after saw-piercing to shape, drilling holes for the stones and so on, a similarly shaped piece is cut from 8 gauge metal, and a simple but neat pattern saw-pierced into it. A length of thin, square wire (12 gauge is sufficient) is necessary for the dividing bars, and finally a piece of 11 gauge *hard* gold is needed for the tongue of the snap. The square wire is cut into two pieces a little longer than the width of the snap, and two smaller pieces for the ends. A glance at Fig. 239 will show where they go.

It is important to realise why these pieces are so placed. When working on a snap such as this, it is always wise to solder the bars on to the back part, and then carry on and make the tongue itself before soldering the back and front of the snap together. The end peg forms a safety device in case the snap should come unfastened for any reason; inasmuch as it will prevent the tongue coming right out from the snap. The distances between the blocks are very important as it may be seen that, in the finished snap, the tongue has to be placed through the space between the end peg and the first pair, and afterwards pushed into place so that the first pair of pegs will fit into the small recesses cut into the sides of the tongue.

The whole snap must work smoothly and easily and yet remain secure and reliable. Bearing in mind these points, the blocks are soldered carefully into place and, by using dividers to mark out the various distances on to the 11-gauge sheet, the outline of the tongue is marked with a scriber. It should be noticed that the thumb-pieces and the ring for attaching to the chain of the necklet are all cut from this piece to avoid the need for soldering, as this would soften the tongue and lose the springiness which is very important to ensure the effectiveness of the snap.

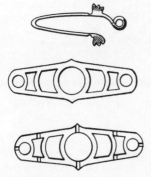
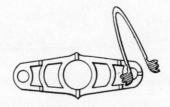

Fig. 240. (left)   Three stages in the manufacture of the tongue and snap. (above) Snap, with top removed, showing the tongue making entry.

After cutting round the outline with the saw, the tongue must be carefully filed to the appropriate width, and the thumb-pieces and ring filed round and correctly shaped. The thumb-pieces are lightly scalloped to make an easy grip for opening. The actual security of the snap depends upon the small recesses cut into the sides of the tongue immediately below the thumb-pieces. These must be the exact width of the blocks soldered in position accordingly, and must not be made too wide or the snap will be loose in use. The whole action of the snap can now be tried. The thumb-piece should be slipped behind the end block (imagining, of course, that top and bottom are both soldered in place) and the tongue hooked through. The tapering tongue can now be pushed down until the two small recesses take their place behind the two side blocks, thus holding the snap in place. From this it can be seen that measurements must be very carefully marked out for the tongue to work efficiently. Fig. 240 will show various stages in the manufacture of these items.

Making a Bracelet

Making a bracelet involves all the principles described so far in this book, and gives plenty of scope for both the designer and the maker. Sometimes the centre piece is a watch framed with diamonds or other gems, with the bracelet tapering steadily towards the back. Alternatively, it may be a bracelet only, comprised of a number of identical sections which form a parallel-sided bracelet, or one which has a centre piece moulded and raised to form an attractive and important front and continued on either side as a tapering bracelet composed of many sections (Fig. 241).

The difference, as far as the maker is concerned, is not very great in either case. Should it be a watch in the centre, a watch case of the appropriate size for the movement is obtained from the case-maker or watch supplier, and the diamond settings are built around it. If the bracelet has an ornate centre

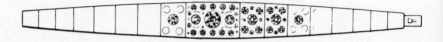

Fig. 241. Front and side view of a tapering bracelet composed of many sections, as it would look when completed.

piece, then this too will be made first as a separate item. To dwell too long on this part of the work would involve a great deal of repetition. It is sufficient instead to mention first the important principles to be applied when making the centre piece of the bracelet, and to follow this with the bracelet itself.

It may be necessary to make a small number of joints in the centre piece itself, to allow it to fit comfortably around the wrist. This is not usual, however, and it is sufficient in most cases to make the centre piece on a slightly curved base appropriate to the curve of the wearer's wrist. The work needs to be as light as is practicable, consistent with strength. The thickness of metal needed is approximately 9 gauge. This will allow sufficient thickness for setting average-size diamonds. One might say that the centre piece will be built as described for necklets, and a very shallow edging or gallery added.

Raised Claw Settings for Larger Stones

It is necessary to describe here a type of setting, often used in this type of work, and which is quite often also used for brooches and necklets, which so far has not been dealt with. This is the claw setting used to raise to prominence individual larger stones in what is otherwise a grain set article. Around the claw setting is a rim of 'daylight' (its usual name), a gap or slight space between the claw setting and its border. To achieve this, a very shallow claw setting is made, or purchased, for the diamond in question, and four very small neat pieces of knife-edged wire are gapped into the back and left projecting a fraction of an inch outside. Into the main part of the setting is saw-pierced a hole slightly larger than the outside of the setting, and the small projections of the setting itself are reduced at the ends until they permit the setting to fit tightly into the hole made to accommodate it. A small paillon of solder at each point attaches the setting in its place.

This need not necessarily be kept for single settings only, but may be useful for several settings joined together, or even for a complete section which demands a 'daylight' round it. The moulding or 'relief' of the centre piece should not be too pronounced, and very sharp or ungainly projections

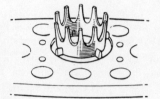 Fig. 242. A claw setting used for giving the centre stone prominence showing the rim of 'daylight' and knife-edged pieces of wire in position.

should be avoided, remembering that its wearer would not appreciate torn clothing which might result from these additions (Fig. 242).

Making the Remainder of the Bracelet

It is necessary, in most cases, that the remainder of the bracelet should follow a similar pattern, tapering towards the back and being made of fairly short jointed sections, the last of which is made into a snap. The overall length of a bracelet is 6¾ in (17 cm) when placed flat. A few important points should be borne in mind when making the joints. They must move only in one direction and, when the bracelet is laid out flat, there should be no sign of the joint at all, each section being close up against its neighbour, and continuing exactly in line, with no suggestion of sideways curve. This accuracy in jointing is very difficult to achieve, but most important.

The bracelet, excluding the centre piece if this is to be made as a separate item, should be made from one piece, and as much work as possible done on this, including saw-piercing all the holes for diamonds and soldering on the edging, before separating the whole into sections. A little extra length will have to be allowed to make up for the closing of the sections after sawing through. The purpose of this will be fairly clear; any attempt to do the whole bracelet by making each section separately would inevitably make the job much more difficult, and would inevitably result in the completed bracelet having slight curves in a sideways direction, or inaccuracies in the continuity of the taper.

The same safeguards apply to the edging. This can be much more easily made and soldered in place as one long piece than in small sections. One can choose between making the edging as a plain narrow edge soldered directly on to the back of the bracelet; or having it separated slightly by a number of small cheniers. The last mentioned is perhaps the neater of the two, but is not so strong. If such a gallery were made, a solid edge would have to be soldered between each section and tube joints made, as these would be the only type which would be strong enough to withstand normal wear, and handling.

Other types of joints which could be used were mentioned in the section dealing with necklets and pendants.

Snaps for Bracelets

The only other part which it is necessary to describe in more detail is the snap fastener. The type of snap fastener that has been described is used only for necklets, whereas the type now to be described would be suitable, if slightly altered and adapted, for either bracelet or necklet. However it can be safely said that it is more suitable as a bracelet snap. This snap can be made, by using one section and making it the snap, or by using the junction of two sections. In the latter case, the two sections will be rigid when fastened, with no flexibility between them. This would not be considered incorrect, as the back of the wrist is, for practical purposes, flat. Therefore no joint is really necessary in that particular section or sections. It will depend entirely upon the size of each section which of these two methods is used; and for the purpose of our practical description, it does not make any real difference. The point to be borne in mind always, is that it should not be *obvious* as a snap. The whole idea is to make it an inconspicuous part of the whole.

This type is called the 'box' snap, and consists of a thumb-piece which, when depressed, will allow a tongue to be withdrawn from the opposite section of the snap. It is best for practical purposes to describe the mechanism and making of the appropriate parts of the snap, and leave it for the reader to decide just how it can best fit into his design of bracelet.

Making a 'Box' Snap

The snap of the bracelet should be made as an integral part of the section, or sections, to be used and 'built in' during manufacture of the bracelet.

The tongue is made from sheet metal of the hardest possible alloy, white 18 ct being the best in all cases, and consists of a piece $\frac{1}{2}$ in (12 mm) long and $\frac{3}{8}$ in (10 mm) wide *if possible*. This is an ideal size which cannot always be adhered to. Usually it has to be smaller, according to the size of the bracelet. Into this, two parallel sawcuts are made with a very fine saw-blade, to two-thirds of its length and dividing the piece approximately into three equal

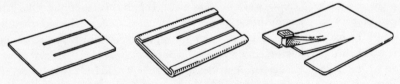

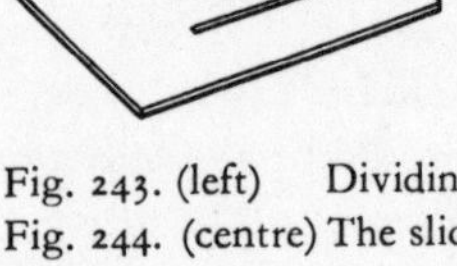

Fig. 243. (left)   Dividing the tongue into three equal sections.
Fig. 244. (centre) The slide shown bent around the tongue.
Fig. 245. (right) The centre of the tongue lifted and with arm fitted.

Fig. 246.   Two views of the snap. Top, after
soldering, and bottom, completed.

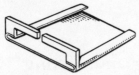

sections (Fig. 243). Next a 'slide' is made, into which this tongue will ride
smoothly. This is done by using a piece of very thin sheet metal, 1 gauge
being sufficient. It should be hard 18 ct alloy, the same length as the tongue
but approximately $\frac{1}{8}$ in (3 mm) wider.

Placing the tongue on the centre of this piece and holding it there securely
with flat-nosed pliers, each of the edges which are projecting beyond the sides
of the tongue is carefully bent over to hold it securely, after which it is
forcibly pulled out from the slide now made (Fig. 244). Obviously it is now
too tight for use, but a little gentle filing at the edges of the tongue will
correct that, and it will move easily but firmly in and out of the slide.

The centre section of the tongue is now provided with an arm and thumb
piece of square wire, soldered together and soldered along the centre of the
tongue as in Fig. 245. The centre section of the tongue should be shortened
just a little before soldering on the arm. The purpose of this will be clear
when the next operation is carried out. This is to make a bridge over one end
of the slide, from 6 gauge sheet metal which forms the actual locking piece.

The working parts of the snap are now completed, apart from adjusting
them to work correctly, and, of course, apart from building them into the
bracelet section. The centre part of the tongue is bent upwards a little, and
the action of the snap is that the tongue when pushed into the slide will
force the centre piece downwards as it passes under the bridge, until it can rise
again, having passed right under. This will prevent the tongue from being
withdrawn until the centre part is depressed by means of the thumb pieces
provided. Fig. 246 showing step by step manufacture of the snap will make
this clear.

10. Polishing and Setting

The actual processes of making hand-made jewellery have been covered in detail up to the stage where each article is polished, set with the appropriate stones, and finally finished. There is another very important process of jewellery manufacture, namely that of casting, but as this is in many respects a distinctly separate section of the whole process it would be appropriate to leave it until the polishing and setting processes have been dealt with. (See Chapter 11.)

It should be said at once that polishing and setting are two distinctly separate arts and both quite separate from mounting, making in fact three branches of the trade which one might well consider as three separate trades. It was once the case that a jeweller made the complete piece of jewellery himself, but those days have certainly gone, and craftsmen normally specialise in one of the three branches.

Polishing Equipment
Taking polishing first, this again is divided into two main processes, preparing work for the setters, which is in fact giving the work its initial polishing, and finishing, which is giving the work its final polish and if necessary plating after the setters have finished their part. The equipment needed is a $\frac{1}{4}$ h.p. electric motor capable of doing 2,000 r.p.m. with a double-ended spindle on to each end of which is fitted a tapered thread attachment. The spindles have a left-hand threaded attachment on one end, and a right-hand threaded one at the other. The effect of this is to tighten up the mops or brushes as they revolve against the pressure of the work applied. The whole of the surrounding area of the spindle ends must be enclosed in a dust-

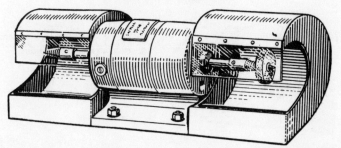

Fig. 247. A double-ended polishing head showing tapered spindles and transparent (celluloid) aperture.

extracting cowl leaving only sufficient space for the operator to work, and provided, where possible, with a transparent (celluloid) aperture through which the work can be seen (Fig. 247).

It will be realised, of course, that a very considerable quantity of polishing material and dust will be thrown off while working, and this is very injurious to the worker continually inhaling it and also renders it impossible to see the result of the work. Another important reason for this is that, during polishing, some minute particles of gold are removed from the work and would be lost if some means of collecting it, together with the dust from the polishing materials, were not available. This is afterwards sent away to the refiners for gold extraction. The equipment for use with this consists of a wide range of felt mops of various sizes including shapes for polishing inside rings, a variety of brushes of different textures and thicknesses and calico mops for finishing.

The polisher must also be equipped with another place for carrying out the hand-polishing part of his work. The most suitable for this is a bench shaped similarly to those of mounters and setters, and provided with a tin tray for materials in use. Attached to one side of this will be a bundle of polishing threads for 'threading' (a process which will be mentioned later in more detail). The bench should also be equipped with small pieces of Water-of-Ayr stone (round and triangular), fine emery-buffs, and blocks of rouge for use with the threads. For the various brushes and mops, it is necessary to have blocks of rouge, or rouge powder, and green rouge block or powder for use on platinum work (Fig. 248).

To complete the polishing department's equipment, an ample supply of hot water, washing soda, bowls, and a place for washing out, together with a boiling-out saucepan or pot, a gas ring or similar means of heating, and methylated spirit is needed. If it is intended to finish work with rhodium plating and gilding, then the appropriate equipment for these must be

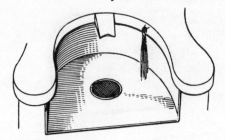

Fig. 248. A special bench for hand polishing jewellery. Note polishing threads on right-hand side.

purchased and placed in a section where they can be kept well covered and away from dust to ensure cleanliness. Polishing is a dirty job and suitable clothing and hand protection should be provided.

Large quantities of work can be dealt with much quicker and easier by obtaining an ultrasonic cleaner. This is a small stainless steel tank with an electronic device called a 'transducer' in the bottom of the tank. When the tank is filled with cleaning fluid and the equipment switched on, ultrasonic waves are produced in the fluid which scours anything placed in it. It is very effective for degreasing to provide chemically clean surfaces and also for cleaning out blind holes and other inaccessible corners of jewellery.

The best way of drying all finished work is to use specially prepared materials—box-wood sawdust or special drying compounds—which can be obtained from jewellery equipment suppliers. When the work has been cleaned, whether by a washing out process or by ultrasonic cleaning, it should be placed immediately in a bowl containing a fairly large quantity of one of the drying materials mentioned, which should be kept slightly warm. In just a short time the work will be completely dried without any deterioration of the polishing and finishing.

Coarse Polishing

Work now finished by the mounter, arrives at the polishing department for preparation. This, as already mentioned, is an initial polishing, or one could say a coarse polishing which in its process shows up any faults which may possibly have been unnoticed by the mounter, such as small 'pin-holes' in soldered joints, small cracks in the metal, or any particularly rough places.

The polisher first rouges the job all over, beginning with some of the more difficult spots which are not easily accessible. This is where the polishing threads are used. Taking as an example scallops in between claws; these, each in turn are rubbed back and forth along the thread (previously rouged) until they are polished inside; other small holes or 'daylights' are similarly treated. Fig. 249 shows this being done. Other small holes or hollowed

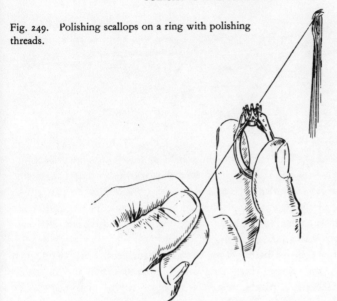

Fig. 249. Polishing scallops on a ring with polishing threads.

surfaces which are difficult of access may have to be smoothed with Water-of-Ayr stone before it is possible even to rouge them. Water-of-Ayr is a very fine and fairly soft lightly abrasive stone which, when used with water, will remove sandpaper marks and other roughness of surface and will render the job easier to polish. After such items have been dealt with, flat surfaces should be checked and very lightly emery-buffed to remove sandpaper marks before going on to use the motor polisher.

It cannot be overemphasised that polishing is an extremely important part of jewellery manufacture, and good or bad polishing can either complete or entirely ruin a piece of work. It cannot make bad workmanship into work of quality, but the reverse can easily happen. Where surfaces are intended to be flat, they must be kept flat for polishing; curved surfaces must be kept in their proper curve; and corners (or angles) which are intended to be sharp and clean and are made thus by the maker, must retain their sharpness when finished. It is extremely easy for these matters to be missed, or carelessly forgotten, and for corners to be rounded off during the rouging or when polishing.

The first stages of rouging on the motor polisher are to deal with those same parts which are more difficult of access; the inside of rings for example are rouged on what is called an 'inside' flat, which is in fact a small tapered

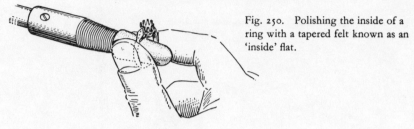

Fig. 250. Polishing the inside of a ring with a tapered felt known as an 'inside' flat.

felt with a rounded end, tapering from about 1 in (25 mm) down to $\frac{1}{2}$ in (12 mm) (Fig. 250). The rouge block is held against this and it becomes impregnated with rouge. The ring can then be placed over it and the inside polished. These felts can also be used for polishing inside domed parts, such as cluster tops, or underneath clip-tops and similar items. The rounded end serves to fit into such curves and hollows and the felt is flexible enough to accommodate itself to variations in shape.

After the more difficult places come the easier surfaces. For flat-polished surfaces, such as the sides of rings, a flat-sided felt is used first and any other similar, easily accessible places, which are flat or slightly curved, can be dealt with in the same way. Then comes the use of small brushes for getting into corners, and then the larger mops for the overall final rouging (Fig. 251). The job should now be free from any traces of sandpaper or emery-paper marks and have a lightly-polished appearance. It will also be clogged with rouge in all its holes, nooks and corners. The final step is to boil it in strong soda water to get it clean and free from rouge, ready for setting. This is important because, if any rouge or other polishing material should be left and possibly trapped behind stones during setting, it will be detrimental to the colour and fire of the stones when the article is finished. This is more particularly so if the settings are not all 'open' settings, that is to say, with holes right through the metal. There are some cases where stones are set with a closed back, for example, flat-back stones, and small rose-cut diamonds.

This completes the preliminary stage of polishing and the work now goes forward to the setter. This is where that specialised part of the work is done which not only secures the stones in place but decorates the otherwise plain surfaces in between stones. More about that later.

Final Polishing
From the setter the work goes back to the mounter if there are any separate pieces to be affixed, such as petals and flowers to spray brooches, spring backs to clips, and such other parts as may have been set and polished while more easily accessible, and then the work returns again to the polishing

  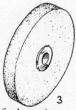

Fig. 251. Showing 1, a large mop for overall final rouging; 2, small brush for getting into corners; 3, a flat-sided felt for flat polished surfaces; 4, tapered felt for polishing the inside of a ring.

and finishing section. Whereas before the concentration was on removing sandpaper and emery-paper marks and to achieve a smoother, more even surface, the accent is now on finishing, and polishing to a bright, fine surface.

This may sound at first likely to be a fairly easy matter, and one is apt to think the polisher has but a small part in the making of a good article of jewellery. This is not so, even though one cannot add much in the way of descriptive work on the processes involved. It is a difficult and important part of the work, and one in which success and final quality can be achieved only by that long steady progress which is experience.

Again then with finishing, as with rouging, the polish must be achieved without losing shape and sharpness, and without making flat surfaces slightly hollowed and rounded. One may say that the polish is given to a ring or brooch or other pieces of work in much the same manner, and in much the same order as the preliminary rouging, but this time using much less rouge. In fact separate sets of felts and calico mops are necessary and little or no work is done with brushes. Platinum is much more difficult to polish to a good finish than gold as the surface has a tendency to drag, and achieves only a medium brightness. The final high polish needs very concentrated effort and patience, and the result is highly rewarding, for a good finish on platinum will remain good without tarnishing for many years.

The work must be finally washed out again to remove any traces of grease and rouge, and here it will depend upon what stones have been set into the article whether they are boiled in soda, washed in methylated spirit, or just washed in warm soapy water. Some stones will not stand up to boiling, and some will stain in methylated spirit. A few details on this point will be added later.

Setting

Gemstone setting, whether the stones be diamonds, sapphires, rubies, emeralds or opals, or the flat type of signet stone like cornelian, bloodstone, onyx or any other gemstone, is an art in itself, needing great skill and experience, and it is for this reason that it has become a separate branch of the manufacturing jewellery trade. There is a tendency in all work these days to specialise in one or other of the departments.

This has taken place in the jewellery trade with the introduction of new ideas and new methods of production, particularly with the 'illusion' type of setting where it is necessary for the setter to be capable of ornamenting the metal surrounding a stone to make it look attractive.

Setting Equipment

Broadly speaking there are three major types of settings: they are claw, millegrain and flush settings, with variations combining more than one type. But before proceeding, mention should be made of the tools and equipment of the setter. The work-bench is a type similar to that used for mounting, namely a semi-circular recess in a strong, thick and solid bench beneath which is hung a leather skin for collecting lemel, resulting from the work of enlarging holes for stones.

A series of sticks, similar to lengths of broom stick, and convenient to hold, have melted on to them a quantity of setter's cement, a wax which softens and becomes pliable when heated, and into which work of various kinds can be pressed and held securely whilst setting is taking place. Also necessary is a clamp in which rings can be secured while the setter works on the top settings. This comprises two pieces of wood, almost semi-circular in section, held together loosely by a brass band or collar, in between which a wedge can be pushed, thus holding the ring securely between the two pieces at the opposite end. It is usual to cover the surfaces which are in actual contact with the rings with very thin leather to avoid any possibility of scratching the work and also to ensure a better grip to avoid slipping (Fig. 252).

The setter must have a very wide range of cutting tools, known by various terms, such as scorpers, spitz-sticks, ball-sticks and others. These names apply to different shapes of cutting surfaces. Broadly speaking, it might be said that scorpers have a flat cutting surface, spitz-sticks a knife-edged cutting surface, and ball-sticks a curved surface. That is only a very brief

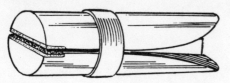

Fig. 252. Clamp—showing leather inserts.

Fig. 253.   A selection of tools for setting.

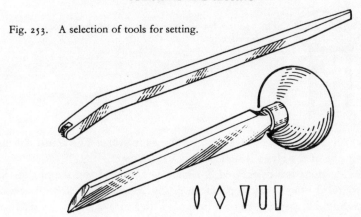

description, and there are many different widths and shapes in each case. Each of these tools is fitted into a small spherical, knob-like handle, convenient to hold in the palm of the hand, and approximately 1 in (25 mm) diameter. The tools themselves, being a convenient length, are rarely more than 2½ in (6.4 cm) long when new. Fig. 253 shows two of these tools.

Another essential for the setter is a flexible shaft electric drill, suspended above his work-place. Into this, fraises of the appropriate shape and size can be fitted. There are many different shapes and sizes of fraises, both ball-type, and pear-shaped, to suit all needs, and the setter should equip himself with a considerable number of these. A good-quality oil stone for sharpening tools is also a necessity. The tools and equipment mentioned are not very many or very costly, but it is the skill with which they are used which brings about the desired result.

Fixing Gemstones in a Claw Setting

With claw settings, whether in a ring, brooch or other article of jewellery, the work is the same. The method of holding the article for convenience will differ. In the case of a ring, it would be secured in a clamp; a brooch would be held on the end of a cement stick (Fig. 254). The mounter will have made the claw setting so that the diamond, or other stone, rests on the top of the claws and, looked at from above, shows about two-thirds of the thickness of the claws round the outside of the stone. The setter must now cut away the claws from the inside and create a rest for the stone a little below the top of them. He must avoid making them too thin at the top, and must also leave the stone resting the same distance from the top all round. This distance cannot be given by any standard measure but it is sufficient to leave a small tip of each

Fig. 254.   A brooch for setting held on the end of a cement stick.

claw which can be pushed over the girdle of the stone. The actual cutting on the inside of the claws is done with a flat scorper.

When the stone has been fitted, it should be removed and the tips of the claws rounded over at the top before finally securing the stone in place. One tip should be partly bent over inwards with a pair of sharp-nosed pliers, and this will act as a stop for the stone, which can now be placed in its setting.

After ensuring that it is correctly resting the same depth all round, the claws may be pushed over on to it, starting with the one opposite to that which was first bent. The stone will now be firm enough for the remaining claws to be pushed gently but firmly down on to it, so that no movement is possible. It remains now for the claws to be carefully smoothed and rounded so that they have no sharp points or rough edges which might catch on the wearer's clothing. This is done first with a fine-cut needle-file, and finally with very fine emery paper. A point which should be noted here is that the filing of claws must be done with extreme care in the case of softer stones. Although diamonds and sapphires and many other stones will not mark if the file should rub along them, there are other stones, such as opal and turquoise, which will. The three stages are shown in Fig. 255.

Fixing Gemstones in a Millegrain Setting

Millegrain setting is the term usually applied to settings where the stone is held in place by a border of very fine grains. Its most notable use is for setting

Fig. 255.   The three stages described in claw setting, with, left, claw set slightly; centre, stone in position; and, right, setting complete.

176

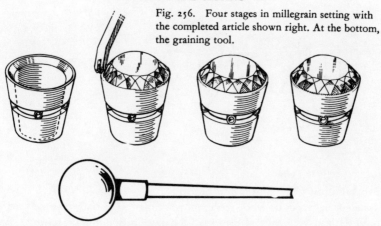

Fig. 256. Four stages in millegrain setting with the completed article shown right. At the bottom, the graining tool.

stones in collets, which are made with a plain, unbroken edge. This type of setting is perhaps not now quite so popular as it has been in past years. With this, as before with claw settings, the setter has to cut away the inside of the collet at the top in such a manner as to leave the stone sunk a little below the level of the top edge. This is done with a ball-stick, its curved cutting edge enabling a smooth, clean cut to be made on the curved inside of the collet. A great deal of skill is needed in setting of this style especially where stones are not very round or have slightly misshapen edges. The work of the setter can improve the appearance of such stones very greatly by the skilful use of the grained edge.

Having made a bearing inside the collet to support the stone, the next step is to push the resulting edge of metal over the edge of the stone to secure it. This is done with the blunt pushing tool used for claw settings, and the edge is pushed a little at a time all the way round the stone, maintaining a near circle. If this edge has been cut too thin, it will buckle during this stage and, if that happens, the result is a very bad and ragged setting which it is almost impossible to correct. This should not happen, and the experienced setter will know just what thickness of metal is required to make a satisfactory job.

When the edge has been pushed over the stone, all round the outer edge is carefully filed, smoothed with emery paper, and finally burnished leaving a clean circle of metal holding the stone. This circle is then milled with the small milling wheel, which is part of the setter's equipment. The wheel is simply a very tiny wheel made to revolve on the end of a small hand tool similar in size to an engraving tool. This is simply run around the edge of metal, creating the small grain appearance known as millegrain.

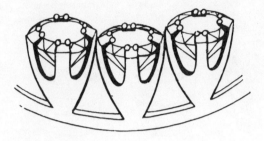

Fig. 257. The finished grains
on the tips of the claws.

Combination Claw and Grain Setting

Some special types of work require a combination of both claw setting and grain setting. Millegrain setting has been described, but grain setting is quite different and does not refer to the setting edge. Firstly it is helpful to deal with setting of coronet clusters, the making of which was described, and which are also often known as 'claw-set clusters'. The fact is that they require grain settings in addition to the claws. Here are the details. The centre stone is claw set and should be dealt with as already explained in relation to claw rings. The stones which surround the cluster have one claw, but the other means of securing the stone is to create grains.

Firstly the hole in which the stone is to be secured is enlarged sufficiently to let the edge of the stone rest a little below the surface. This is best done with a cutting tool which will keep the hole smaller at the base and cut in a small supporting edge without making the top of the hole any larger than is completely necessary to let the stone in. If the sides of the hole are made too steeply angular, the result will be that the edge of gold which is to be used to secure the stone will be too far away from the stone and therefore make the securing much more complicated. Now, having let in the stone, the one claw may be pressed over and then the surrounding surface of the stone is to be cut into little knobs of metal which can be pressed over the edge of the stone. These can then be made into neat grains with a grain tool of the appropriate size, which is shown in Fig. 257 with the setting as described.

Fixing Stones in Flush Settings

The flush setting used for bloodstone signets and similar work, in effect a polished flat edge surrounding the stone, is begun as for millegrain setting. Usually the setting is gold instead of platinum, and the stones to be set are very much larger. With these, a bearing is cut for the stone so that it will rest just below the edge of the setting. A very close fit is essential so that no

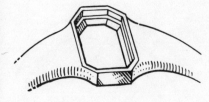

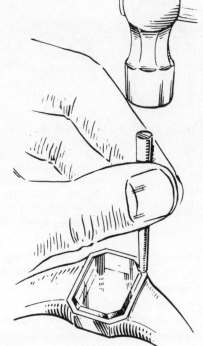

Fig. 258. (above)   A bearing is cut for the stone so that it rests a little below the edge of the setting.

Fig. 259. (right)   The punch, while being hammered, is moved slowly along the edge of the ring.

Fig. 260. (below)   The stone set in position and the metal surrounding it smoothed and finished off.

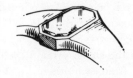

space is left between the edge of the stone. This time the metal is wider and thicker, to push it over by hand would be extremely difficult (Fig. 258).

To complete this operation satisfactorily, a small, flat-edged, steel punch is used and it is usual to have an assistant to hammer this punch steadily and consistently as required. The method adopted is for the setter to hold the ring in the clamp with the left hand, and with the right hand to hold the punch steadily on the setting edge. The assistant then taps lightly upon the punch with a small hammer while the setter moves the punch slowly along the edge, steadily pushing the edge of metal over the stone and securing it in position. This edge now has to be carefully filed smooth and flat and emery buffed, before burnishing and polishing. The effect should be a flat border of metal approximately $\frac{1}{16}$ in (1.5 mm) wide, surrounding the stone. A variation is to have, instead of a flat border, a neat hollowed border; an effect which is obtained by using a curved-edge scorper very skilfully and cutting down a semi-circular hollow all round the stone, leaving, of course, the edge which secures the stone quite intact (Figs. 259 and 260).

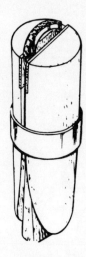
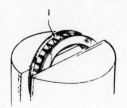
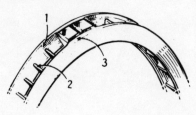

Fig. 261. (left)   The ring in the clamp with one-third of it projecting.

Fig. 262. (centre)   The bearing for the stones is cut deep enough (noted by the figure 1) to allow the girdle of the stones to rest a little below the surface.

Fig. 263. (right)   The three stages in setting: (1) metal cut away to make a channel; (2) spacing bars must clear stones; (3) edge of metal turned over stones.

Setting Stones in an Eternity Ring

As I have now adequately dealt with the three main types of setting, several different combinations and variations of these might well be mentioned and described. One example is the type of setting used for eternity rings, having square or rectangular stones set in them. This is known as calibre setting, which means that an edge or rim is burnished over the stones around the outer edges without any metal separating the stones from each other.

Eternity rings are made with two flat circular sides, separated by shallow bars of metal which do not reach to the outer edge of the ring. The ring is held in clamps, with about one-third projecting to enable the setter to work upon it (Fig. 261). This part is set first, and afterwards the ring is turned in the clamp to enable another section to be dealt with. The inner edges of the setting surfaces are cut to form a channel, or bearing, upon which the stones can rest. This must be cut deeply enough to allow the girdle of the stones to rest a little below the edge of the ring (Fig. 262).

The cutting is done with a flat scorper. This has a fairly wide cutting edge. When a channel has been cut sufficient for several stones, these are placed in position and the edge is very gently pressed over the girdle of the stones (Fig. 263). Great care is needed to avoid 'crimping' the edge in this operation. It must be done a little at a time on each side of the stones, using the brass pushing tool until the stones are quite secure.

When the whole ring has been set, the edges can be lightly filed and burnished to present a smooth and even edge of metal holding all stones securely in place as in Fig. 264. It may, of course, be that one or two stones

Fig. 264. The stones in position with an edge of metal pressed over the girdle of each and smoothed off.

Fig. 265. A ring to be set with brilliants in the clamp.

will have to be cut by the lapidary to enable a complete circle of stones to be achieved. But that will depend upon the size of the ring, and the number of stones available of the appropriate length and width.

Setting Brilliant Cut Stones

An eternity ring to be set with baguette cut diamonds would be treated exactly the same, but one which is set with the normal brilliant cut (round) diamonds, is different. This requires a true millegrain setting, in which many very important points have to be observed. In this case there will be metal between the stones, and the amount should, as far as practicable, be kept to a minimum consistent with strength. It could be said that the stones should be as close together as possible, but the mounter is responsible for that to a greater extent than the setter. Both must be guided by the number of matching stones available, the finger size of the ring, and the number of stones which it is possible to set in the circumference of such a ring.

To carry out the actual setting, the ring must be held in the clamp as before, to enable about one-third of the ring to be dealt with at one time (Fig. 265). The holes for the stones are enlarged with fraises until the girdle of the stones drops just a fraction of an inch below the surface of the ring, almost immeasurable in inch fractions. If the stones are not cut perfectly round, and this is quite often so, of course, then each stone must be dealt with individually, and each hole cut as necessary with the ball-stick to accommodate any variations in shape.

With the stone in position, the next step is to secure it with a grain of metal cut up from between the stones in four different places. This is always referred to as 'raising grains', because the operation does raise a cutting of metal above the surface and just over the edge of the stone. It can now be seen that when several diamonds have been secured, the effect will be that of having four grains pushed up between each pair of stones, two securing the edge of each diamond (Fig. 266). One more grain is now raised in the centre of these four, which should be capable of overlapping the edge of both dia-

Fig. 266. (left) Stones held in place
in an eternity ring by grain setting.
Fig. 267. (right) Ring set with stones
and millegrained.

monds. Should the diamonds be placed too far apart, however, this will not be possible and some variation may have to be made, i.e., the raising of more grains.

These 'grains' are merely in the roughly cut shape, and will have to be moulded into shape by the use of the graining tool. This is a small steel tool with a concave end, and fitted with a knob-like handle with which it can be pushed on the grain to mould it into a smooth and burnished tiny dome of metal. Each of the grains will be dealt with in this fashion, and then all stones should be held securely in place.

There is still, however, a considerable amount of metal to be dealt with along both edges of the ring. This is cut into a shallow V-shaped channel parallel to, and quite close to, the edges of the setting surface. Finally the outer edge is milled with a millegrain wheel. Great care must be taken to keep these edges quite straight and absolutely parallel, because any defect will show very badly in the finished ring (Fig. 267).

Fixing Stones in an 'Illusion' Setting

Another, and very skilful, variation of the three main types of setting is that of 'illusion' setting. This is very much in use to-day when the cost of articles of jewellery is so inflated that the jeweller must produce the most appealing display of reasonable size with the smallest diamonds, thus keeping down the cost to within reach of the greater number of purchasers. The purpose is not to deceive the purchaser into thinking he has something bigger than is in fact so, but to give importance to what would otherwise be a very insignificant diamond. In the centre of a setting of average size is a small diamond; the setter then has skilfully to cut up the surrounding metal into suitable patterns, and secure the stone in place.

The ways of doing this are many and varied, but one typical example will suffice to show the general principles. The hole is enlarged with the fraise and the diamond placed in it, a little below the surface as before. This time a six-point star is cut, using the diamond as its centre, and by cutting toward the diamond six grains can be raised. These will be small grains, and some metal will actually be cut away in forming the star, leaving sufficient only for the size of the grains required. The edges of the star can be grained with the millegrain wheel to form an outline.

Further cutting is now done with a narrow flat scorper on the outside of the star to form another grain between each point of the star. This will be moulded into shape with the graining tool in the same way as the other grains; but in this case, they will serve for ornamentation only, and not to secure the stones. Around the outside of the star, a circle can now be neatly cut, and its outer edge milled with the millegrain wheel. This should beat the edge of the metal surround, unless an exceptionally large amount of metal is to be decorated, in which case two rows of milling, or perhaps a small row of grains cut up, should be sufficient (Fig. 268).

Fig. 268. Enlarged view of an illusion setting. To be successful the setting must blend with the stone.

When dealing with larger pieces of jewellery, the methods are principally the same, but artistry lies in the way in which metal is cut up and used to achieve the desired effect. For instance, the leaves of a spray brooch can really be made to look like leaves with small veins cut along them in appropriate directions, and grains raised, or rows of milling wherever suitable. All of that is the setter's art, and no amount of description can replace the years of experience needed to know how a particular piece will look best when finished. The same applies to brooches and clips, necklet snaps, and any other article which requires setting. Quite often there is a lot of space between stones which has to be ornamented or 'cut up' by the setter. This has to be done in such a way that it adds to the beauty of the article, and does not look like a lot of space which no one knew how to fill!

11. Casting

Casting for the jewellery trade is not new by any means, as originally all items were cast, very roughly but nevertheless cast, in moulds of clay or sand as long ago as Greek and Roman times. The result was not good, according to our standards, and steadily improved techniques were employed for fashioning all goods by hand until eventually the methods described in earlier chapters resulted.

During the last few years however, owing to the need for faster methods of reproduction of any particular pattern or parts of rings and other items, casting techniques have again been developed and are an important, in fact essential, part of modern jewellery manufacture.

Centrifugal Casting
The method used is centrifugal casting, and it is used for reproducing, from one master pattern, a limitless number of replicas in the desired metal. The whole process is rather expensive, and is not suitable economically for a very small number of reproductions. However, once a workshop is equipped, the saving in time and cost is invaluable.

Practically any design can be cast, however intricate and however detailed. The whole process, described very briefly, consists of the making of a master pattern, from which a rubber mould may be made. In turn this is used for quantity production of wax replicas. These are then set up on a base or cone of wax. The next operation is to produce this set of waxes in metal. This is done by pouring a destructible mould around the waxes, and when this has solidified the waxes are burnt out, leaving a moulded shell. This shell is then filled with molten metal and, when cool, is destroyed. This description is only the procedure in bare outline, but it will serve as a guide through the various processes as they are described in detail.

Making the Master Pattern

The first operation is to make the master pattern. A very important point which must be remembered from the start is that the casting will be approximately 2 per cent smaller than the master; it is therefore important to make the master that appropriate amount larger than the required dimensions of the casting. A master can be made from a variety of materials, e.g. Perspex, lead or similar; but undoubtedly the best material for the jeweller's purpose is one of the stronger and more malleable metals which will withstand the heat of many soldering temperatures. Examples of these are copper or brass, or even one of the more precious metals, if desired.

It must be remembered that, once made, a master pattern will remain available for making as many replicas as will ever be needed. The moulds will wear, but not the master pattern; and if considerable care and time are used in making it, the manufacturer will be well rewarded by the subsequent quality of the castings. Whether it be a complete ring, a ring head, a brooch, or another part of a piece of jewellery, however intricate, castings of excellent quality can be made from it. They should require but little work afterwards; depending upon the skill and care with which each stage is carried out.

A few important details can be described by taking one particular and very much used sample of ring head, a three-stone claw ring. The method of making is precisely the same as that described earlier in this series.

1. Avoid unnecessary sharp angles and corners by lightly rounding off the extreme sharpness of the inside edges of scallops. This will not in any way spoil the appearance of the finished work (Fig. 269), and will help to avoid damage to the rubber mould when made.

2. Avoid extremely thin parts. Where it is desired that only a very thin strip of metal should show, it should, wherever possible, be made a little thicker at the back or inside, as the case may be (e.g. scallops as Fig. 270). This will help in avoiding breakages of delicate wax replicas.

Fig. 269. For casting, avoid sharp corners; sharp edges should be rounded off.

Fig. 270. Extremely thin parts should be avoided. Whenever possible metal should be a little thicker.

3. Avoid very small holes or piercings, as the smaller the hole the more difficult it is to produce a clean finished casting.

4. Finish the pattern with the finest and smoothest possible emery paper. This is to achieve a hand-polished surface and helps very considerably in obtaining a good, smooth surface on the finished casting. There is, in fact, no reason why a casting should not result with a surface fine enough to be polished without preliminary cleaning and smoothing, but this will depend, alas, upon many other factors.

Position of the Sprue

Having made the master pattern, a stem or 'sprue' as it is termed, must be attached in a suitable place. Here one must visualise a cavity in a mould, exactly like the master pattern, and, to form the casting, this cavity must be filled with molten metal. It therefore follows that a channel must be made in the mould through which the metal may flow to reach and fill the cavity. This channel is formed by the sprue. Choosing the position of the sprue must depend upon the pattern and bulk of the casting. Broadly speaking, one must choose a position from which it can be cut from the casting without damage to the casting itself. However it is also necessary to choose a position which will provide sufficient space for the metal to flow freely; this will be usually at the thicker part of the piece.

It is often advisable and very convenient to have a double sprue or, better still, one which divides into two channels and joins the master pattern at two strong and convenient points. In the instance of a three-stone ring, with which we are dealing, it is a good plan to join the sprue to each end of the back bezel as shown in Fig. 271. Discretion must be used regarding the thickness of the sprues. Guiding factors are that sufficient molten metal must be able to flow through into the casting very quickly before the metal begins to cool. To allow this to take place, very thin sprues are better avoided. On the other hand, the sprues as well as the pattern are cast, and unnecessary wastage of metal must be avoided, hence one must not go to the other extreme and provide very thick sprues.

It is a very important point to bear in mind that, after the mould has been made from the master pattern, the wax replicas and sprues are made as one piece. This avoids any unnecessary wastage of time when preparing the waxes for casting; whereas if no thought is given to this and separate sprues have to be made and added to each wax, a lot of time is inevitably wasted.

Making the Rubber Mould

Now to make the rubber mould from the master pattern. There are actually

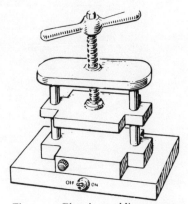

Fig. 271. Metal should be run into both sides of the mould by a divided sprue.

Fig. 272. Electric moulding press.

a variety of moulding materials available, but the one principally used and, in fact, the only one with which we need to be concerned, is uncured rubber sold specifically for this purpose. Before starting, one must have a moulding press of suitable design; again this can be purchased from suppliers of casting materials (Fig. 272). Briefly, the press consists of two electrically-heated plates of steel capable of being pressed together with considerable pressure, and thermostatically controlled to a temperature of approximately 145 °C (293 °F). Also necessary are moulding frames of varying size and thickness to accommodate the variety of master-pattern sizes which will undoubtedly be made. Each frame consists of two separable halves with guiding pegs to keep both halves correctly aligned. Fig. 273 shows this.

Making the mould is now comparatively simple. The lower half of the frame is placed on a sheet of thin metal a little larger than itself and pieces of rubber are cut to fit into the lower half of it (rubber is usually supplied in sheets of approximately $\frac{1}{8}$ in (3 mm) thick), and sufficient pieces are placed in to fill it. These need not be an exact fit, just approximate will be sufficient. The master pattern is placed on the top layer with the end of the sprue

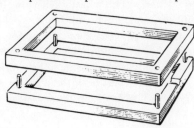

Fig. 273. Frame for making the moulding, showing guide pegs.

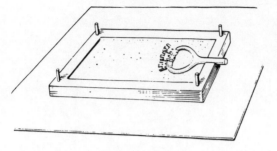

Fig. 274. The master pattern placed in position.

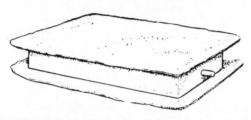

Fig. 275. The mould after it has been under the press, and before trimming.

projecting into the recess provided (Fig. 274). The top half of the frame is placed in position, and care taken to ensure that none of the rubber is caught between the two halves, as it is necessary that they should fit very closely together.

More sheets of rubber are now laid on top of the pattern until the frame is filled, and then one further piece of rubber is laid on to overfill the frame by about ⅛ in (3 mm). This ensures that when pressure is applied in the vulcanising press, the rubber will be pressed into the smallest and most intricate parts of the pattern. The mould is now placed between the plates, and the current switched on, the top plate of the press being screwed down to exert just a little pressure on to the rubber. As the temperature increases the wheel or bar of the press is steadily tightened until the temperature has reached approximately 120°C (248°F) and full pressure has been reached, that is with the press screwed down as tightly as possible.

The mould is left now to vulcanise completely throughout for an appropriate length of time according to its thickness. This is easily calculated by using half an hour for ½ in (12 mm) and *pro rata*. When sufficiently 'cooked', the press is switched off and the mould allowed to cool sufficiently for the two halves of the moulding frame to be separated and the mould removed.

If sufficient rubber has been used, a thin layer of it should be overhanging the mould (Fig. 275), having been squeezed out with the pressure applied. This surplus can now be neatly trimmed off with a pair of scissors and the mould is ready to be cut open.

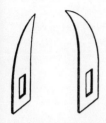

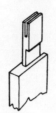

Fig. 276. Surgical blades of various shapes, with holder.

Opening the Rubber Mould

Having enclosed the master pattern in a solid block of rubber, the next operation is to cut the rubber open in such a manner that the model may be removed. The cut should also allow the wax replicas of the model to be removed without breaking them. Surgical blades of various shapes are obtainable and will cut the rubber. It is essential that these very sharp blades are available for use, and that a supply of them is at hand, as they lose their sharpness quite quickly (Fig. 276). Should the cutting edge make contact with the master pattern, it will lose its sharpness at once.

Cutting is perhaps the most skilful operation of the process as upon it will depend the success of the waxes made from the mould. An important part of the cutting is to ensure that indentations or irregularities are deliberately cut to ensure that the two halves of the rubber mould align accurately, thus ensuring that the waxes are correctly made. It is wise to start cutting by the sprue which is protruding from the rubber block. By cutting a little each side and following down the sprue to the model itself and by holding the two halves stretched apart, it is possible to keep to the centre of the model.

It is very difficult to describe fully, exactly *how* the mould should be cut to enable waxes to be removed without breaking them, as once again, this is a matter of experience, both in cutting a mould, and in using it. Only practice can decide just how each particular pattern is best dealt with. In principle, one must aim at separating the two halves in such a manner that the top half can be lifted off completely, leaving the wax in the bottom half of the mould. The next operation is to cut into the bottom half sufficiently to form a 'core', which can be lifted to release any under-cutting of the model. Assume, for example, that we are dealing still with the three-stone ring head, the core must be lifted to enable the wax head to be pulled out. Fig. 277 shows the general principle more clearly. The rubber will stand up to a very considerable amount of stretching, and advantage should be taken of this during the cutting operation.

Making the Wax Replicas

The mould is now completed and ready for making wax replicas. For this a

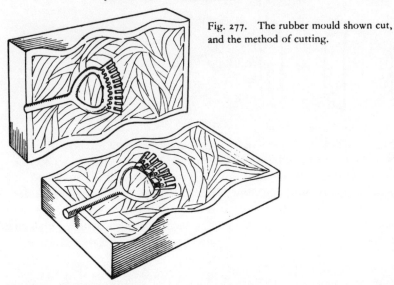

Fig. 277. The rubber mould shown cut, and the method of cutting.

wax pot is essential, which, briefly, is an electrically-heated pot containing wax, the temperature being closely controlled to the most efficient working temperature of the wax in use. The pot is filled with compressed air at approximately 8 lb per sq in and has a spring-loaded nozzle from which the wax is ejected into the mould. Fig. 278 shows, diagrammatically, the essentials of a pot.

Little experience is required to make waxes, but reasonable care in handling the moulds is well rewarded in the quality of waxes made. The mould is dusted lightly with a very fine film of powder (talcum powder or french chalk), to prevent the warm wax from sticking to the rubber. The two halves are placed together and held firmly, between two thin metal plates of approximately the same size as the mould, by using thumb and forefinger of each hand. The sprue hole of the mould is then pressed against the nozzle of the wax injector and wax is forced into it (Fig. 279). A few seconds suffice to fill most moulds, but if the mould is held there a second or two longer than necessary, it is an advantage; inasmuch as it will allow the wax replica in the mould to cool off and solidify while still under pressure, thus reducing the amount of possible shrinkage. If the sprue hole in the mould is made a good fit on the nozzle of the injector, wax will not be spilled when the mould is full.

After allowing a few minutes for the wax to cool off and solidify, the mould is then opened. This is done by lifting off the top half, starting by the sprue

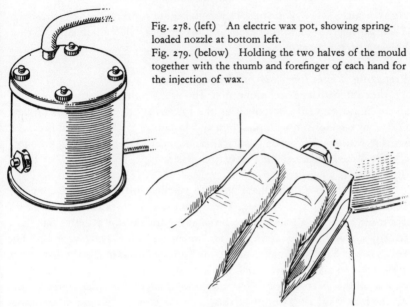

Fig. 278. (left)   An electric wax pot, showing spring-loaded nozzle at bottom left.
Fig. 279. (below)   Holding the two halves of the mould together with the thumb and forefinger of each hand for the injection of wax.

and gently opening until the two halves are separated. This will leave the wax model in the lower half of the mould. Starting at the sprue the wax can now be lifted gently on its core and withdrawn from the mould. The result should be an exact replica of the master pattern. In actual fact, it is not always just so because, if the mould is not held firmly enough, wax may be forced in between the mould halves in some places. The result is a wax with what are known as 'flashes' in various places (Fig. 280). The best plan with this is to put the wax aside for remelting rather than to try to clean it by flicking off the flashes. Perfect waxes are essential for good casting, and it is much better to scrap a number of them than to permit them to go forward for casting, and have to scrap the castings at a later stage.

When a sufficient number of waxes have been made, the next part of the process depends upon the metal in which the casting is to be made, as there

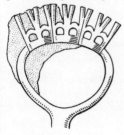

Fig. 280.   If the mould is not held firmly together it results in 'flashes' of wax in various places. Such a wax should be remelted.

are two main types of casting technique, quite different from each other. There are many variations of each, and an operator will undoubtedly develop his own particular variations.

Preparing Waxes for 'Low-heat' Investment

To proceed with one technique first: this is the one for casting gold and silver, more generally described as the lower melting-point metals (lower, that is, by comparison with platinum and palladium). The major differences are that with the first group (gold) larger quantities can be cast at a time, and the investment material used is of the plaster type, but more about those differences as we proceed.

The waxes have to be made up into suitable formation for casting, by setting them up on a disc of wax. These wax discs, or bases as they are termed, are made by using a base former supplied by the casting material suppliers, usually circular, about $2\frac{1}{2}$ in (6.4 cm) diameter and slightly concave. The base is then fixed to a metal base plate (simply by warming the base plate sufficiently to make the wax stick to it). Next, by using a heated strip of metal or a small low-heat electrical soldering iron, the waxes are placed one by one on the base (Fig. 281). In doing this, both the base and the end of the sprue must be slightly warmed so that they will join very securely and smoothly. The waxes can be fairly close together but a limit should be set and, in general, a space of not less than $\frac{1}{8}$ in (3 mm) should be left between them. The length of the sprue should also be varied, thus making it a little easier to set the maximum number of waxes upon one base by careful placing.

When the waxes have been set up, they must be prepared for the next process, which is investing. They must first be cleaned to remove any powder adhering from the mould, or any very small scraps of wax 'flash' which might be present, or which might have been broken away from one of the waxes.

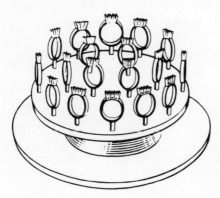

Fig. 281. Finished waxes are fixed to a metal base plate in preparation for the investment material.

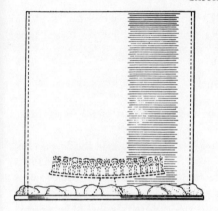

Fig. 282. A flask with the waxes in position. Plasticine seals the base to the flask.

This is done by carefully holding the whole upside-down in a small bowl of cleaning agent. One of the modern detergent liquids will serve this purpose very well. By gently swirling the waxes in the liquid, dust and powder are removed. Finally they must be rinsed in clean water to wash away the detergent from the surface of the waxes. If this remained, it might well spoil the quality of the investment used.

After allowing the waxes to drain off and getting rid of surplus water bubbles from any fine holes in the waxes, the metal base plate must be dried thoroughly, and then lightly smeared with a household type grease such as Vaseline, or similar. This is to stop the investment from sticking to the base. Care must be taken to avoid putting grease on any of the waxes and, obviously, care is needed throughout the whole time of handling of these delicate objects as the slightest mishap can break pieces off them, wasting many hours of work. A metal flask is now placed over the waxes and allowed to rest in one of the grooves of the metal base. The size of the flask must be chosen to allow at least $\frac{1}{2}$ in (12 mm) of height above the highest waxes, and $\frac{1}{2}$ in (12 mm) all round the outside. The flask is now held to the metal base, and the join between them sealed by squeezing a strip of Plasticine all round (Fig. 282).

Making the Investment

The waxes, when mounted and surrounded by the metal flask, are ready for the investing material to be prepared. As the castings are in gold, it is well to use what is generally known as a plaster-type investment, that is to say one which has a base of plaster of Paris. Investments are commercially produced and it is not worth while for the jewellery manufacturer to concern himself with trying to make his own. It is better to use one already marketed, as it will save him a great deal of difficulty. The actual formula which each supplier uses is different, but broadly speaking one may say that all plaster-type investments have these characteristics:

1. They set very quickly;
2. The temperature to which they may be fired must be held to specified limits; and
3. A retarding agent is either used as an integral part of the investment, or is to be added by the user.

Each supplier will, of course, give details on how to obtain the best results with his materials.

The investment powder and water must be prepared in their correct proportions, and then mixed quickly and smoothly, either with a mechanical mixer or by hand according to the quantity being used. It should be emphasised here that no advantage is gained by trying to mix a large quantity because the investment would begin to set before the whole process was complete, and would result in very poor quality castings. An average maximum of five flasks using about 1 lb (450 g) each is advisable.

Having mixed the investment, it must be poured speedily and carefully into the flasks, avoiding pouring directly on to the waxes, but rather around the sides of the flasks. As soon as sufficient has been poured, the flasks are put under the top of the 'lid' of the vacuum plant and the pump set in motion to remove the air bubbles trapped in the investment and in between the waxes. When the dome or lid of the vacuum plant is completely evacuated, the investment expands with removal of the air pressure, releasing all air within the investment and allowing it to be pumped out. As soon as the maximum amount has been pumped out, the vacuum is released and the investment sinks down and packs tightly around the waxes. This operation must be timed with care as there is the possibility of the investment beginning to set and not packing down as tightly as it should.

Removing the Waxes
After removal from the vacuum plant, the flasks must be set aside and left undisturbed until the investment has set. This takes from 5 to 15 minutes. The investment then, although obviously containing moisture, will be set hard and the copper base plate, on which the waxes are set, may be removed by simply twisting it free. This will leave the waxes, on their wax base, firmly set in a solid mould. All the waxes are then completely removed from the mould, leaving instead a series of cavities which retain the impression of the wax models. This is done by placing the moulds in a de-waxing oven, on a fairly low heat, which allows the wax to drip away into a pan placed under-

neath. A steady heat is necessary because any sudden rapid heat would cause uneven expansion and cracks to develop in the mould. This process usually takes about 2 hours.

The de-waxing oven is not necessarily an expensive production, and improvised ones can be very satisfactory—an old gas cooker will serve very well. When the wax has been thoroughly drained out, the moulds are transferred to a furnace. This should have been lighted a little in advance at fairly low pressure, to allow it to reach a temperature around that of the de-waxed moulds (approximately 100°C, 212°F). This will avoid any sudden change of temperature when the moulds are transferred. From then onward, the temperature of the furnace is steadily increased over a period of 2 hours or so, until the correct limit is reached. With most investments this is between 700°C and 750°C (1292–1382°F). Care should be taken to avoid the moulds becoming overheated as this would cause the surface of the moulds to disintegrate, resulting in very coarse surfaced castings.

The maximum temperature should be maintained for 1 hour, by which time all traces of wax should have been removed. It wou d at first appear unnecessary to maintain anything like such a high temperature to remove comparatively low melting-point wax, but some of the wax soaks its way into the investment and this must be completely removed to make a success of the castings.

The moulds can then be allowed to cool off steadily down to the lowest temperature required for casting. This is variable, according to the metal being used and also to the investment; but 350°C (662°F) is a fairly good average. It is possible to cast at considerably lower temperatures, but it is not advisable because the metal, when cast into the moulds, may cool off too rapidly before reaching the extremities of the intricate parts of the mould.

Preparing Waxes for 'High-heat' Investment

Before proceeding with the actual casting, the other type of investment should be dealt with, up to the same stage. When setting up waxes for casting in high melting-point alloys, that is platinum or palladium, it should be remembered that a very much smaller quantity of metal (2 oz (60 g) is a good average) can be cast. It is therefore necessary to use a different method of setting up, using a much smaller number of waxes. It is also very important to keep the travelling distance of the molten metal down to a minimum to avoid cooling off before reaching the extremities of the mould.

A good method is to have a small cone of approximately $\frac{3}{4}$ in (20 mm) diameter at its larger end, $\frac{1}{2}$ in (12 mm) diameter at its smaller end, and $\frac{3}{4}$ in (20 mm) high, on to which to set the waxes (Fig. 283). Instead of using a

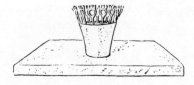

Fig. 283. Method of setting up waxes for investments to be used for platinum and palladium.

copper base plate, as when setting up for gold, the small cone is set on a piece of absorbent asbestos sheet, approximately $\frac{1}{4}$ in (6 mm) thick, and the waxes set on to the wider end of the cone. Up to 20 is a reasonable average when dealing with heads for rings or similar items. The assembly is washed and rinsed and a flask placed around it, but this time a lining of absorbent asbestos is pressed, while very wet, around the inside of the flask. This *must* be pressed firmly on to the sides of the flask. A space of approximately $\frac{1}{2}$ in (12 mm) should be left at top and bottom. This asbestos lining is to allow for expansion of the investment when heating. An extension of gummed paper should be added at the top of the flask, and the flask itself secured to the asbestos base either by Plasticine or melted wax.

Making the 'High-heat' Investment

The investment used does not contain plaster and is known by the general term of 'high-heat investment'. The high-heat investments are very different from the plaster type and a different technique is necessary. With this, as with the plaster type, instructions for mixing and the quantity of water to be used are given by the suppliers, and may vary a little with each particular batch. The procedure does not vary greatly, however. These investments do not set quickly and haste is not necessary with the preparation. A good thorough mixing spread over perhaps half-an-hour is an advantage. Usually, it is necessary to add the investment powder to the water quite slowly, and allow it to mix thoroughly as each additional quantity is added. When the correct proportions have been mixed, they should be left, stirring in the mixer, for 10 minutes or so before pouring. There is no danger at all of the mixture starting to set.

The pouring is done in just the same way as with plaster investment, care being taken to avoid pouring directly on to the waxes. After pouring, the same procedure for removing air is carried out in the vacuum plant. The whole is then left undisturbed to set for at least a day, after which the asbestos base is removed, leaving the waxes invested in a solid mould.

The process of removing the waxes must, in this case, be carried out much more slowly, and the heating to casting temperature must be very slow and up to approximately 800 °C (1472 °F). The heating should be spread over

8 or 9 hours, or even more if possible. If this precaution is not observed, there is a great danger of cracked moulds and coarse castings.

The Casting Process

Casting metal into a mould is done on a specially constructed machine, simple in principle and in operation, but depending, nevertheless, on the judgment and skill of its operator. Centrifugal force is relied upon to send the molten metal into every part of the intricate design and pattern of the model, and also to eliminate gas bubbles and porousness.

The machine (a commercial product, Fig. 284) is, very briefly, a balanced arm on a central pivot, with a shaped crucible D for melting the metal. It has a hole at one end, which is placed against the mould E, and a counter-balance weight A at the other. The arm is constructed so that it may be wound in a clockwise direction, against a spring, and held in position by some form of ratchet; so that, upon release, the whole arm will spin anti-clockwise and force the molten metal into the mould. Whether platinum, palladium, gold or silver is being used, the principle is the same; although there are several machines produced and each has its certain advantages.

The temperature at which the metal is cast, and the temperature of the mould at the time of casting must depend upon a number of factors such as type of investment, the metal being cast, the fineness of the items being cast, and so on.

Take first the palladium-platinum group of metals for which high-heat investment has been used. As described earlier, the moulds are heated up to a temperature of around 850°C (1562°F) for the required length of time, after which they may be allowed to cool off to around 700°C (1292°F). If cooled off too far, it may be that the metal, when cast, will not reach the finer parts of the moulding as the metal itself will be cooled off too rapidly by the lower temperature of the mould.

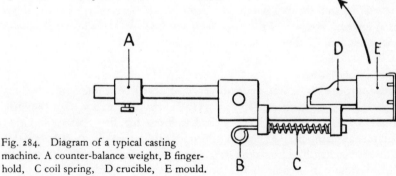

Fig. 284. Diagram of a typical casting machine. A counter-balance weight, B finger-hold, C coil spring, D crucible, E mould.

Preparing the Machine

The machine is 'wound up' on its spring and set for operation. A small crucible of refractory material suitable for high temperatures is placed in the fitting at the end of the arm (hole towards the outside), the mould is then placed in position at the same end, and both are held by the spring C which pushes the crucible and mould together against the stop plate at the end of the arm. The metal is then placed in the crucible preparatory to melting. Judging the quantity of metal required is not very difficult and need not be an absolutely accurate calculation. Sufficient is needed to fill a good portion of the base as well as the actual casting, thus providing a bulk of metal and adding pressure when the metal is cast. On the other hand, if too much is used, some must splash over when the machine is released. Broadly speaking, $1\frac{1}{2}$ to 2 oz (40–60 g) of platinum or palladium is as much as can be used for each cast. Melting is done with an oxygen and coal gas blowtorch, which is capable of producing a very fierce hot flame, using fairly high oxygen pressure. The hottest part of the flame is just a little beyond the sharply defined inner blue zone of the centre of the flame.

Casting Platinum

No flux is needed when casting platinum as the metal is not subject to oxidisation, and stays 'clean' at all stages of melting, so the job of casting is primarily one of getting sufficient heat to make the metal flow freely. Platinum melts at around 1750°C (3182°F) but considerably more heat is needed to make it fluid enough to cast. Because figures and temperature measurements convey little or nothing in practical casting, the only real guide to the right time to cast the metal is its colour. Obviously, dark welding goggles are absolutely essential when dealing with such high temperatures, and even then the brightness becomes a glare. It is difficult to define the colour of the metal ready for casting, but perhaps the best description is 'pearly white', when viewed through the dark green goggles of the operator. When this colour has been reached, the arm of the machine is released and spins in an anti-clockwise direction, forcing the metal into the mould.

Casting Palladium

Palladium casting is not quite so easily achieved. Although it melts at a slightly lower temperature (approx. 1550°C, 2822°F), it is a more sluggish metal, and more 'treacly' when melted, and requires the same casting temperature as platinum. Palladium is subject to oxidisation and to overcome this a flux is needed. The best time to add this to the melt is when the metal is just beginning to become molten, and only a small quantity is used. Heating is then continued until complete fluidity is obtained and the metal has a clean surface, completely free from scum or skin which is present in the early stages of melting. By carefully manipulating the torch, the metal is washed around in the flux to help in achieving this cleanness, after which the flame is held quite steady in the centre of the melt until maximum heat is reached and the metal is ready for casting. The machine must be released immediately the correct casting temperature has been reached, without losing any of the heat.

Removing the Castings

When the machine has finished spinning (in practice, of course, the operator will allow it to spin for a few minutes and then carefully slow it down and stop it) the mould is removed from the machine and allowed to cool a little more, but not very much. It should then be steadily immersed in a bucket or tub of water, which will cause the investment to break away freely and will leave the castings surrounded by only a little of the investment material. This is removed by placing them in hydrofluoric acid; a *very dangerous* acid to use, and one which should at all times be handled carefully and with rubber gloves to avoid splashes on the hands. The acid itself should be placed in a polythene or rubber container and kept where its fumes can escape into a chimney or flue of some kind. This is because the fumes are very dangerous and most unpleasant to breathe.

After the castings have been cleaned, they should, upon close inspection, show a fine, smooth surface, free from air bubbles and any trace of porosity. Many factors enter into this, however, and a great deal will depend upon the quality and grain size of the investment used. This is a matter over which the operator has no control, but he does have control over all the other factors which affect castings.

After cleaning and inspection, the castings are cut off from the base and the base is returned to the scrap box for future use.

Casting Gold

Casting gold into a mould is similar in principle to casting palladium but the heat required is not nearly so great. After the mould has been prepared and cooled down to the appropriate temperature, the remaining procedure will depend upon the quality of gold to be cast. In most cases 400°C (752°F) is sufficiently hot for the mould, but the temperature to which the metal is heated will vary according to the alloy. White gold needs greater heat than yellow golds and the higher the quality the greater the temperature required. This means that 18 ct white needs to be hotter than 9 ct white before casting.

Although the principle is similar, the actual procedure for casting gold is rather different from that for casting palladium. Whereas with palladium it is necessary to keep the mould up to its high temperature, and the mould is put into the casting machine before melting is begun; with gold, in addition to allowing the mould to cool off, melting is completed and the metal heated up to almost casting temperature *before* the mould is put into the machine. This obviously makes it necessary to have an assistant available to bring the mould from the furnace and place it into the casting machine, while the operator temporarily takes the torch flame away to avoid burning the assistant. The purpose of leaving the mould until the metal is melted, is to avoid overheating the mould again. This would be done by the heat which passes through the end of the crucible (via its exit) during the actual melting process.

This is important with plaster-type investments, because an overheated mould or one which has been subjected to localised overheating from the torch, can cause a much coarser surface on the casting. This does not apply to the same extent with silica-based investments.

A few important points, which must be observed while melting gold, are necessary to avoid 'burning' the metal, or some of the alloy which it contains. Firstly, it is necessary to find the correct proportion of oxygen to coal gas, again according to the particular gold being cast. This is a matter only decided by experience and no hard rule can be laid down. Generally speaking, oxygen pressure should not exceed 25 lb (11 kg) per square inch, and even then it should be used with care to avoid sudden heating of some of the metal. It is wise to apply gentle heat, spread over as much of the metal as possible, and gradually heat up the whole of the metal, rather than to apply a smaller fierce flame which will melt only a smaller area, and thus run the risk of burning the metal in so doing.

Melting should be done with a covering of flux over the metal to assist flow and absorb surplus oxygen. A number of commercial types of flux are available, beside the well-tried powdered borax. All serve equally well. The metal should be freely flowing, and its surface clean and bright before releasing the machine to force the metal into the mould.

After the mould has been allowed to cool a little, it can be quenched in water and the investment will break away fairly cleanly. Final cleaning can be done with hydrofluoric acid and water, 50 per cent solution.

The general details of casting have now been dealt with and described. The various types of investment for the various metals to be cast are commercial and details should be obtained from the suppliers; this also applies to the whole of the equipment needed which includes wax injectors, wax removal leathers and casting machines. There are many varieties available to deal with small or large quantities of metal, and the actual casting machines now available include fully electronic ones which melt the metal by means of an electronic furnace instead of using gas-torches: they are very safe and convenient. The important points, which I have already dealt with, are the real craftsmanship of making master patterns. The ability to create the best quality of castings comes from experience and using equipment correctly in all respects. It will no doubt be clear that casting by the centrifugal casting system is for quantity production and reduces the cost of hand-making regular production patterns.

Retrieving Lemel

It is very important that the lemel—which includes filings, scrapings, drillings and other waste metal—produced by the mounters, setters and repairers should be very carefully kept and not thrown away. When a reasonable amount has been amassed, it should be sent to a bullion merchant; no specific weight is usually required by them. The bullion merchant will melt it down and divide it into pure gold, silver, platinum, palladium, etc.: he will then weigh these, pay you at the going rate, and resell the metal.

Any unusable scrap gold, etc, could also be included in this metal sold; however it should be remembered that, if you do any casting, this scrap could be melted and recast by yourself.

Do not ignore the floor sweepings and used sandpaper that is discarded by workers. It should be collected and stored for sale to a bullion merchant; he will be able to retrieve enough precious metals to make it worth your while. Lastly, some lemel remains on the hands of the workers and is washed down the sink when they clean their hands. It is possible to hire a special tank from a gold-dealing company which catches this lemel; the company will empty the tank from time to time and purchase the resulting metal. The tank works by filtering all water from wash basins, washing equipment, etc., and is well worth having if you have several men at work.

12. Repairs and Jobbing

After some years of wear, or perhaps after unfortunate accidental damage, many items of jewellery require repairing. Rings often need to be changed in finger size when purchased as a gift, or when its owner changes weight. This work also requires skill, experience and careful behaviour to avoid further damage and to ensure that the result of the repairs, etc is worth while. One very important understanding that the craftsman must have is about which stones set into jewellery will accept the heat of soldering without suffering, and which (the majority) will accept very little heat without being ruined.

Suppose a ring requires sizing and therefore soldering at the back of the shank: if the shank and the ring are not extremely heavy and thick, stones can be protected. However, if a ring or any other article has to be soldered fairly close to the stone, then it is not possible to protect the stone and it would have to be unset before repair and reset afterwards.

Gemstones that Tolerate Heat

Here are the stones which will accept heat such as is produced by soldering very close to them. They survive although the stones may have become red hot during the process. Diamonds are very good. If a claw-set ring has a claw broken off, it can be repaired and a new claw soldered to it with the diamond remaining in the ring—it will not suffer damage. Sapphires, rubies, spinels, either real or synthetic, and garnets will accept similar heat if they do not possess internal, natural inclusions. If they do, then it is possible for the inclusion to expand and split the stone. Small stones very rarely have inclusions that can do such damage but it is wise to examine large stones carefully with a magnifying glass before taking the risk of using such heat. Generally speaking these are the only stones which will accept this amount of heat. It helps to protect the stones if they are covered with a moist coating of borax and then steadily dried and heated. It is *essential* that the article containing the stones is allowed to cool off properly before being placed into the sulphuric acid to clean it up. If the stone is placed into any cool liquid while it is still hot, it will probably split or be seriously damaged.

The majority of other gemstones will accept warmth but not great heat: for example, emeralds and the whole range of quartz stones, such as amethyst, citrine, smoky quartz, onyx, bloodstone, etc. It is essential that they must not be suddenly cooled from warmth. It is also essential that no soldering or great heat be allowed near these stones. In some repairs, they would have to be unset; but if the heat is a reasonable distance away, it is wise to cover them with a specially purchased chemical paste, known as 'Cool Heat' which is a protector against heat, before soldering the back of the shank, etc.

Finally there are some stones which are even more delicate such as opals turquoise, pearls. Very great care must be taken to avoid very much warmth with these stones. These must not be put into sulphuric acid to clean the article, otherwise they will be damaged and discoloured.

When dealing with gold, silver or platinum items, it is important that a solder of the same quality is used. As already stated, there are various melting points available in all qualities, mostly known as hard, medium or easy, and one should consider which is to be used according to the job being done.

Sizing Rings

When altering the finger size of a ring, it is wise to check first to see if there is a joint in the shank already. Do this by warming it so that any soldered joint becomes visible. If it does, then it is correct to cut through that joint and remove a portion, if making the ring smaller; or to open up the ring and to add a section if it is to be made larger. If a ring of good thickness only has to be enlarged one size, it is acceptable to stretch it by tapping the shank on a triblett and then refinishing the shank. However, if it is to be increased by more than one size, then it is correct to add a section of gold, the gold being the same standard as the ring.

If the ring has no join in the shank, then it must be sawn through, avoiding damage to the hallmark, and dealt with as above. The solder used should be medium, and the joint should be cleaned up inside and outside the ring. The whole ring is then refinished to look as new as possible. By doing this, the joints will be strengthened and hidden.

It is also very important to realise that some rings which require to be sized are probably cast rings. These are a very good and useful part of jewellery manufacture nowadays, permitting the repeating of popular patterns; but they should *not* be stretched on the special stretching equipment as used by many jewellery shops and jobbing jewellers. The reason for this prohibition is that they may crack, break or be severely damaged. Being cast, the gold has not been rolled to its appropriate thickness, etc, as manufactured rings are, and is therefore more fragile and more easily broken by operations such as stretching. It is more correct, and safer, to size as described above by adding gold.

It is also important to know that, when sizing a silver ring, it spreads the heat of soldering more than gold does. It can therefore be more dangerous to gemstones which are vulnerable to high temperatures. It is a good idea to leave a fair amount of space between the new joint and the mounted stone when soldering silver rings. It is more essential to use 'Cool Heat' on many silver rings than to use it on gold ones.

Strengthening Shanks

Many rings wear at the back of the shank, especially when they are worn with a wedding ring, until they become thin and weak. When such a ring is submitted for repair and strengthening, the same quality of gold should be used. The best way to do this is to cut off the worn section, file across so that both ends are flat, then create a section the same finger size and file both sides flat in preparation for soldering. The best way to assess the finger size is to place the ring and the new section on the size stick and make it about half size smaller than is finally required, to allow for the process of filing up and finishing. To solder the two sections together, it is best to hold them with binding wire and again use medium solder to fix them (Fig. 283).

Always check the stones which are set in the ring. If they are diamonds, sapphires, rubies or garnets, there is no problem; the stones will accept the heat. If however they are fragile stones such as opals, they would have to be unset if fairly close to the joint. If the joint is a reasonable distance away, it might be possible to use the chemical cooler.

After soldering is completed, allow the ring to cool and remove the binding

Fig. 285. A ring tied with binding wire in preparation for soldering after it has been re-sized.

wire before putting the ring into sulphuric acid to clean and remove the oxidised blackness. Remember that iron or steel wire used for binding must never touch sulphuric acid because they will combine with each other. After the ring has been cleaned and dried, proceed to file out any surplus solder from inside it, correct the shape and size and then file the outside of the ring to remove the visibility of the joints; lastly sandpaper, polish and finish.

New Claws for Claw-set Rings

Diamond rings that are claw set, whether single-stone, three-stone or five-stone, sometimes have their claws worn away by many years of use. A claw can also be broken off by accident. The best means of repairing them is to keep the diamond, sapphire or whatever in the setting while repairing, but if there is a centre stone or side stones which cannot accept extreme heat, they must be unset and the ring repaired without them.

The best means of adding new claws is as follows. The metal used must be the same as the claw setting, e.g. platinum or 18 ct white gold. File off the top of the claws at an angle and cut off pieces of metal the same width as the claws and long enough to provide sufficient metal for setting the stone safely. Use borax liquid to place the new pieces in position and hold them there, add a paillon of fairly easy solder touching both the new tip and the claw. This can be done with all the claws that have to be retipped in order to solder all together in just one session, see Fig. 284.

After the ring has cooled and been cleaned in the acid, use the appropriate setting tool to press the claw tips down to the stone. Then file off the surplus, round off the tips, smooth with sandpaper, polish and finish.

General Information

It is obvious that repairs required vary very considerably. Here are a few points to be observed and considered:

1. Soft solder, which is lead solder, should not be used on any jewellery. The only exception is an article such as a very old carved brooch, badly worn and weak, which requires a new joint or catch and where it is not possible to unset the cameo. Otherwise remove the cameo, repair the mount

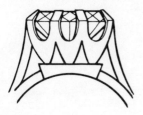

Fig. 286. A ring whose claws have been retipped and finished.

with gold solder and then reset again. Fortunately it is rare not to be able to unset the cameo but, if soft solder has to be used, it can be covered with gilding solution to make the job look better. It should be copper-plated with a special solution obtained from jewellery chemical suppliers and then gilded.

2. If an article has been prepared with soft solder and should not have been, the best means to correct it is to dissolve the bad solder off the job by immersing it in hydrochloric acid. This will require about 24 hours probably. The repair can then be completed with gold solder as it should have been originally.

3. Gilding and rhodium plating are very important and useful for finishing. These are technical processes and special solutions are needed which are not created personally by the jeweller. The solutions are obtainable from bullion dealers, and the equipment in which to use them are also supplied by equipment sales people. The methods are explained quite simply in the literature supplied with the equipment.

Index